Library and Information Centres

Red doles Lane

Huddersfield, West Yorkshire

HD2 1YF

This book should be returned on or before the latest date stamped below. Fines are charged if the item is late.

You may renew this loan for a further period by phone, personal visit or at www.kirklees.gov.uk/libraries, provided that the book is not required by another reader.

NO MORE THAN THREE RENEWALS ARE PERMITTED

D1439853

800 654 260

PENGUIN BOOKS

What Every Parent Needs to Know

Miranda Thomas started teaching in 1990, coinciding with the very first national curriculum. She was the Chair of Governors at her local primary school in Wiltshire and is now a secondary school governor. Miranda has seen her own five children through primary school.

Toby Young is the outspoken columnist who wrote the international bestseller How to Lose Friends and Alienate People. A high-profile and passionate education reformist, he has co-founded four schools, including three primaries, and is Director of the New Schools Network, a charity that helps people set up schools. Toby has four children.

What Every Parent Needs to Know

How to Help Your Child Get the Most out of Primary School

Toby Young and Miranda Thomas

PENGUIN BOOKS

PENGUIN BOOKS

UK | USA | Canada | Ireland | Australia
India | New Zealand | South Africa

Penguin Books is part of the Penguin Random House group of companies
whose addresses can be found at global.penguinrandomhouse.com.

First published by Viking 2014
Revised edition published in Penguin Books 2017
001

Set in 10/13 pt Quadraat OT
Typeset by Jouve (UK), Milton Keynes
Printed in Great Britain by Clays Ltd, St Ives plc

A CIP catalogue record for this book is available from the British Library

ISBN: 978–0–241–97539–8

www.greenpenguin.co.uk

Contents

Appendices

Acknowledgements

We consulted numerous educational books in the course of writing this one, including the series of guides published by Civitas called *What Every Child Needs to Know: Preparing Your Child for a Lifetime of Learning*, which we'd thoroughly recommend, as well as the excellent series published by Michael O'Mara with titles like *Where On Earth? Geography Without the Boring Bits* and *Thirty Days Has September: Cool Ways to Remember Stuff*. We talked to lots of teachers about how the national curriculum is likely to be taught, including Phil Bagge, Caroline Lander, Emma Lennard, Rebecca Liddington, Matthew Faulkner, Michael Schumm and Natalie de Silva, all of whom were very generous with their time. We spoke to some of the people involved in drafting the 2014 national curriculum, including Nick Gibb, John McIntosh and Alex Standish, as well as several civil servants at the Department for Education, including Alistair Kelsey and Caroline Barker. Special thanks are due to Michael Tidd, a teacher and blogger, who fact-checked everything for us and made lots of useful suggestions about how to improve the text, as well as Jon Brunskill, who fact-checked the paperback edition. Above all, we'd like to thank our spouses, Caroline Bondy and Martin Thomas, and our nine children, Sasha,

Ludo, Fred and Charlie Young and Joseph, Fred, Flora, Honey and Sylvie Thomas. Their suggestions, comments and criticisms, while not always gently put, were always helpful.

Toby Young
Miranda Thomas

Prologue:
How to Use This Book

In 2008 the Secretary of State for Children, Schools and Families commissioned Sir Jim Rose, a former Ofsted inspector, to carry out a review into the primary school curriculum. Among the recommendations Sir Jim made in his report, which was published in 2009, was the following: 'It is apparent that a guide to the primary curriculum, in plain language, would be of considerable help to parents and enable them to give more support at home for their children's learning at school.'

This is the book you hold in your hand.

Our aim is to help parents of primary school children understand what it is their children are learning in the classroom and what they can do at home to help. To that end, we've taken the ten main subjects your child is learning – or will be learning – in primary school and set out a year-by-year breakdown of what your child will be taught in each one, along with lots of suggestions of things you can do to complement this. We've also included separate sections on School Dinners, Grammar and Punctuation, Phonics, Times Tables, Reports and Assessment and Special Educational Needs, as well as a range of Appendices that cover things such as how your child should form letters when practising their handwriting.

As our starting point, we have used the Early Years Foundation Stage (EYFS) Framework, which covers the nursery stage of your child's education as well as their first year of primary school (Reception), and the national curriculum for English primary schools introduced in September 2014, which covers Year 1 to Year 6. You can find both documents on the Department for Education's website (www.education.gov.uk). We've also spoken to lots of teachers and drawn on our own experience as parents.

When writing the hardback edition, which was published in 2014, we had to speculate about how the new national curriculum would be taught, but for this edition we've spoken to a number of teachers about how it is being taught in their schools. Of course, that doesn't mean we've got it right in every case.

The vast majority of state primaries in England – 90 per cent, at last count – teach the national curriculum, but a few schools don't. Academies and free schools aren't obliged to follow it and most prep schools will follow the common entrance curriculum to prepare children for transfer to private secondary schools at the age of eleven or thirteen. Those state primaries that are legally required to teach the national curriculum are those that are funded by local councils, i.e. community schools, foundation schools, voluntary aided schools and voluntary controlled schools. If you're not sure what sort of school your child is at (or will be going to), check its web address. If it ends in sch.uk, chances are it teaches the national curriculum – and most academies and free schools will also follow this curriculum, even though they're not required to.

By law, every state-funded school in England must offer a curriculum that is 'broad and balanced'. What that means in the case of local authority schools is that they'll teach the 'core' subjects specified in the national curriculum – English, maths and science – as well as the 'foundation' subjects – art and design, computing, design and technology (DT), geography, history, music, physical education (PE) and, from Year 3 onwards, languages (usually French or Spanish). In addition, they'll teach religious education (RE) and personal, social and health education (PSHE).

In this book we've focused on the three core subjects and all the foundation subjects apart from PE. We haven't included any information about RE or PSHE, since these subjects sit outside the primary national curriculum, and we've left out PE, since there's not a lot you can do at home to complement what your child is being taught in PE, beyond the obvious, such as taking them swimming on Saturday mornings.

At present, the majority of primaries spend every morning teaching English and maths (often referred to as 'literacy' and 'numeracy') and teach everything else in the afternoons. Until recently, schools were expected to devote two hours a week to PE (though only about half of primaries met that target), and most devote one period a week to science and one to RE. Beyond this, it's hard to say exactly what they'll do, and the national curriculum doesn't specify how much time should be devoted to each subject. Clearly, primary schools don't have enough time left in the week to teach the remaining six subjects (seven, if you include languages) as discrete disciplines, and because the foundation subjects aren't assessed in any of the mandatory tasks and tests schools will inevitably spend less time thinking about how best to teach them than English or maths. Some schools dedicate one period a week to PSHE, some to art and design, some to DT, some to music, and some will dedicate a separate period to each. Many schools used to 'embed' information and communication technology (ICT) so it was taught across the curriculum rather than as a stand-alone subject, but that is becoming less common because ICT has been replaced by computing in the current curriculum, which is considerably tougher. Although the digital literacy aspects of computing may still be largely embedded across other subjects, such as English, the new requirement to teach children how to code is likely to follow a discrete, structured scheme of work. If children are going to be taught to write programs, computing needs to be a stand-alone subject.

When it comes to geography and history, a large number of primaries have continued to do what they did under the old curriculum, which is to teach both subjects under the general heading of Topic, stressing the cross-curricular links between the two. (Some schools use the term Humanities.) Typically, schools assign two periods a week to Topic and teach a history 'unit' in one and a geography 'unit' in the other, changing the unit every half-term or so. Alternatively, they study one unit twice a week for a term, then another unit the next.

Until recently, some schools embraced what was known as the 'creative curriculum', with teachers emphasizing the cross-curricular links between as many subjects as possible, believing that this helped children to retain what was being taught and made them more creative. (There's not much evidence for this.) In these schools, it was quite common to teach all the foundation subjects under the general heading of Topic (with the exception of PE), including science. The current curriculum allows schools to continue to do this – and some schools will take advantage of this freedom because they won't want to abandon the 'creative curriculum' – but most schools have now moved towards a more subject-specific approach, especially as they move through Key Stage 2. So expect your child's school timetable to look something like this, with only history and geography being subsumed under Topic:

Day	8.40–9.10	9.10–10.20	Assembly	Break	11.00–12.05	12.05–1.20 Lunch	1.20–1.40	1.40–2.55	2.55–3.15
Mon	Reading	Literacy	Class assembly		PE		Reading	Topic/PSHE	Story
Tue	Reading	Literacy	School assembly		Maths		Reading	Music/Topic	Show and Tell
Wed	Phonics/ Handwriting	Literacy	Key Stage assembly		Maths		Reading	Art/Design	Story
Thur	Reading	Literacy	Singing		Maths		Reading	Science	Story
Fri	Reading	Literacy	School assembly		Maths		Reading	Spelling and PE	Story

Year 1 timetable taken from the website of Bathampton Primary School in Bath

It's impossible to know exactly which geography and history units schools will teach in Topic in each year because teachers organize the content of the national curriculum in different ways and there's some flexibility about which units to teach. But the majority of teachers are teaching many of the same units that they taught under the old curriculum – not just in geography and history, but in other subjects, too. The current curriculum is less prescriptive than the old one, granting teachers much more latitude about how to teach the specified subject matter (which is itself quite broad-brush). There are some new areas of study, such as ancient civilizations, which you can expect your child to study at some point in Key Stage 2. But it's naïve to expect many teachers to tear up all the lesson plans, worksheets and marking schemes they were using up until 2014 and start again from scratch.

Your child will also encounter the word 'topic' in other subjects. In art, for instance, they may tell you they've just started a new 'topic' called 'Henry Moore'. When used in this way, it's just a synonym for 'unit' or 'subject' and shouldn't be confused with Topic (upper case 'T'), which is typically presented as a subject or theme in its own right and allotted one or two periods a week.

There's one other thing you should know, which is that the Department for Education divides up the seven years your child will spend at primary school into three different stages. Most primaries follow this model. In Reception, your child will be in their final year of the Early Years Foundation Stage (EYFS), which also covers the years they spend in nursery; in Years 1 and 2, they'll be in Key Stage 1; and in Years 3, 4, 5 and 6, in Key Stage 2. Some primaries also distinguish between Infants (four- to seven-year-olds) and Juniors (seven- to eleven-year-olds). To clarify, Infants = Reception + Key Stage 1; and Juniors = Key Stage 2.

Key Stage:	EYFS	Key Stage 1	Key Stage 2
Year Group:	Reception	Year 1, Year 2	Year 3, Year 4, Year 5, Year 6
Age Group:	4–5	5–6, 6–7	7–8, 8–9, 9–10, 10–11

The primary national curriculum covers Years 1–6 and the seven foundation subjects are divided up into Key

Stage 1 and Key Stage 2, with no differentiation beyond that. It simply says what children are supposed to know at the end of each Key Stage and leaves it up to the teacher as to how to teach it, including what order to teach it in. Consequently, you'll find some repetition in the summaries of what your child will be doing in those seven subjects, though we've done our best to find out which parts of each subject will be taught in each year in both Key Stages, at least in most schools. Some guesswork is inevitable, but less has been involved in describing what will be taught in English, maths and science because the national curriculum goes into more detail in these core subjects, setting out the programmes of study year by year. For that reason, we've begun each chapter with the three core subjects and followed up with the foundation subjects in alphabetical order.

All schools are supposed to include information about the curriculum they'll be teaching on their websites, so if you want more detail about what your child will be learning that's a good place to start. However, some schools won't bother and those that do may not include enough detail to be of much use. (Or the detail they include will be out of date.) Not many schools publish a year-by-year breakdown of what children will be doing, which, in our experience, is what parents want. If the school's website doesn't provide you with the granularity you're looking for, we suggest contacting the head teacher and asking them if they can give you a more detailed breakdown. They should have a collection of 'curriculum maps' setting out exactly what your child will be learning in each subject in each year which they may be willing to share with you.

As you leaf through this book, you'll see some passages in bold, many of them in bullet points. These are precis of what it says in the national curriculum. In each section we've tried to summarize the programmes of study included in the current curriculum and then describe how they're likely to be taught. Following that, we've described what you can do at home to complement what your child is learning at school. (We've included what the national curriculum says about the 'Purpose of Study' and 'Aims' of each subject in the Appendix that starts on p. 458.)

The two exceptions to this rule are maths and science, where the material doesn't lend itself so easily to precis. So you won't find many passages in bold in those sections.

We hope you'll find this book useful. We're bound to have got a few things wrong. Some of these mistakes will be unavoidable, because there is no set way of teaching the specified programmes of study and teachers will, quite rightly, be taking advantage of the new freedom they've been given. In addition, some primaries in rural areas will put children of different ages together in the same class because there won't be enough children to teach them in different year groups. In these schools, the content children study in each subject will vary according to the age range within each class. But, for the most part, there will be a right answer – how most schools introduce children to computing in Year 1, for instance – and we'll have just got it wrong. So please email us to let us know what mistakes we've made and, hopefully, we can correct them in future editions. There will also be lots of games/exercises/etc. which you've done at home that we don't know about, so please email us any suggestions along those lines as well. Our email address is tobyandmiranda@gmail.com.

Finally, please don't think you have to do *everything* we suggest. Plenty of children are exhausted when they come home from school, particularly younger ones, and the last thing they want to do is some educational 'exercise' with Mum or Dad. (Some of them will have already spent an hour in an after-school club.) That's fine – let them veg out in front of the television. Between us, we have nine children and, while we've done most of these after-school activities with them at one time or another, we've never done all of them with any one of them. If we had, we'd probably have driven the child mad. But, as a general rule, your child will engage in these activities willingly for the simple reason that they'll want to spend time with you. That won't be true for ever. Before long, they'll prefer spending time with their friends, so enjoy your child while you can. These are the golden years and some of the most precious moments you spend together will be when you're introducing them to the world and showing them all its treasures.

Toby Young
Miranda Thomas

Introduction:
The National Curriculum

The fact that no one has written a parents' guide to the national curriculum before is puzzling, given that the national curriculum was created by the 1988 Education Reform Act and first used in schools in 1989. One reason may be that it keeps being revised, which threatens to render any guide obsolete by the time it's published. When we first wrote this book we hoped that the latest version of the national curriculum, which came into effect in 2014, would remain in place long enough for a single edition to prove useful. While the curriculum itself hasn't changed in the past three years, some of the tests your children are expected to take have, so we've updated the 'Reports and Assessment' section to reflect this, and made other minor changes throughout the text.

It's understandable that successive British governments should try to influence what children are taught in schools. Teachers often complain about politicians' constant tinkering with the national curriculum and compare Britain unfavourably to Finland, where there's more continuity in education policy. But the total population of Finland is just over half that of London, and

more than three-quarters of Finns are members of the
Evangelical Lutheran Church of Finland. In a country as
populous and diverse as ours, with dozens of different
social, ethnic and religious groups all vying to influence
public policy, education will always be a political football. As it is, the national curriculum applies only to
England, with Wales, Scotland and Northern Ireland
being responsible for education in their regions, and,
even in England, it doesn't apply to all schools. Private
schools aren't obliged to teach it, and neither are academies or free schools.

Nevertheless, the national curriculum applies to the
overwhelming majority of English primary schools, and
there are four reasons for being optimistic that it won't
be changed again in the near future.

Firstly, it's really not that different from the pre-
2014 version. Among primary school teachers, the
consensus is that the only subjects that changed significantly were English and maths. Science, geography and
history changed a bit, while the other foundation subjects (art and design, DT and music) barely changed at
all. Yes, the language was different in these subjects –
phrases such as 'the best in the musical canon' were
new – but the broad outline remained similar. Apart
from that, the big differences were that languages were
made compulsory in Key Stage 2, with schools allowed
to teach ancient languages as well as modern; and ICT
was replaced with computing, with the emphasis shift-
ing from digital literacy and understanding how to use
apps such as PowerPoint and Excel to teaching children
how to write programs and use open computer networks
such as the internet. Here's a slide that one primary
school teacher used in a presentation he gave on the new
curriculum when it was first introduced:

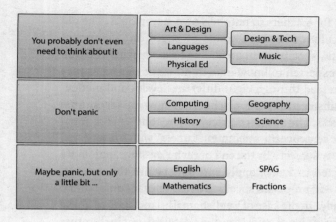

You probably don't even need to think about it	Art & Design	Design & Tech
	Languages	Music
	Physical Ed	
Don't panic	Computing	Geography
	History	Science
Maybe panic, but only a little bit ...	English	SPAG
	Mathematics	Fractions

Secondly, it commands a measure of cross-party support. Michael Gove, the Secretary of State for Education when the national curriculum was rewritten, was a polarizing figure and the first draft provoked a fierce public debate when it was unveiled in 2013. But many of its more controversial aspects were toned down in response to expert criticism. For instance, if you flick through our summary of the new history curriculum, you'll see that it contains much more than 'patriotic stocking fillers so beloved of traditionalists', which is how it was originally described by Richard Evans, a history professor at Cambridge University. Under 'Aims', it says that all pupils should 'know and understand significant aspects of the history of the wider world' and that these should include 'the nature of ancient civilizations', 'characteristic features of past non-European societies' and the 'achievements and follies of mankind'. Not much evidence of Little Englandism there.

Thirdly, the current national curriculum is a much shorter document than its predecessor, leaving more room for teachers to put their own stamp on it. The old curriculum contained reams of pages on 'attainment targets', specifying in great detail exactly what children were expected to know in each different subject as they progressed through eight different 'levels', and meticulous instructions for teachers on how to assess that progress. The current curriculum, by contrast, has just a single sentence on 'attainment targets', which is repeated in every subject: 'By the end of each Key Stage, pupils are expected to know, apply and understand the matters, skills and processes specified in the relevant programme of study.' In the case of English, maths and science, these 'programmes of study' are quite detailed, but in the other subjects they take up no more than a page or two. (In art and design, for instance, the 'subject content' is only 120 words long). Because the current curriculum is less prescriptive about what should be taught and completely agnostic about the manner in which it should be taught, it can accommodate a broad range of views without the document having to be revised each time there's a change of government.

Finally, the new curriculum isn't nearly as 'Victorian' as some of Michael Gove's opponents suggested. On the contrary, the emphasis on building up children's factual knowledge – which has been wrongly described as 'rote learning' – is underpinned by the latest research in cognitive science and supported by a good deal of empirical evidence.

Let's look at the 'rote-learning' charge. To begin with, there's almost no material in the current curriculum which children are expected to learn by rote, with the exception of times tables (and maybe phonics), and that was also true of the old curriculum. Yes, it's a 'knowledge-rich, subject-specific' curriculum (Gove's words), but the manner in which this is taught is a far cry from the Gradgrindian stereotype that was conjured up by Gove's critics – rows of children sitting in front of a blackboard. Unlike the old curriculum, the current one isn't prescriptive about how teachers choose to deliver its content and teachers have continued to teach in the gentle, child-friendly way they're used to. In terms of content, the main difference is that children are now supplied with a 'schemata' in each subject. That is, they begin by learning some basic factual knowledge, which can then be built upon in a logical, systematic way. In geography, for instance, this means learning the names of the seven continents, the five great oceans, the four points of the compass, the difference between latitude and longitude, the rudiments of map-reading and so on.

Critics contrast this knowledge-building approach with a skills-based approach in which children are taught all-purpose abilities such as 'problem solving', 'critical thinking' and 'creativity'. However, this is a false dichotomy. The consensus among cognitive scientists after three decades of research into the development of the human brain is that you can solve problems in a particular subject only if you already know quite a lot about that subject. Higher-order thinking skills such as 'problem solving' and 'creativity' aren't abstract, stand-alone abilities that can be taught instead of subject knowledge, as some people mistakenly believe. Nor does teaching children factual knowledge inhibit the emergence of these skills. On the contrary, children begin to develop these skills in a particular subject only after they've memorized a good deal of facts about that subject. There's no reason to believe children won't begin to think creatively and analytically about, say, music or design and technology in primary school, but they won't be able to acquire those skills without learning about those subjects. The development of these higher-order thinking skills in any subject goes hand in hand with learning a lot of facts about that subject. This is how the cognitive scientist Daniel Willingham puts it:

> Data from the last thirty years lead to a conclusion that is not scientifically challengeable: thinking well requires knowing facts and that's true not just because you need something to think *about*. The very processes that teachers care about most – critical thinking processes such as reasoning and problem solving – are intimately intertwined with factual knowledge that is stored in long-term memory (not just found in the environment).[1]

There's a substantial body of evidence that the knowledge-building approach is more effective than one that dispenses with subject knowledge and skips straight to higher-order thinking skills such as problem solving. For instance, the American state of Massachusetts introduced a curriculum much like the current English national curriculum into its public schools in 1993, and the results were astonishing. Scores in the standard tests taken by ten-year-olds and fourteen-year-olds – the National Assessment of Education Progress (NAEP) – shot up and, in 2005, Massachusetts children became the first to top the league tables in all four NAEP categories. When the biannual tests were repeated in 2007, Massachusetts topped the table again, as it did in 2009, 2011, 2013 and 2015.

Some critics of the knowledge-building approach

---

1. Daniel T. Willingham, *Why Don't Students Like School?* (San Francisco: Jossey-Bass, 2009, p. 28).

claim it's suitable only for white, middle-class children – that the current curriculum is designed in Michael Gove's own image. Yet the evidence from America suggests otherwise. As a result of its curriculum reforms, Massachusetts saw the attainment gap between children from different social and ethnic backgrounds narrow further than in any other state between 1998 and 2005. Between 2002 and 2009, the NAEP scores of African-Americans and Hispanics improved faster than those of white children, and children from low-income families made similar gains. 'If you are a disadvantaged parent with a school-age child, Massachusetts is the state to move to,' wrote the American educationalist E. D. Hirsch in 2008.[2]

The reason for this is obvious. Children of educated, middle-class parents pick up a good deal of knowledge in the home and that gives them a head start over their less fortunate peers when they begin their schooling. Unless the school compensates for this by adopting a knowledge-building approach, disadvantaged children will struggle to catch up. This was the finding of two Kansas psychologists, Betty Hart and Todd Risley, who set out in the mid-eighties to find out why a government programme designed to help children from low-income families wasn't doing much to improve their grades. They looked at how parents talked to their babies, and visited forty-two families every month, spending an hour recording conversations between parents and their children. Then they spent the next six years transcribing and analysing everything that was said and revisited the children at the age of nine to see how they were getting on at school.

2. Quoted by James Stergios, Charles Chieppo and Jamie Gass, 'The Massachusetts Exception', *City Journal*, summer 2012.

They concluded that the most important environmental factor in the development of young children's cognitive abilities – and their subsequent academic performance – is how many different words are spoken to them per hour. Hart and Risley discovered that children in professional homes hear, on average, 2,153 words per hour, children from working-class homes an average of 1,251 and children from welfare homes just 616. 'Extrapolated out, this means that in a year children in professional families heard an average of 11 million words, while children in working-class families heard an average of 6 million words and children in welfare families heard an average of 3 million words,' they concluded. 'By age four, a child from a welfare-recipient family could have heard 32 million words fewer than a classmate from a professional family.'[3]

It's partly as a result of Hart and Risley's research – which has never been successfully challenged – that there's so much emphasis on enlarging children's vocabulary in the new national curriculum. As you'll see when you leaf through this book, schools are expected constantly to teach children new words, not just in English, but across all subjects. (We've included a glossary of the vocabulary your child will be expected to learn in computing in an Appendix.)

There's no doubt that the current primary curriculum is ambitious. One of its stated aims is to introduce children to 'the best that has been thought and said', from a phrase coined by Matthew Arnold. However, it would be wrong to think that a knowledge-based education is suitable only for children at private schools or in the top half

---

3. Betty Hart and Todd R. Risley, *Meaningful Differences in the Everyday Experience of Young American Children* (Brookes Publishing: 1995).

of the ability spectrum. As the example of Massachusetts shows, all children can benefit from this approach, regardless of background or ability. To dismiss it as right-wing or conservative just because it's championed by Michael Gove would be a mistake.

We'll leave you with the words of Robert Tressell, author of The Ragged-Trousered Philanthropists, a seminal text of the British labour movement. We think this sums up the spirit of the national curriculum:

What we call civilisation – the accumulation of knowledge which has come down to us from our forefathers – is the fruit of thousands of years of human thought and toil. It is not the result of the labour of the ancestors of any separate class of people who exist to-day, and therefore it is by right the common heritage of all. Every little child that is born into the world, no matter whether he is clever or dull, whether he is physically perfect or lame, or blind, no matter how much he may excel or fall short of his fellows in other respects, in one thing at least he is their equal – he is one of the heirs of all the ages that have gone before.

Reception

Introduction

Reception is not treated as a stand-alone year in a child's development, but as the final year of what's known as the Early Years Foundation Stage (EYFS).

The national curriculum doesn't begin until Year 1 in primary school, by which time children are already five years old. In 2010, shortly after the Coalition was formed, an attempt was made by Nick Gibb, the Conservative Schools Minister, to expand the national curriculum to encompass Reception, but he was thwarted by Sarah Teather, the Lib Dem Minister for Children and Families. Consequently, Reception remains part of the EYFS. There's a legal document setting out what children should be learning from the moment they're born until the age of five, the 'EYFS Framework', and state-funded nurseries, pre-schools, Reception teachers and registered child-minders are all legally obliged to follow it.

The EYFS Framework sets out seven areas of learning and development. These are divided into three 'prime' areas: Personal, Social and Emotional Development (PSED); Communication and Language; and Physical Development; and four 'specific' areas: literacy;

mathematics; understanding the world; and expressive arts and design.

The seven areas

All seven areas of learning and development are held to be important and interconnected.

The three prime areas are regarded as crucial for igniting children's curiosity and enthusiasm for learning and for building their capacity to learn.

The four specific areas include teaching children the skills and knowledge they'll need if they're to start learning the national curriculum in Year 1. They grow out of the prime areas and provide important contexts for future learning.

PRIME AREAS

Personal, Social and Emotional Development (PSED)	Making relationships
	Self-confidence and self-awareness
	Managing feelings and behaviour
Communication and Language	Listening and attention
	Understanding
	Speaking
Physical Development	Moving and handling
	Health and self-care

SPECIFIC AREAS

Literacy	Reading
	Writing
Mathematics	Numbers
	Shape, space and measures
Understanding the World	People and communities
	The world
	Technology
Expressive Arts and Design	Exploring and using media and materials
	Being imaginative

PSED involves helping your child to develop a positive sense of themselves and others; to form positive relationships and develop respect for others; to develop social skills and learn how to manage their feelings; to understand appropriate behaviour in groups; and to have confidence in their own abilities.

Communication and Language focuses on giving your child an opportunity to experience a rich language environment; to develop their confidence and skills in expressing themselves; and to speak and listen in a range of situations.

Physical Development is about providing opportunities for your child to be active and interactive; and to develop their coordination, control and movement. Your child should also be helped to understand the importance of physical activity and to make healthy choices in relation to food. (Crisps are not one of the 'five a day'!)

Literacy involves encouraging your child to link sounds and letters and begin to read and write. Your child should be given access to a wide range of reading materials (books, poems and other written materials) to ignite their interest.

Maths is supposed to provide your child with opportunities to develop and improve his or her skills in counting; understanding and using numbers; calculating simple addition and subtraction problems; and describing shapes, spaces and measures.

Understanding the World is an attempt to help your child make sense of their physical world and community through opportunities to explore, observe and find out about people, places, technology and the environment.

And, finally, expressive arts and design is about enabling your child to explore and play with a wide range of media and materials, as well as providing opportunities and encouragement for sharing their thoughts, ideas and feelings through a variety of activities in art, music, movement, dance, role play, and design and technology.

Throughout Reception, your child's teacher will probably observe the following principles:

- Playing and exploring: they will encourage your child to investigate and find out things for themselves, to 'have a go'

- Active learning: they will help your child concentrate on the task in hand, to persevere when the going gets tough and be proud when they achieve something

- Creating and thinking critically: they will try and get your child to come up with their own ideas, make links between the things they're learning and choose their own way of approaching different tasks

Don't be too alarmed if this all sounds a bit intense. There's likely to be an emphasis on play right through to the end of Reception. Teachers are expected to allow children to choose a range of activities and 'play' for nearly 50 per cent of the school day in Reception.

Our approach

For the Reception chapter of this book, we've combined Communication and Language and Literacy under the general heading of 'English' and left out Physical Development and PSED. Why have we left these out? As we explained in the Prologue (see p. xiii), we haven't included the physical exercises your child will be doing in school – known as PE from Year 1 onwards – because there isn't much you can do at home to complement these, beyond the obvious. And we haven't included PSED and PSHE because, like RE (religious education), it doesn't form part of the national curriculum. Schools are legally obliged to teach RE, and most will teach PSED and PSHE (personal, social and health education) as well although it's non-statutory, but how they teach it will vary so much from school to school that it falls outside the scope of this book. Our aim is to tell you what your child is likely to be doing in the classroom from year to year and how you can complement it at home and, in the case of PSHE and RE, we simply don't know.

In addition to English, we've included sections on maths, Understanding the World and expressive arts and design in this chapter. Understanding the World includes material from a range of subjects (geography, history, science), as does expressive arts and design (art, design, drama, movement and music), but we haven't broken them down into subsections because that won't be how they appear in your child's timetable. In all likelihood, they'll simply appear as 'Understanding the World' and 'expressive arts and design' or 'EAD'. (These might be referred to by your child's school as 'Knowledge and Understanding of the World' and 'Creative Development', which is how they used to be described in the EYFS Framework until it was revised in 2012.)

Below a brief description of what your child will be learning in these classes, we've set out the early learning goals in these categories, as stipulated in the EYFS Framework, and some suggestions of what you can do at home to help your child attain these goals. By no means all children will reach them by the end of Reception and you shouldn't treat these goals as a checklist to see whether your child is developing 'normally'. However, these are the goals your child's Reception teacher will have in the back of his or her mind. (Usually 'her'.)

In the English and maths sections of this chapter, we've listed the suggestions about what you can do at home under different headings: 'After school', 'Every day', 'Games', 'Car journeys'. We think this is appropriate here, since you'll be spending quite a lot of time trying to accustom your child to the idea of learning and instilling good habits in them. But from Year 1 onwards, we've put all these activities together under the general heading of 'What can you do to help?' At most schools, children will start being given homework in Year 1, building up (in some schools) to as much as an hour a night by the time they approach their Key Stage 2 tests in Year 6 (see 'Reports and Assessment' on p. 53). Just getting them to do that will be demanding enough, without burdening you with suggestions of how you can fill car journeys with educational activities. Unless they're talking books, of course, which can be fun.

You'll have to judge how much time to devote to these extracurricular activities – how much is appropriate for your child. As a general rule, girls are more willing to engage in these sorts of activities than boys in Reception, and children born in the first nine months of the academic year will have a greater tolerance for them than 'summer babies'. But it will also vary tremendously from child to child because children develop at different rates. What is universally true is that no child, however ready to learn, will want to do *anything* when they get home from school before they've been given a 'snack' (usually something sugary and unhealthy). Woe betide the parent who tries to get their child to do any of these activities on an empty stomach.

Baseline test

The Department for Education announced in 2014 that children in Reception would be expected to take a new 'baseline test' in the first week and, in 2016, many of them did. However, the Department subsequently announced that it wouldn't be using the 2016 'baseline test' data to measure progress in schools, so the future of these tests is now uncertain. If your child does take one, it won't be a written exam, but a teacher-led assessment of your child's 'baseline' abilities in literacy, reasoning and cognition. For more information on this, see 'Reports and Assessment' on p. 50.

Before You Start

You'll be amazed how much you can teach a young child. Take the following extract from a letter written by the nineteenth-century biologist Francis Galton at the age of four to his elder sister Adèle: 'I can read any English book. I can say all the Latin Substantives and Adjectives and active verbs, besides 52 lines of Latin poetry. I can cast up any sum in addition and multiply by 2, 3, 4, 5, 6, 7, 8, 9, 10, 11 . . . I read French a little and I know the Clock.'

That's a little ambitious even for the pushiest of parents, but here's a list of rudimentary skills that your child is expected to have when they start 'big school'.

- They should be 'toilet-trained', i.e. able to go to the toilet by themselves, wipe their own bottom and wash their hands afterwards. Not every child will be able to do this, but you shouldn't make life any harder for Reception teachers than it already is. Wiping children's bums is not what they got into teaching for!

- Make sure they can get undressed and dressed by themselves so they can change in and out of their PE kit. This means being able to do up and undo buttons and zips, and put on their PE shoes (Velcro straps are much easier than laces). Because so many children haven't learnt these basic skills, a forty-minute PE lesson often means thirty minutes of dressing and undressing (no exaggeration), leaving only ten minutes for physical activity.

- They should be able to recognize their own names. A bit obvious, perhaps, but a 2013 report by the Centre for Social Justice revealed that one of the reasons some children fall behind in school is because they start Reception unable to respond to their own names.[1] Ideally, your child should not just recognize their own name when it's called out by the teacher, but when it's written down, too.

- Given that they'll be embarking on a phonics reading programme almost immediately, it's helpful if your child is already familiar with the alphabet. There are lots of excellent alphabet books, such as *Alphabet* by Alison Jay, which is beautifully illustrated, *ABC* by Quentin Blake and *Alligators All Around* by Maurice Sendak. These books tend to use the name of the letter, and in upper case, whereas your child will be learning letters by the sounds they make rather than their name, but teachers we've spoken to aren't bothered by this – any form of letter awareness is a positive. The 'Alphabet Song' is helpful, too (the letters of the alphabet sung to the tune of 'Twinkle, Twinkle, Little Star').

- Ditto for maths and the numbers 1 to 20. Again, there's a range of good books that introduce young children to numbers. We'd recommend *Counting* by Alison Jay, a companion volume to *Alphabet*. Counting rhymes are also helpful in teaching children how to recite numbers out loud: 'One, two, three four five / Once I caught a fish alive / Six, seven, eight nine ten / Then I let it go again.'

- Your child should be able to sit still for up to forty minutes – or at least remain seated in one place

1. *Requires Improvement: The Causes of Educational Failure*, The Centre for Social Justice, September 2013.

without getting up and wandering off. This can be a lot harder for boys than girls. Calm time spent with your child playing games, doing jigsaw puzzles or just drawing and painting helps.

There are other things you can do, too:

- Visit the school with your child before they start so it's not an unfamiliar environment on their first day.

- If possible, meet your child's Reception teacher beforehand. If they offer you a 'home visit', take them up on it.

- Read your child bedtime stories in which the characters are starting school, such as *Busy School* by Melanie Joyce.

- Make sure all your child's stuff is marked with name tapes or, if that's not practical, permanent pen.

- Have your child memorize your mobile phone number. If, God forbid, they ever get lost, they can ask someone to call you. (Admittedly, it's easier said than done.)

- Teach your child to write their own name.

- Try not to burst into tears when you drop them off on their first day. Crying can be contagious and you don't want to set off the other parents!

Learning to Read and Write: A Short Guide to Phonics

All the skills of language are essential to participating fully as a member of society; pupils, therefore, who do not learn to speak, read and write fluently and confidently are effectively disenfranchised.

These days all primary schools teach children to read by using the phonics system, starting in Reception, so we thought we'd include some information about it here. Phonics is widely recognized as the most effective way of teaching young children to read and is particularly helpful for children aged four to seven.

Phonics

Phonics teaches children how to:

- recognize the sounds that each individual letter makes

- identify the sounds that different combinations of letters make, such as 'sh' or 'oo'

- blend these sounds together from left to right to make a word.

Methods of teaching reading have evolved over the years. With increasing research into what works and what doesn't, it has become clear that many children who seemed to be able to read quite well came unstuck when faced with a new word in an unexpected context. It turned out that they were relying on visual recognition of whole words and had no back-up plan for *decoding* new letter combinations. Phonics solves this problem by teaching children how to *decode* words – to work out how to say them rather than guess. This is the first important step in learning to read. Writing, by contrast, requires them to *encode* sounds into letters and groups of letters.

Your child will be using vocabulary that may be unfamiliar to you: 'phoneme', 'grapheme', 'digraph', 'split digraph', etc. It's worth understanding what these words mean. You may also be interested to see the full list of forty-plus phonemes they'll be introduced to in their first few years at school (see below). Some schools give parents leaflets on phonics or invite Reception parents in and explain it to them.

- A **phoneme** is a sound, distinct from others, e.g. 'd', 'r', 's', 'ch', 'oy'.
- A **grapheme** is a letter or combination of letters that represent that sound, e.g. the phoneme (sound) 'ay' can be represented by any of these graphemes: 'ai', 'ay', 'a-e', (as in 'bait', 'may', 'late').
- A **digraph** is a grapheme consisting of two letters, e.g. 'sh', 'ai', 'ay' (these last two each represent the same phoneme).
- A **split digraph** is a grapheme of two letters that are not next to each other, e.g. 'a-e' (as in 'lane', where both the 'a' and the 'e' are needed to make the right phoneme (sound), but are separated by the 'n').
- A **tricky word** is one that doesn't follow the rules, that is not spelt phonetically, e.g. 'he', 'laugh', 'why'.
- **Segmenting** is breaking up words into their individual sounds to spell a word.
- **Blending** is putting individual sounds together to read a word.

- **Sound talk** is the process of saying each phoneme in a word in order to blend or segment.

What makes English hard to learn to read, apart from the large number of tricky words, is the bewildering number of graphemes (letters) that can represent one phoneme (sound). And what makes English so hard to spell is the need to learn which grapheme to use from the dizzying choice available in any one word. (Is it 'lait', or 'layt', or 'late'?)

And, to finish, grapheme-phoneme correspondences vary. The grapheme 's' corresponds to the phoneme 's' in the word 'see', but it corresponds to the phoneme 'z' in the word 'easy'.

Which means it's far from easy.

International phonetic alphabet

CONSONANTS		VOWELS	
/b/	bad	/ɑː/	father, arm
/d/	dog	/ɒ/	hot
/ð/	this	/æ/	cat
/dʒ/	gem, jug	/aɪ/	mind, fine, pie, high
/f/	if, puff, photo	/aʊ/	out, cow
/g/	gum	/ɛ/	hen, head
/h/	how	/eɪ/	say, came, bait
/j/	yes	/ɛə/	air

CONSONANTS	
/k/	cat, check, key, school
/l/	leg, hill
/m/	man
/n/	man
/ŋ/	sing
/θ/	both
/p/	pet
/r/	red
/s/	sit, miss, cell
/ʃ/	she, chef
/t/	tea
/tʃ/	check
/v/	vet
/w/	wet, when
/z/	zip, hens, buzz
/ʒ/	pleasure

VOWELS	
/əʊ/	cold, boat, cone, blow
/ɪ/	hit
/ɪə/	beer
/iː/	she, bead, see, scheme, chief
/ɔː/	launch, raw, born
/ɔɪ/	coin, boy
/ʊ/	book
/ʊə/	tour
/uː/	room, you, blue, brute
/ʌ/	cup
/ɜː/	fern, turn, girl
/ə/	farmer

How will this be taught at school?

Most schools choose one or two phonics programmes and stick to them fairly rigidly. Examples include:

Floppy's Phonics Sounds and Letters: Oxford University Press
Jolly Phonics: Jolly Learning Ltd
Letterland Phonics (rev. edn 2013): Letterland International Ltd
Letters & Sounds: Department for Education
Phonics Bug: Pearson
Phonics International: Debbie Hepplewhite
Read Write Inc.: Oxford University Press
Sound Discovery: Synthetic Phonics Ltd
Sounds-Write: Sounds-Write Ltd

Most schools have a lesson every morning called 'Phonics' in Key Stage 1, where children are grouped by level into small clusters working on new phonemes, graphemes or tricky words. Often the work they're doing in a phonics class seems simplistic – they may be reading at a higher level than their phonics lesson suggests. But there is a method behind the sequence of activities, and it has been shown to work.

In Reception, and in nursery, too, there is a huge emphasis on teaching your child speaking and listening skills. These include being able to sit still during 'carpet time' and raise their hand when they want to speak. In this context, though, the skill in question is the ability to listen to a word and hear the sounds that make it up. This skill is regarded as a vital precursor to learning to read.

Phonics will be taught in 'letter sets', with about a week spent on each set, as in the example below:

Set 1	s, a, t, p
Set 2	i, n, m, d
Set 3	g, o, c, k
Set 4	ck, e, u, r
Set 5	h, b, f, ff, l, ll, ss
Set 6	j, v, w, x
Set 7	y, z, zz, qu

Then they will move on to graphemes such as:

Consonant digraphs	ch, sh, th, ng
Graphemes	ear, air, ure, er, ar, or, ur, ow, oi, ai, ee, igh, oa, oo

Some words are decodable and can be 'sound talked', such as 'and', 'it' and 'in'.

Others are tricky and cannot be 'sound talked', such as 'the', 'no' and 'go'.

This latter group needs to be learnt by sight and then applied in context so children know each word off by heart and understand its meaning.

The children may be taught to follow these steps:

Step 1: Recognize and read the words
Step 2: Say a sentence, using each word
Step 3: Have a go at spelling and writing the words

In Year 1 (or possibly earlier), the daily phonics lesson usually involves a small group of children clustered on the carpet or at a table around the teacher or teaching assistant. They will be shown a sequence of cards with a grapheme on the front, e.g. 'ew', and a picture on the back of, say, someone eating beef stew. They will be familiar with this card. They will then be asked to chant 'ew, chew, stew', and will move swiftly on to the next card. A particular grapheme or group of graphemes is thus embedded and the children can then be introduced to a new one. The teacher often uses a wipeable white-board and marker pen, but the children don't write during this part of the lesson.

Next will come group and individual reading of a short book that embeds the new grapheme. Children read to each other and love bossily correcting each other's errors, pouncing on inaccuracies. They will discuss the book in some detail. Clever questioning and prompting by the teacher gives opportunities for the development of lots of important skills – speaking, listening, observa-tion, comprehension, prediction, inference, etc.

There will be a large chart of graphemes on the class-room wall and it will be referred to often.

The phonics programmes available differ in their approach – *Jolly Phonics* associates hand motions with phonemes, *Letterland Phonics* makes characters of each letter and so on – but the same phonemes and graph-emes are taught in roughly the same order. As a parent, you get no say in the matter and will, with any luck, think your school has chosen an excellent scheme. Some par-ents like to buy some of the supporting material which all the schemes offer for home use: books, flashcards, posters, games, etc.

Towards the end of Year 1, all children undergo a phonic screening check. This is a short, light-touch assessment to confirm whether individual children have learnt phonic decoding to an appropriate standard. The purpose of this test is to identify those who need extra help so they can be brought up to speed quickly. (See 'Reports and Assessment' on p. 51.)

By the time a child's reading has taken off, what may still be called 'Phonics' in school will have morphed into a structured spelling and vocabulary programme. This may happen in Year 2, or further up the school.

What can you do to help?

● Encourage your child to play with language by playing rhyming games or memory games, such as: 'Mrs Magnolia went shopping and she bought . . .' (Take turns to add an item to her list when what's already been added has been successfully recited.)

● Encourage your child's speaking skills by asking them to tell you the story of something that happened to them recently (playing with a friend, visiting a relative or a museum, for example).

● Practise listing words that start with a chosen letter – your child could choose the letter, and you take turns to come up with different words.

● Use bath crayons to draw letters on bath tiles and get them to use a flannel to rub off the ones you call out.

● Play simple Bingo or Lotto games to practise recognizing letters and words. Make your own Bingo board of squares, write the letters or words to be practised in them, and write the same letters or words on separate pieces of paper. Draw these from a hat, and whoever has that word on their board can cover the space with a counter. First to complete the board – and shout 'Bingo!'; that's very important – wins.

● Use letter-picture cards (cards with simple pictures and a corresponding letter, for example, the letter 'b' with a picture of a ball; there are lots of sets available).

● Play blending and segmenting games. For example, ask what word is a blend of 'f', 'a' and 't' (answer: 'fat'), or 'm', 'a', 'sh', 'ee' and 'n' (answer: 'machine'), or how you would segment 'brick' (answer: 'b', 'r', 'i' and 'c').

● Above all, read to your child and with your child. Reception-age children can't get enough short stories with good illustrations. They love to catch you out missing a sentence (or a page) of a book they know backwards. Year 1 children particularly like traditional rhymes and fairy tales. Many beginner books have lots of rhyming words and repetition, e.g. the Dr Seuss books, which make them easy to read (for the child) and therefore fun to do together. Well, fun the first time.

● There are plenty of phonics apps, such as Read Write Phonics, Twinkl Phonics Suite and abc PocketPhonics, Forest Phonics, Mr Thorne Does Phonics.

● There's lots of information on phonics online. You can search for 'phonics' on the Department for Education website at www.gov.uk/dfe or go straight to www.gov.uk/schools/collections/phonics, where the first link is to 'learning to read through phonics: information for parents'.

English

There will be a part of the day, usually in the morning when energy levels are high, set aside for phonics (sometimes referred to as 'literacy hour'). During this period, your child will sit on the carpet in a semicircle gathered around the teacher and be expected to stay still and concentrate. They will focus on a new or revisited 'phoneme' (see 'Learning to Read and Write: A Short Guide to Phonics' on p. 11). They will usually then sit at a table and complete a worksheet, or practise letter shapes, either using pencil and paper or a small wipeable board.

At some point during the day your child will listen to a story and answer questions. They may be asked to contribute a piece of news, or be invited to ask another child a question about news they've just heard. In such ways and many others, they will address the goals set out below.

Don't worry if this sounds too much like hard work. Remember, there will also be plenty of time set aside for play.

The early learning goals in English are as follows:

Listening and attention

By the end of Reception your child should be able to:

- sit quietly in a lesson and concentrate on what the teacher is saying without fidgeting or talking

- follow stories and be able to anticipate key events and answer questions about the text

- listen to what others are saying and respond appropriately, even when engaged in another activity.

Understanding

By the end of Reception your child should be able to:

- follow a story without pictures or props

- listen and respond to ideas expressed by others in conversation or discussion

- follow instructions involving more than one idea or action

- answer 'how' and 'why' questions about their experiences and in response to stories

- understand humour, e.g. jokes, nonsense rhymes, slapstick.

Speaking

By the end of Reception your child should be able to:

- develop their vocabulary

- use language to organize and clarify their thinking, ideas, feelings and experiences

- express themselves effectively, demonstrating an awareness of what a listener requires to understand what they're saying

- use past, present and future forms accurately when talking about events that have happened or are about to happen

- develop their own narratives and explanations by connecting ideas or events.

Reading

By the end of Reception your child should be able to:

- name and sound out all the letters of the alphabet

- read and understand simple sentences

- use phonic knowledge to decode regular words and read them aloud accurately

- read some common irregular words

- use vocabulary and forms of speech from the books they've read

- enjoy an increasing range of books

- demonstrate understanding when talking to others about the books they've read.

Writing

By the end of Reception your child should be able to:

- write their own name and other things, such as labels and captions

- write common words in ways that match their spoken sound, e.g. 'cat'

- write some irregular words, e.g. 'the'

- begin to write simple sentences that can be read by themselves and others

- begin to spell some words correctly.

What can you do to help?

Reading to your child

The most important thing you can do at home is to read aloud to your child. Einstein said, 'If you want your children to be intelligent, read them fairy tales.' You should discuss what you're reading with your child, both as you go along and at the end. You can ask them to guess what will happen next, retell the story, make up a different ending, tell you who their favourite character is and why . . . and so on.

Reading to your child is important for a variety of reasons. At a very basic level, you are teaching your child how to read a book: to start at the beginning, to turn the pages over one by one, to read from left to right and top to bottom.

Listening to someone read also helps your child begin to understand that words are made up of distinct sounds. This is an important precursor to reading. It also teaches them that the letters on the page have a meaning – different letters make different sounds. Numerous studies have shown that reading to your child is the way you can help them learn to read – and quite a lot of the time they spend in Reception will be sitting on the floor listening to a teacher read them a story.

Reading continues to be an important part of a child's education because it is a way of 'feeding' the brain. The experience of reading, or being read to, activates and exercises many areas of the brain. The memory makes connections between the things the child knows already and the topic of the story and its content. The child integrates new information learnt through reading, further strengthening and improving their network of knowledge.

Reading to your child will help him or her with all of the five categories listed in this section: listening and attention, understanding, speaking, reading and even with their writing.

AFTER SCHOOL

● Most children come out of school hungry, so it's a good idea to have a snack ready.

● Your child is unlikely to be set formal homework in Reception. The length of the school day is hard enough for them to cope with as it is and they'll be tired by the time they get home. However, from quite early on in their first term they will come home with a reading book at an appropriate level. For some children, this will be a book without a single printed word, which can be somewhat surprising for the parent. The idea is to get the child used to turning pages from front to back and noticing that the 'story' unfolds sequentially. You should try and get into the habit straight away of sitting down with your child and their reading book every day, or almost every day – it'll only be for five or ten minutes in Reception. Whether you should do this straight after school, or after a break, or in the morning before they go to school, is up to you.

EVERY DAY

● There's plenty you can do at home to help your child to write. One of the most common reasons children struggle with writing is that they haven't developed their fine motor skills and find handwriting very challenging. This is particularly true of boys. Play-Doh, puzzles, beading, Lego and playing with stickers will all help develop their fine motor skills as, in each case, accuracy with their fingers is required. And that helps writing.

● Always correct the way your child holds their pencil if they are not doing it properly.

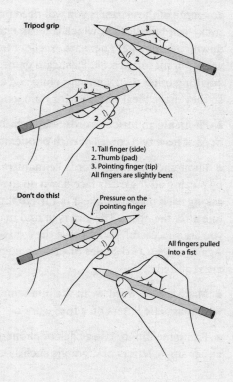

Tripod grip

1. Tall finger (side)
2. Thumb (pad)
3. Pointing finger (tip)
All fingers are slightly bent

Don't do this!

Pressure on the pointing finger

All fingers pulled into a fist

- Use the letter shapes in the Appendix on p. 473 when showing your child how to form letters. For more inspiration, look at the following website: http://handsonaswegrow.com/30-kids-activities-materials-for-promoting-fine-motor-skills/.

- Get your child writing. Most children love the sense of ownership that comes with writing their name on something, even if it's a pebble. Encourage them to label their pictures, or to write shopping lists. Don't worry too much about poor letter formation or spelling at this stage.

GAMES

For some of these games you will need phoneme and tricky-word flashcards, which you can either buy, download or make. There are excellent free printables on www.phonicsplay.co.uk. Flashcard games don't need anything other than you, your child and a pack of cards, so they make ideal activities for train journeys.

- Phoneme and tricky words Snap (obviously, you will need at least two copies of each phoneme/tricky word).

- Phoneme and tricky words Pelmanism. This is played by putting all the cards face down on the table and then asking each player to take it in turn to flip two cards over, one after the other. The aim is to find matching pairs; if you are successful, you remove the cards from the table. Again, at least two copies of each phoneme/tricky word are required.

- Make simple words with the phoneme flashcards or with magnetic letters on a fridge door.

- Phoneme Bingo. Use a pack of phoneme cards, with either single letters or digraphs such as 'sh' or 'ch', or make your own. Make up a Bingo square and play as you would normal Bingo.

● The Tray Game. Put various items on a tray and give your child thirty seconds or a minute to memorize them, then cover the tray and have them either verbally list all the ones they can remember or, when the child is a bit older, write them down. This kind of memory game may improve your child's 'working memory' (a concept exactly like RAM in computers – a mental workspace or notepad, the 'place' where we manipulate information, perform mental calculations and form new thoughts).

● Jigsaw puzzles will help develop gross and fine motor skills, hand-eye coordination, memory and shape recognition.

● Encourage your child to start writing at home: shopping lists, thank-you letters, cards (which they can also make) and so on.

● Children of this age often enjoy putting on a show. You might find watching these shows rather painful, particularly as the concept of 'the end' seems hard for young children to grasp. However, the process of putting on a show is a good way to reinforce your child's understanding of storytelling and their ability to articulate and organize language. Unless they have older siblings whose examples they can follow, you could start them off by suggesting a simple story (it could be a book or film they know well) and acting it out with them with the help of some props, such as a pile of old clothes in a dressing-up box. They'll soon get the idea, but be warned: they'll prefer to extemporize rather than rehearse and these 'plays' can be interminable.

CAR JOURNEYS

● Play rhyming games. For example, you can take turns to choose a word and then come up with as many words that rhyme with it as possible. Rhyming helps children become phonemically aware. For example, when they recognize that 'cat' rhymes with 'mat' they are recognizing the 'at' diagraph and learning that you can swap the first sound or letter to make new words while retaining the latter segment of the word.

● Listen to CDs in the car (stories and children's songs). This will help children follow stories without pictures. Singing songs reinforces their rhyming knowledge.

● Play I Spy but, rather than saying 'beginning with the letter "B" ', say 'beginning with the sound "b" ' and make the sound 'b' rather than saying the name of the letter. This game again develops phonemic awareness.

● A good game to play on long journeys is the Number-plate Game. The idea is that you have to spot every letter in the alphabet on car number-plates, starting with the letter 'A' and working your way through to 'Z' in the correct sequence. If two or more children are on the same letter, the one who spots it first – and shouts it out – wins.

Maths

In Reception your child will be exposed to numbers, counting and the language of maths (as described below) on a daily basis. There will be a portion of the day, usually in the morning when energy levels are high, when children do maths (often called 'numeracy'). Children will sit, probably on the carpet, clustered around the teacher, and be expected to sit still and concentrate. They will count, take turns to 'add one' and learn how to write a new number. Then they will sit at a table and do some written work, such as practising writing numbers, or play a mathematical game. Maths will come into the language used in the classroom throughout the day.

The early learning goals in maths are as follows:

Numbers

By the end of Reception your child should be able to:

- count from 1 to 20, recognizing and naming the numerals

- place the numbers 1 to 20 in the correct sequence and say which number is one more and which is one less than any other number in the sequence

- add or subtract two single-digit numbers by counting on or back

- solve problems involving doubling, halving and sharing

- count an irregular arrangement of up to ten objects

- use the language of 'more' and 'fewer' to compare two sets of objects

- begin to use the vocabulary involved in adding and subtracting in practical activities and discussion.

Shape, space and measures

By the end of Reception your child should be able to:

- use everyday language to talk about size, weight, capacity, position, distance, time and money, and to compare these properties for different quantities and objects, e.g. this brick is heavier than this feather

- identify certain common shapes, e.g. circle, square, rectangle, triangle and oval

- distinguish between two-dimensional and three-dimensional shapes, e.g. square and cube, and name them correctly

- recognize, create and describe patterns

- explore characteristics of everyday objects and shapes, using mathematical concepts to describe them

- use everyday vocabulary to describe the relationship between shapes, e.g. 'next to', 'in front of', 'behind'

- begin to tell the time by looking at a watch or clock.

What can you do to help?

EVERY DAY

Incorporating the language and concepts of maths into daily life is helpful and relatively easy.

● Count – anything – with your child: How many stairs? How many peas on your plate? How many seconds does it take to brush your hair?

● Reinforce the concept of one more or one less at mealtimes: How many fish fingers will you have if I give you one more? Similarly, with smaller and bigger: Who's got the biggest chip? (Try to avoid Who's got the biggest chip? competitions becoming a nightly ritual. They can quickly become very tedious!)

● Use mathematical language. Most of it will (and should) be incidental, but should prove helpful to your child when faced with mathematical concepts and problems at school.

● Sorting and classifying are important mathematical concepts. Ask your child to 'help' with the laundry: to pair up the socks, put all the blue T-shirts in one pile and the red ones in another and so on.

● Use positional language such as 'above', 'below', 'behind' or 'next to'. Encourage your child to speak in full sentences when explaining where something is: 'The butter is behind the water jug'; 'The remote control is on the shelf under the table'; 'The chocolate is hidden in Mummy's secret place.'

● Beading is an activity that helps children with their fine motor skills and can introduce them to the concept of patterns: two blue beads followed by two red beads, etc. In general, developing your child's fine motor skills is a good idea. A longitudinal survey of 2,700 American school children, following them from kindergarten to eighth grade, discovered that the next best predictor of later academic achievement after size of vocabulary was a child's fine motor skills.[2]

2. E. D. Hirsch, 'Primer on Success: Character and Knowledge Make the Difference', Education Next, Vol. 13, No. 1, winter 2013.

• Baking is a good way to introduce many mathematical concepts – measuring, halving, doubling. You can also get cookie cutters in the shapes that your children will be expected to learn in Reception, such as squares, triangles, oblongs, etc.

GAMES

• Play the Coin Game. It improves memory and sequencing ability as well as attention and concentration – and children enjoy it because it's fast-paced and fun. First, you'll need a small pile of assorted coins, a cardboard sheet to cover them and a stopwatch (or a regular watch with a second hand). Choose five of the coins from the pile, e.g. three one-pence pieces and two five-pence pieces, and put them into a sequence. Now tell your child to look carefully at the coins arranged on the table. Cover the coins with the cardboard, start the stopwatch and ask them to make the same pattern, using the coins from the pile. When they have finished, mark the time with the stopwatch and remove the cardboard cover. Write down the time it took them to complete the pattern and whether or not they were correct. If they didn't complete it correctly, have them keep trying until they do. You can increase the difficulty of the patterns as you go and include more coins of different values. You'll see your child's concentration and sequencing ability improve the more they play.

• Positional language ('above', 'below', 'behind', 'on', etc.) is also part of maths – so Simon Says, or some variation of it, is always a good game to play.

• There's an app called 123 Tracing which helps younger children learn how to do just that by using the touchscreen of a tablet. Your child will be introduced to numbers and shown how to draw them with their finger. The numbers fill the screen, so are suitably large-format, and the tracing points are well laid out.

● Another good app is Wee Kids Math. It has lots of colourful games to teach children about numbers and basic mathematics. Good for children just starting to learn their number shapes and order (0–20), as well as those starting out on addition and subtraction. However, it's a bit babyish for those who've grasped these concepts already.

CAR JOURNEYS

● One very simple game involves getting each of your children to pick an exotic make of car – say, Porsche or Ferrari – and inviting them to predict how many they're likely to see on the rest of the journey. They count them up and, when you reach your destination, the child whose prediction is the most accurate – not the child who's spotted the most – is the winner.

Understanding the World

There aren't subjects called 'geography', 'history' or 'science' in Reception. Instead, your child is likely to start studying all three, as well as RE, under the general heading of 'Understanding the World'. In all likelihood, two or three periods a week will be allocated to it.

Your child will probably spend the morning doing English and maths (as well as having assembly and break and structured play in the classroom). In the afternoons, as well as more play, some time will be set aside to help them reach the goals in the Understanding the World section of the EYFS Framework set out on p. 4, whether through stories, pictures, displays, various collections of bits and pieces or school trips to museums and the like.

How much knowledge your child is taught in Understanding the World will vary from school to school, with some schools focusing on fun activities, such as studying 'mini-beasts' (ants, earwigs, spiders, etc.), and others bringing forward some of the subject matter specified in the national curriculum in geography, history and science.

Typically, the geography and history components of Understanding the World will involve getting your child to talk about their family; making simple maps of their neighbourhoods; beginning to understand seasonal change; distinguishing between the North and South Poles and identifying them on a globe; copying the flags of different countries, including the United Kingdom; learning some rudimentary facts about the British constitution, such as the relationship between the Prime Minister and the monarch; and thinking about different types of transport and how they've changed over time.

The science component will involve your child learning about his or her body, including the names of different body parts and the difference between a healthy and an unhealthy diet; studying the life cycles and habitats of different animals and insects; growing plants and vegetables from seed; and, in all likelihood, being introduced to the rudiments of climate science and the concept of 'sustainability'.

The early learning goals in Understanding the World are as follows:

People and communities

By the end of Reception your child should be able to:

- talk about past and present events in their own lives and in the lives of family members

- appreciate that other children don't always enjoy the same things as they do and be sensitive to this

- understand similarities and differences between themselves and others, and among families, communities and traditions.

The world

By the end of Reception your child should be able to:

- understand similarities and differences in relation to places, objects, materials and living things

- talk about the features of their own immediate environment and how environments might vary

- make observations of animals and plants, explain why some things occur and talk about changes.

Technology

By the end of Reception your child should be able to:

- recognize that a range of technology is used in places such as homes and schools

- select and use different technologies for particular purposes.

What can you do to help?

- Read your child stories set in other countries or cultures and talk about the similarities with and differences to theirs.

- Pretend you're a natural philosopher: collect leaves, sticks and nuts and name them. Draw around leaves or make leaf rubbings (put paper over a robust leaf and gently shade with the flat of a crayon so the 'skeleton' of the leaf shows). Identify different species of plants, trees and wildflowers.

- Most children love animals, so a visit to the zoo or the local pet shop or farm is usually popular and prompts all sorts of observations and questions.

- A good way to learn about the huge variety of different bird species is to play the Royal Society for the Protection of Birds' Bird Bingo. It's beautifully illustrated by Christine Berrie and features sixty-four species of birds from around the world.

- If you live in London – or even if you don't – it's worth making a trip to Kew Gardens. There are plenty of interesting places to explore, such as the greenhouses and the allotments, and the Treetop Walk is both fascinating and completely safe, even for four-year-olds. It also has an excellent children's play area called 'Climbers and Creepers', complete with its own cutting-and-sticking room. To cap it all, the gift shop sells Venus flytraps – guaranteed to fascinate even the most jaded child.

- Buy or make a glass ant farm or wormery and study the creatures inside. Make your child responsible for looking after them and ensuring they don't die. Add other 'mini-beasts', such as caterpillars, and observe what happens. Search 'build an ant farm' on www.wikiHow.com.

● Organize a nature scavenger hunt. If you're going for a country walk, write down a list of things for your child to find on a sheet of A4 – a pine cone, a buttercup, an oak leaf, etc. – and then have them run along in front of you, searching for all the items.

● For a few pounds you can buy a kit that enables your child to power an LED light by inserting some copper and galvanized nails into some lemons. For example: KidzLabs lemon clock and KidzLabs envirobattery.

Expressive Arts and Design

Expressive arts and design, or EAD, covers the whole gamut of 'creative' subjects – art, design, drama, movement and music. Typically, two or three periods a week will be devoted to it.

An example

To give you an idea of the range of things your child will do in EAD over the course of a year, take the following list of activities from a Reception class at a West London primary school:

GETTING STARTED

- Identify the three primary colours
- Distinguish between light and dark versions of the same colour

- Identify the primary colours used in Mondrian's paintings
- Learn how to produce secondary colours by mixing primary colours
- Produce a range of self-portraits, using pencils, pastels, collage, watercolours and poster paint
- Sing along to the 'Funny Faces' song from *The Gruffalo Song and Other Songs*

SCULPTURE

- Study sculpture and other 3D art forms
- Study a range of sculptures by Henry Moore and Degas
- Make a sculpture using salt dough and moulding tools
- Paint the sculpture

CHINESE NEW YEAR

- Study origami
- Find out about the Chinese New Year
- Make an origami dragon
- Study dragon masks used in Chinese New Year celebrations
- Make a dragon mask
- Study dragon dances
- Create and perform a dragon dance

PAINTING

- Explore still-life images in the work of van Gogh, Cézanne, Walton and others

- Observe and draw fruit

- Observe and draw sunflowers

MARY POPPINS

- Study kite design

- Sing 'Let's Go Fly a Kite' from *Mary Poppins*

- Make a kite

- Perform own version of 'Let's Go Fly a Kite'

THE OLYMPICS

- Go on a school trip to the Olympic Park and study the different buildings there

- Design an Olympic stadium

- Create an Olympic Park out of cereal packets and the like ('junk modelling')

- Make a sculpture of a famous Olympian and their equipment, e.g. a canoe

- Study different football kits

- Design a football kit

Early learning goals

EXPLORING AND USING MEDIA AND MATERIALS

By the end of Reception your child should be able to:

- sing songs, make music, dance

- use a variety of materials, tools and techniques in art, sculpture and design

- understand the way colour, design, texture, form and function combine across a variety of different media.

BEING IMAGINATIVE

By the end of Reception your child should be able to:

- use what they've learnt about media and materials in original ways, thinking about uses and purposes

- represent their own ideas, thoughts and feelings through design and technology, art, music, dance, role play and stories.

What can you do to help?

● You'll probably already have an 'arts and crafts' cupboard at home containing paints, glue, children's scissors, coloured card, glitter, beads, etc., so you don't need any advice from us on this front. But it's worth bearing in mind that lots of galleries and museums set aside rooms for children to do cutting-and-sticking activities, with most of them providing expert advice from dedicated helpers. For instance, the Fleet Air Arm Museum in Somerset – definitely worth a detour if you're motoring along the A303 – has an area where children can design and make their own paper aeroplanes and see whose can fly the furthest. In London, the Tate Modern and the Royal Academy, among many others, have regular children's activities. Wherever you live, there'll be a museum or gallery somewhere near that will set aside some time (or space) for children. A great resource for finding galleries and collections near you (and other stuff, too) is the Arts Council website artuk.org.

● Art galleries and exhibitions can be a bit of a trial with a young child, but there are things you can do to make it fun. Instead of waiting until the end to buy half a dozen postcards, buy them at the beginning, hand them to your child and tell them they have sixty minutes to find all six of the pictures on the cards. If you have more than one child, turn it into a competition.

● Colouring in may strike your child as a bit babyish, but there are colouring-in books and then there's *Art Masterpieces to Colour: 60 Great Paintings from Botticelli to Picasso* by Marty Noble. Your child can colour in the black-and-white line renderings of these sixty masterpieces, using crayons, felt-tip pens, watercolours, acrylic paint . . . whatever they like. The originals are reproduced at the front so if your child wants to copy the paintings they can do that, too. Colouring in is not the waste of time it often appears to be to adults. It develops fine motor skills, improves focus and concentration and can help fix a picture in a child's memory.

● Children love construction toys and there's no reason to confine yourself to Lego. For the traditionalists among you, Meccano is still going strong (though mums and dads will have to lend a hand) and for those who want to try something new there's K'nex. K'nex requires a bit more patience than Lego, but the cars, helicopters, robots, etc., you can build are robust and beautiful and look like proper design prototypes.

Reading List

There are so many wonderful books to read to your Reception-age child that it's hard to know where to start. Your child will quickly form favourites and ask for them to be read over and over and over again. You will be happier to oblige with some than others. (The Thomas and Friends books are almost supernaturally dull and the message of each one is 'know your place', but children love them.) The illustrations can be as important as the text at this stage. If you get fed up with the books you own, go to the local library as often as you can. Your child will enjoy picking books out to borrow, although they're usually very bad judges, so you'll have to master the art of 'losing' their choices on the way to the librarian's desk. Here are some that our children have liked (divided into the EYFS subject areas for Reception but otherwise in no particular order), but there are plenty more.

English

Peter Rabbit books by Beatrix Potter
Mr Men and Little Miss books by Roger Hargreaves
Olivia books by Ian Falconer
Noddy books by Enid Blyton
Mog books by Judith Kerr
Thomas and Friends books based on the Railway Series by the Revd W. Awdry
Elmer stories by David McKee

Hairy Maclary books by Lynley Dodd
Peepo by Allan & Janet Ahlberg
Beware of the Storybook Wolves by Lauren Child
The Story of Ferdinand by Munro Leaf
The Jolly Postman by Allan & Janet Ahlberg
Funnybones by Allan & Janet Ahlberg
Each Peach Pear Plum by Allan & Janet Ahlberg
The Ghost Train by Allan Ahlberg & Andre Amstutz
A Balloon for Grandad by Nigel Gray
Avocado Baby by John Burningham
Mr Gumpy's Outing by John Burningham
A Dark, Dark Tale by Ruth Brown
Giraffes Can't Dance by Giles Andreae & Guy Parker-Rees
Rover by Michael Rosen
Little Rabbit Foo Foo by Michael Rosen
We're Going on a Bear Hunt by Michael Rosen
The Pigeon Finds a Hot Dog! by Mo Willems
Don't Let the Pigeon Drive the Bus! by Mo Willems
Lost and Found by Oliver Jeffers
The Tiger Who Came to Tea by Judith Kerr
The Cat in the Hat by Dr. Seuss
Going to School: Usborne First Experiences
A Walk around a School by Sally Hewitt
My Favourite Nursery Rhymes by Tony Ross
The Very Hungry Caterpillar by Eric Carle
The Gruffalo by Julia Donaldson & Axel Scheffler
A Squash and a Squeeze by Julia Donaldson & Axel
    Scheffler
Stick Man by Julia Donaldson & Axel Scheffler
Monkey Puzzle by Julia Donaldson & Axel Scheffler
Peace at Last by Jill Murphy
Zagazoo by Quentin Blake
All Join In by Quentin Blake
Babar by Jean de Brunhoff

Where the Wild Things Are by Maurice Sendak
Dear Zoo by Rod Campbell
Harold and the Purple Crayon by Crockett Johnson
Goodnight Moon by Margaret Wise Brown
The Enormous Crocodile by Roald Dahl
Father Christmas by Raymond Briggs
The Snowman by Raymond Briggs
Rosie's Walk by Pat Hutchins
Owl Babies by Martin Waddell & Patrick Benson
What Do People Do All Day? by Richard Scarry
There was an Old Lady Who Swallowed a Fly by Pam Adams
Tinga Tinga Tales by Claudia Lloyd
Operation Alphabet by Al MacCuish & Luciano Lozano
The Enormous Turnip by Alexei Tolstoy

Maths

Ten Monkey Jamboree by Dianne Ochiltree
How Many Sharks in the Bath? by Bill Gillham
Five Little Monkeys by Zita Newcome
Read and Learn: Finding Shapes
Reading Roundabout: My Money by Paul Humphrey

Understanding the World

The See Inside series of Usborne flap books
My First Book of Bugs and Spiders: TickTock Books
Come and Play with Us: Oxfam
Come and Ride with Us: Oxfam
Come and Eat with Us: Oxfam
Come Home with Us: Oxfam

Expressive Arts and Design

Amazing Art Attack Stuff by N. Buchanan
A Year in Art: The Activity Book by C. Weidemann
I Spy Colours in Art by L. Micklethwait
Looking at Pictures: An Introduction to Art for Young People
  through the National Gallery Collection by J. Richardson

Reports and Assessment

Reports and How to Translate Them

In every academic year you'll probably receive one long report with detail about your child's progress and attainment (two different things) in every subject, usually at the end of the summer term. You may also get a short, tick-box sort of affair as an interim measure midway through the year. When you receive a report, there'll be an accompanying letter inviting you to make an appointment with the school if you want to discuss anything. In addition, schools hold at least one parents' evening a year, though these are usually before they send out the school reports.

The comments in the long report are where the teacher has the opportunity to show you how well they know your child. Every school has a carefully thought-through policy on report writing – what should and shouldn't be included, how much needs to be written, whether teachers can copy and paste from a 'comment bank', whether negative comments are helpful or not, etc. – and these policies will vary.

Schools will also differ on the information they deem useful for parents, such as whether to include your child's reading age and the results of non-statutory tests your child may have taken, for instance, NFER tests.[1]

All schools are statutorily obliged to produce an EYFS profile at the end of Reception. It was supposed to become optional in 2016, but it didn't. The EYFS Framework is statutory and Ofsted will continue to refer to it when assessing your child's school. In addition, your child will do a phonics check in Year 1 and various 'national curriculum tasks and tests' in Years 2 and 6 (more on these tests below). How much additional testing schools do and what tests they use will differ, but it's a safe bet that the school will accumulate more data about your child than it will share with you. There's nothing sinister about this; it would be impractical to pass on the results every time a school carries out an assessment because it happens so frequently and, for the most part, the data are recorded in a technical format that non-teachers wouldn't be able to decipher. (Even some teachers have difficulty under-standing it.) If you want to see all the data a school has on your child you can submit a 'subject access' request to the school and the governing body must ensure that the data is made available for you to view within fifteen days. If you would like a copy of the data, you can request that, too, and the governing body has to provide that within fifteen days as well. Governing bodies can charge for copies, but it must be at cost.[2]

Before the current national curriculum came into effect in 2014, primary school teachers were obliged to assign every child a national curriculum level in English,

1. National Foundation for Educational Research: reading and maths tests for children in Years 3, 4 and 5.
2. For more information on how to do this, see http://schoolrecords. wordpress.com.

maths and science at the end of each Key Stage, with all children expected to have reached level 2 by the end of Key Stage 1 and level 4 by the end of Key Stage 2. (They didn't just base this on test results, but on classwork and homework as well.) Each level was subdivided into 'a', 'b' and 'c', with 'a' being the highest and 'c' the lowest. (These were known as 'sublevels'.) The expected levels across all subjects for each year group were as follows:

Year 1	Year 2	Year 3	Year 4	Year 5	Year 6
1b	2b	2a/3c	3b	3a/4c	4b

Ofsted inspectors used these levels when judging how well schools were doing, with all the children in the school expected to progress between one and two levels in Key Stage 1, and two levels in Key Stage 2. If you have a child at primary school, you may be used to seeing these levels, because some teachers use the same combination of numbers and letters on school reports to indicate how your child is doing – if not in each subject, then possibly in English and maths.

Since the introduction of the current national curriculum in 2014, which is not linked to these levels, most schools have stopped using them and moved to their own assessment methods. The exact form the assessment takes will vary from school to school, depending on how they're choosing to teach the national curriculum. Hopefully, your school will decode its assessment method for you before passing on any information about how your child is doing.

All children at taxpayer-funded primary schools, including academies and free schools, will do national curriculum tasks and tests in Year 2 and towards the end of Year 6 – what used to be called 'SATs' (Standardized Assessment Tasks) and in many schools still are. (The Year 2 tests may be phased out in due course.) The performance of all primary school children in England in the Key Stage 2 tests will be recorded in the school league tables and, for the most part, passed on to the secondary schools they go to in a 'common transfer file'. (Some schools also pass on your child's results in the Key Stage 1 tests.) If the secondary school in question has setting or streaming in Year 7, your child's results may affect what set or stream they're put in, but that may also be affected by their performance in a different test that the secondary school will set within your child's first week or so. Key Stage 2 data will also be used to calculate a secondary school's Progress 8 data – a measure of how much progress children make that's calculated by comparing their Key Stage 2 results with their GCSE results in eight subjects.

Some information about progress and attainment in your school will be available online. Schools are obliged to put their most recent Ofsted reports on their website, and you can see where your primary sits in the league tables by entering the name of the school on www.gov.uk/school-performance-tables.

Statutory Reports, Tasks and Tests

Examples of Key Stage 1 and Key Stage 2 tests can be found at www.gov.uk/government/collections/national-curriculum-assessments-practice-materials (or Google 'sample SATs papers').

Reception: baseline tests – currently on hold

In September 2016, the Department for Education was due to roll out some national tests for Reception-aged children in England. The purpose of these 'baseline tests' was to assess each child's level of development at the beginning of their formal schooling so it would be possible to measure how much progress they've made when they're tested again at the end of their primary school education. However, these particular tests have been abandoned and may be replaced by another test in Reception, pending the outcome of a consultation.

Reception: EYFS profile

This profile summarizes and describes your child's attainment at the end of the EYFS (i.e. at the end of Reception) with respect to seventeen Early Learning Goals (ELGs), with your child assessed according to whether they're 'emerging', 'expected' or 'exceeding' in each category. (You can ask to see this profile – and if you do schools are obliged to show it to you – but it's not normally given to parents.) Each goal relates to one of the seventeen elements of the 'Seven Areas' in the table on pp. 2–3. (They encompass the subdivisions of the three prime areas of learning: Personal, Social and Emotional Development (PSED); Communication and Language; and Physical Development; and the four specific areas of learning: literacy; mathematics; understanding the world; and expressive arts and design.) We refer to these goals in the various sections of the Reception chapter.

The profile also includes a narrative on how your child demonstrates the three characteristics of effective learning: playing and exploring (how they investigate and experience things, and 'have a go'); active learning (how well they concentrate and keep persevering if they encounter difficulties); and creating and thinking critically (how they develop their own ideas, make links between ideas and develop strategies for doing things).

Year 1: Phonics check

This check will take place in June and is designed to assess your child's phonics knowledge. It consists of a list of forty words, half real and half not, which your child will be asked to read to a teacher. The purpose of including nonsense words, e.g. 'vap', 'pim', 'jound', is that your child won't have seen them before and therefore won't be able to read them using their memory or vocabulary. Instead, they'll have to use their decoding skills.

Administering the test usually takes between four and nine minutes per child. If your child struggles to answer the questions, the teacher will stop the test. It's designed not to be stressful. Your child will have done similar tests before and, in all likelihood, they won't realize they're being 'tested'. (The Department for Education insists on calling it a 'check' rather than a 'test'.)

The school should tell you how your child has performed in the phonics check, informing you of their score out of forty and whether or not they have met the standard. If your child has found the test difficult, the school will probably put various 'interventions' in place to support them, such as one-to-one tuition or small-group work, and tell you what you can do at home to help. Children who have not met the standard in Year 1 will retake the test in Year 2.

Year 2: Key Stage 1 tests

At present, the Key Stage 1 tasks and tests can be done at any point in Year 2, but they are usually done in May. Your child will do a task or test in reading, in maths and in spelling, punctuation and grammar. Your child's teacher is obliged to assess how your child is doing in reading, writing, maths, speaking and listening and science, and these tests are designed to help the teacher make this assessment. Often, children aren't aware they're being tested as the 'test' consists of being asked to perform a task in the course of a normal lesson. The results of the tasks and tests inform a teacher's overall assessment in each subject.

Although the tests are set externally, they are marked by teachers within the school. Instead of the old national curriculum levels, children are given a scaled score. Their raw score – the actual number of marks they get – is translated into a scaled score, where a score of 100 means the child is working at the expected standard. A score below 100 indicates that the child needs more support, whereas a score of above 100 suggests the child is working at a higher level than expected for their age. The maximum score possible is 115 and the minimum is 85.

Teacher assessments are also used to build up a picture of your child's learning and achievements. In addition, your child will receive an overall result saying whether they have achieved the required standard in the tests (your child's actual results won't be communicated to you unless you ask for them). The Department for Education wants 85 per cent of children in each primary to reach the expected standard, a higher standard than was expected before 2016.

Schools are obliged to pass on these assessments to

their local authorities, but they're not obliged to pass them on to secondary schools in your child's 'common transfer file'. Some will; some won't. Whether the school passes on all or some of this information to parents will vary – many will just give an aggregate grade in English, maths and science – but parents must be provided with *all* of this data on request.

In March 2017, the Secretary of State announced that the Department for Education would be holding a consultation on whether the Key Stage 1 tests should be abandoned in favour of a newly designed baseline test in Reception. However, if the tests are scrapped it's unlikely to be before 2024.

Year 6: Key Stage 2 tests

Key Stage 2 tasks and tests are taken over the best part of a week in mid-May when your child is in Year 6. The tests were overhauled in May 2016, and were sat by the first Year 6 cohort in June of that year.

They consist of three papers in English and three in maths. The English papers are a forty-five-minute grammar and punctuation test, a fifteen-minute aural spelling test of fifteen words, and a one-hour reading test comprising a single paper with questions based on three passages of text. The maths tests consist of two forty-minute reasoning papers and a thirty-minute arithmetic paper in which children will answer questions involving addition, subtraction, multiplication and division.

Finally, some schools are selected to take part in a 'sampling test' in science in Year 6. This consists of three papers of approximately twenty-five minutes each. These aren't usually taken by everyone in your child's class and the children who are asked to take them will be selected at random. The results are fully anonymized, so no one will ever know how your child does. The results will not be used in the school league tables and won't be passed on to schools or parents.

As in KS1, your child will be given a raw score – the actual number of marks they get – which is translated into a scaled score, where a score of 100 means the child is working at the expected standard. A score below 100 indicates that the child needs more support, whereas a score of above 100 suggests the child is working at a higher level than expected for their age. The maximum score possible is 115 and the minimum is 85.

What can you do to help?

Don't get too worked up about all this testing. In most schools, the big push will be at the end of Key Stage 2, because your child's performance in those tests affects the school's standing in the league tables. Your child will be asked to do practice papers at school from the beginning of January and, in some cases, will be given them as homework. If that happens, you'll have to decide how much help to give them, bearing in mind that they aren't supposed to have help when they do the tests for real, although some schools bend the rules a bit. There's no reason for your child to get stressed out about them because they won't have much impact on their future and won't affect whether your child gets into a particular secondary school. On the other hand, you might not want to tell your child that if they're not taking the tests seriously enough.

Some comprehensives, academies and free schools have 'fair banding' admission arrangements whereby all the applicants are sorted into different bands according to ability. Typically, the top 25 per cent are placed in the top band, the middle 50 per cent in the middle band and the bottom 25 per cent in the bottom band. The school then applies its oversubscription criteria to each band, making sure it ends up with a mix of children from across the ability spectrum. However, the band your child is placed in isn't related to how they do in their Key Stage 2 tests – not least because the fair-banding 'sorting hat' spins its magic long before those tests are taken. It's determined by how your child performs in a dedicated test they'll be asked to do at the school in question, usually in November of Year 6. For academically selective schools, whether grammar or independent, your child will have to take a separate test, usually referred to as 'Common Entrance' or 'the 11+'.

Year 1

Introduction

The start of Year 1 should be an exciting time for your child. They should have none of the nerves that may have accompanied their start in Reception and will probably be pleased to be back with their class, telling stories of their summer exploits. In Reception they may well have been taught by a phonics specialist, but their Year 1 teacher is likely to be more of a generalist because, by now, they should have mastered the basics of phonics and be on their way to becoming a proficient reader. For most primaries, Year 1 is when your child will embark upon the national curriculum.

English

The overarching aim in English in the national curriculum is, not surprisingly, to promote high standards of language and literacy. There is a strong emphasis on children's spoken language, reflecting a determination to improve standards of verbal communication. Spoken language also underpins the development of reading and writing. The quality and variety of language that pupils hear and speak is vital for developing their vocabulary and grammar and their understanding for reading and writing. Spoken language is not formally taught in any one lesson, but rather across the board in all aspects of school life. In the current national curriculum there is a requirement for children to learn and recite some poetry by heart.

The English curriculum is divided into reading and writing. Reading is further subdivided into word reading (what we think of as reading) and comprehension (understanding what you have read). Writing is subdivided into transcription (spelling and handwriting), composition and, finally, vocabulary, grammar and punctuation.

To summarize:

- Reading = word reading; comprehension

- Writing = transcription (spelling and handwriting); composition; vocabulary, grammar and punctuation

We will tackle each of these subdivisions, explain what sort of thing your child will be doing and how you can help, with the exception of the last, which we've dealt with in 'Grammar and Punctuation' on p. 375. (For the 'Purpose of Study' and 'Aims' of the English curriculum, see p. 458.)

Reading

Children arrive in Year 1 with a year's worth of phonics learnt in Reception under their belt. They build on this now, learning to read sentences and books, and they need to be helped to understand what they've read. Comprehension is a term that covers much more than the meaning of the individual words. For instance, your child will learn to identify which words in a passage tell them that the man is angry or that the fly escaped from the frog.

WORD READING

By the end of Year 1 all children should be able to read aloud those books that are consistent with their developing phonic knowledge, as well as some common exception words (i.e. the many that aren't spelt phonetically, such as 'who'). They should be able to recognize all forty-plus phonemes (including as examples 'sh', 'igh', 'ing') and be able to cope with endings such as '-ed', '-er' and '-est'.

Building on work in Reception, children in Year 1 will continue to sound out phonemes and blend together the sounds to form different words, in more and more new combinations. As an example, your child will start by making the word 'cat' from the sounds 'c', 'a' and 't', and then move on to making the words 'high' and 'shore' from 'h' and 'igh' and 'sh' and 'ore' respectively. So although your child may instantly recognize many familiar words, they can now begin to decipher lots of new words using their grasp of grapheme-phoneme correspondences (which groups of letters represent which sounds). They don't have to rely on guesswork. Your child will be encouraged to progress from doing this out loud to blending phonemes silently in their head, and will be given plenty of extra practice if they find this hard.

All schools send children home with reading books at

an appropriate level, depending on how far they've progressed within the school's particular phonics scheme. How often these are changed varies from school to school. Almost all schools follow one or two reading schemes, so competitive parents and children have a pretty good feel for where their child comes in the reading pecking order because the books have clearly marked levels. Children read aloud from their current book on a one-to-one basis with the teacher or teaching assistant at least once a week and in some schools more often.

Some children will progress to 'chapter books' by the end of the year (as distinct from shorter, heavily illustrated books), and will therefore no longer be dependent on pictures to keep their attention and help them to guess words they're finding hard to decode. This is not to suggest there's anything wrong with illustrations – as motivators and discussion points, they're not to be sniffed at. Some children may even be promoted to 'free readers', able to choose a book they fancy from the class bookcase or school library rather than being offered the next one in the reading scheme. Huge kudos attaches to reaching this starry level. In a typical Year 1 class of thirty there will be about five free readers by the end of the year.

The class will listen to stories and longer books read by the teacher throughout the year.

Those who start the year a bit behind in reading will listen to and discuss the same books as the rest of the class in the hope that their vocabulary and grammar will continue to develop at the right level. Expect them to be given extra attention to get them up to speed.

What can you do to help?

● Read with your child every day, if at all possible. Show an interest in the book in their book bag. Fake enthusiasm for the next in the series. (Never easy, particularly with the Oxford Reading Tree books, although things do look up once the 'magic key' starts glowing.) Go to the parent–teacher events when the teacher explains how they teach reading, so you understand and don't make errors such as calling letters by their names rather than the phonic sound they make before your child is ready. Write comments in the 'reading record' – there'll be one of those in the book bag, too – so the teacher knows you're doing your part and your child sees that you're taking it seriously.

● Be endlessly patient and encouraging. Say things like, 'Oh, I love that page, can we have it again?' and 'How have you got so good at this?' Bribe them if necessary. Make it so that having to read their reading book with you every day is non-negotiable, absolutely normal, not a punishment, just a part of life. Most children relish the one-to-one attention.

● Correcting mistakes is a bit of a minefield. It's hard to judge how quickly to jump in with the word they're struggling over, when to insist on accuracy, how often to remind them to pause after commas – and to pause for even longer after full stops. (Again, a working knowledge of how they are taught phonics helps.) Even experienced readers-with-children find it hard to be consistent as it's important to take the child's mood into account. It's always good to get the child to change their voice when different characters are speaking – it's more fun and helps with comprehension.

● When is the best time to read with your child? Children are often tired after a hectic school day, so it's usually better to let them unwind with some TV/screen time or by kicking a ball around before getting them to sit still and concentrate. However, for the very unwilling reader it's often better to treat the reading as an immediate extension of the school day – we've known parents who tackle the task in the car outside the school to get it done before the tempting distractions of home arise. Others swear by the early-morning post-breakfast slot. If at home, be in a quiet room alone with the child, with the carrot of the TV programme or playground to come once the dreaded task is over. Don't leave it until bedtime. Having said that, all bets are off if your child volunteers to read to you. If they do that, drop everything and sit down with them, regardless of what time of day it is.

● Encourage your child to look at writing everywhere – the sides of buses, on advertising hoardings, signposts, McDonald's. Play 'I bet you can read at least two words on that bus,' or 'What's in this aisle of the supermarket?'

● Give your child a highlighter and ask them to circle twenty instances of the word 'the' in a newspaper article (or just ten if they can't count to twenty yet). Ask if they can do it in the time it takes you to finish some task, like sewing on a name tag, or in a race with a friend/sibling.

COMPREHENSION

In Year 1 children are expected to develop pleasure in reading, motivation to read, vocabulary and understanding. They should learn to appreciate rhymes and poems and to recite some by heart. They should be taught to understand both the books they can read and those that are read to them. Ideally, they should be able to check that the text makes sense to them as they read and correct their own inaccurate reading. They should learn to discuss the significance of the title and events and predict what might happen next in a story on the basis of what's happened so far.

A lot of time in Year 1 is spent listening to books being read by the teacher with the obvious benefits for your child of extending their vocabulary and beginning to understand how written language can be structured. For instance, they should start to appreciate how a surprise can be used in a story for dramatic impact or how the facts are presented in a piece of non-fiction, with the author using slightly more formal language.

What can you do to help?

- Read to your child, often, from a wide variety of sources – stories, poems, cereal packets . . . anything. Ask their opinion: 'What's going to happen next?' 'Who is your favourite character?' 'Why?' When they read to you, it's often clear that they are concentrating so hard on decoding the words that they haven't taken in the meaning of the text. As we said in 'Word reading', ask them to repeat sentences in the voice of the character once they've worked out the words and their meaning. Encourage them to do it by doing it yourself, exaggerating the different accents to make them laugh. This encourages them to keep going and improves their comprehension.

- Learn a funny poem together. Let your child choose one and let them see you trying to learn it alongside them. And don't just correct them when they can't remember it perfectly – get them to correct you, too.

Writing

This usually develops more slowly than reading because children have to concentrate first on turning the sound into the right letter or combination of letters, then on physically mastering the pencil, and then on remembering what they want to write next. Children this age can be surprisingly forgetful. Any time spent in a class of Year 1 children includes agonizing stretches of silence while they try to remember what they were so itching to say when they raised their hand as high as they could and squirmed with desire to be picked. The same happens when they sit down to write. They practise planning a whole sentence before starting to write, but find it really hard to remember what the end was going to be once they've got the first few words down.

TRANSCRIPTION

a) Spelling

In Year 1 children learn to spell simple words, name the letters of the alphabet in order and write from memory simple sentences dictated by the teacher.

Spelling is harder than reading because the phoneme-grapheme correspondences which underpin spelling are more variable than the grapheme-phoneme correspondences which underpin reading. If this makes little sense to you, it's because you didn't concentrate hard enough when reading 'Learning to Read and Write: A Short Guide to Phonics' (see p. 11). Tsk, tsk.

For example, when a child reads the word 'tr-ai-n', it could only be 'train', but several different graphemes (letters required to make a sound) could be used to make the blend of phonemes (sounds) in 'train'. It could be spelt 'trane', or even 'trayn', as far as a new reader is concerned. There's no way around this – spelling has to be learnt. There's plenty of evidence to show that the more a person reads, the better they become at spelling, because wrongly spelt words look wrong if you're subliminally familiar with the correct versions.

b) Handwriting

In Year 1 children learn to sit correctly at a table holding a pencil comfortably and correctly, form lower-case letters in the correct direction, form capital letters and form the digits 0–9. (See the Appendix 'How to Form the Letters of the Alphabet' on p. 473 for the correct way to write the different letters.)

Handwriting needs one-to-one attention. Given the pupil–teacher ratio in any class, it's obvious that practice at home will help, but it's important that the helpful adult knows how the school likes it to be done, so do check the handwriting guide in the Appendix on p. 473, which most primaries will follow. It's also important to make sure your child is using a pencil or pen that isn't too big and is holding it correctly. Handwriting cannot be practised enough, but the line between encouraging accuracy and giving free rein to any form of written expression is hard to judge. Remember that boys' fine motor skills tend to develop later than girls'.

If your child is left-handed bear in mind that it is harder for them: the arm is coming in towards the body rather than moving away, and this is more work. Left-handed children who are taught how to write with their left hand (rather than just allowed to do so, unsupervised) won't develop a needlessly uncomfortable, inefficient, slow or messy way of writing that could be a lifelong hardship. So it is especially important for parents and teachers to understand how to teach left-handed children to write correctly. The position of the writing paper, that of the arm and wrist, and the grip on the writing instrument are all important. There are lots of helpful books (try *Improve Your Handwriting* by Rosemary Sassoon). Left-handed children, once they're using pens, may benefit from pens specially designed for them.

COMPOSITION

In Year 1 children learn to say out loud what they are going to write about, compose a sentence orally before writing it, put sentences in a sequence that forms a short narrative, reread what they've written to check that it makes sense, discuss what they've written with the teacher or other pupils and read aloud their writing clearly enough to be heard by others.

Some children give the impression of being born able to hold a pencil the right way. They are the lucky ones for whom the physical act of handwriting comes easily. They have less of a dread of writing and so often seem, initially, to be the best at composition. But once basic mastery of pen-to-paper has been achieved, most children love writing (unless there is pressure for it to be neat or correctly spelt). As a parent it is vital to perfect the art of interpreting crazy versions of phonetic spelling in order to appreciate the brilliance of your child's jottings. 'What on earth is this meant to say?' is an unhelpful, confidence-knocking question. All writing should be encouraged – stories, diaries, shopping lists – and, at this early stage, be aware that even the occasional gentle spelling tip can be off-putting. Having said that, reminders about full stops, capital letters and question marks are generally helpful because an enormous amount of nagging is required before the message sinks in (hopefully by the end of Year 3). You might as well help the teacher by starting early.

What can you do to help?

To some children, the invitation to write a story – 'Anything you like, literally *anything*' – is thrilling. They start young and in one form or another keep at it for years. A pristine new notebook is there to be written in (often abandoned soon after, but never mind). Others find it a chore, and you need to come up with some ruses. Here are some ideas:

● Spy games often result in carefully folded bits of paper with secret notes, secret rules and secret codes written on them.

● Children enjoy writing lists, such as their most-yearned-for toys, favourite meals they wish they could have that week and presents they'd like to get for Christmas or their next birthday.

- If your child has done a drawing, ask them to add their name and a title, like a proper artist.

- Make a book. Staple together a few small pages and rule some lines on each page. Get your child to draw an illustration and below it write a sentence or two on each page, creating the perfect present for a grandparent or a friend. Get them to decorate the front with glitter/stickers as an added incentive.

- Ask them to write something funny in the condensation on the car or bathroom window.

Maths

Mathematics is essential to everyday life, critical to science, technology and engineering, and necessary for financial literacy and most forms of employment. A high-quality mathematics education therefore provides a foundation for understanding the world, the ability to reason mathematically, an appreciation of the beauty and power of mathematics, and a sense of enjoyment and curiosity about the subject.

Your child should be fluent in the fundamentals of mathematics by the time he or she leaves primary school. All too often, children hear adults happily affirming that they have always been really bad at maths and that they hated it at school. Don't do this! Your child will pick up a message that it's fine to be bad at maths, even a source of pride. It's not fine at all – a facility for dealing with numbers is an essential skill. If children are made to feel at home with the conventions and procedures of mathematics at an early age there is no reason for any anxiety about the subject to arise. To make them feel comfortable, they need lots of lively exposure to mathematics and lots of practice. In primary school your child will have a maths lesson every day.

Maths is more than adding, subtracting, times tables and fractions. It covers concepts of shape and position, pattern recognition, measurement of time as well as space, and problem solving. Many schools don't refer to 'maths', but use the word 'numeracy', and call a one-hour maths lesson 'numeracy hour'.

The principal focus of maths teaching in Key Stage 1 is to ensure that pupils develop confidence and mental fluency with whole numbers, counting and place value (the value a digit has depends on whether it is in the place for units, tens, or hundreds, etc.). They will work with numerals, words, the four operations (add, subtract, multiply, divide), shapes and measuring tools.

Maths is taught in a very different way to how we learnt it at school. Some schools offer 'Maths for Parents' evenings and will invite an expert (or a class teacher) to teach parents how their children are going to be taught and these are really worth attending. Ask your school to lay one on if they don't already.

The national curriculum sets out what your child should learn in Year 1 under the various headings below. (For the 'Purpose of Study' and 'Aims' of the maths curriculum, see p. 459.)

Number and place value

Your child should learn to count up to 100 (forwards and backwards, beginning with any given number) and to read and write numbers from 0 to 100 in numerals and 1 to

20 in words. They will learn to count in multiples of 2s, 5s and 10s. They should be able to identify one more and one less than a given number. They will be taught to identify and represent numbers using objects (such as pencils or coins) and to use a number line (a horizontal line with, say, 1 to 20 written in numbers at even spaces from left to right), a useful tool for helping to add and subtract.

Addition, subtraction, multiplication and division

Your child should learn to read, write and interpret mathematical statements involving addition (+), subtraction (−) and equals (=) signs, to add and subtract one-digit and two-digit numbers up to 20, including 0, to solve one-step problems that involve addition and subtraction, using objects and pictorial representations, and work out missing-number problems such as $7 = ? - 9$.

Your child will learn to represent and use 'number bonds' and related subtraction 'facts' (such as $7 - 2 = 5$) for numbers which add up to a number between 1 and 20.

A 'number bond' (sometimes alternatively called an 'addition fact') is a simple addition sum which has become so familiar that a child can recognize it and complete it almost instantly, in the same way they soon will with times tables. For example, $5 + 2 = 7$. A child who knows this number bond should be able immediately to fill in any one of these three numbers if it were missing and they were given the other two, without having to work it out.

Number bonds are often learnt in sets for which the sum is a common round number such as 10 or 20. The most vital set to master as early as possible is the pairs that add up to ten. Having acquired some familiar number bonds, children should also soon learn how to use them to develop strategies to complete more complicated sums, for instance, by navigating from a new sum to an adjacent number bond they know, i.e. $5 + 2$ and $4 + 3$ are both number bonds that make 7; or by strategies such as 'making 10', for example, recognizing that $7 + 6$ is the same as $7 + (3 + 3)$, which is the same as $(7 + 3) + 3$, which is the same as $10 + 3 = 13$. A child who fails to memorize a set of number bonds at an early stage in primary school may later struggle to achieve accuracy and efficiency in computation.

A child should learn new vocabulary including 'put together', 'add', 'altogether', 'total', 'take away', 'distance between', 'difference between', 'more than' and 'less than'.

Through grouping and sharing small quantities, your child will begin to understand multiplication and division, doubling numbers and quantities (of water, say, or sugar) and how to work out simple fractions of objects, numbers and quantities.

Fractions

Your child should learn the meaning of 'half' and 'quarter' as fractions of discrete quantities (a handful of sweets) and continuous quantities (a jug of water) by using shapes, objects and quantities. They are likely to connect halves and quarters to the equal sharing (into two or four parts) of sets of objects (sweets) and to measures (water), as well as recognizing and combining halves and quarters as parts of a whole.

Measurement

Children will deal with length, mass, volume and time. They will probably start by comparing (longer/shorter, heavier/lighter, etc.) and move on to measuring and recording. This will be using non-standard units at first, e.g. the number of cups of sand it takes to fill the bucket, and then, in order to become familiar with standard measures, they will begin to use measuring tools, such as a ruler or weighing scales. (For the pedants among you, the pairs of terms 'mass' and 'weight', and 'volume' and 'capacity', are used interchangeably at this stage.)

Your child will start to use the language of time, including telling the time throughout the day, first using 'o'clock' and then 'half past'.

Geometry

Your child should learn to recognize and name rectangles (including squares), circles and triangles, cuboids (including cubes), pyramids and spheres.

They should use the language of position, direction and motion, including 'left' and 'right', 'top', 'middle' and 'bottom', etc. They will probably learn to make whole, half, quarter and three-quarter turns in both directions and connect the expression 'turning clockwise' with the movement a hand makes around a clock.

Is that all?

No. The paragraphs above cover what all children are supposed to learn according to the national curriculum. The fact that hexagons are not mentioned doesn't mean children won't be able to describe a hexagon, recognize one or spell the word. Many children in Year 1 will be able to count beyond 100 and some will be able to perform prodigious feats of mental arithmetic.

What can you do to help?

- There's a lot you can do to help your child get off to a flying start. There is fun to be had playing games to do with pattern recognition, sorting of objects and awareness of shape which your child won't necessarily think of as 'maths'. You can (and probably do) use the language of maths often in everyday life. Encourage comparison language, e.g. 'I'm shorter than Dad'; 'This bag is heavier than that one', and make sure your child completes the sentence ('heavier than', rather than just 'heavier'). There are endless opportunities to count up and down and in 2s, etc.

- Shape Lucky Dip. Cut squares, rectangles, circles and triangles of various sizes from card. Put them in a paper bag. Get your child to plunge their hand in, pick a shape and, just by feeling it, tell you what it is. Then ask them to take it out to see if they're right. Or you could ask your child to find you a particular shape and they then have to put their hand in and try and pull out the right one just by feeling around. Extend to pentagons, hexagons, etc.

- Pattern Trains. Use building blocks to make a pattern in a long line, e.g. big brick, little brick, and ask your child to continue the pattern. Extend to, for example, big-big-little-big-big-little. Use whatever is at hand – poker chips of different colours, coins, beads, pasta of various shapes, etc. Ask your child to invent patterns for you to continue. (This could become quite addictive at a very high level – it's a classic IQ test.)

- Pelmanism. Make a set of twenty matching pairs of cards with shapes and their names in various colours, place them face-side down on a table and then take turns flipping over a card and finding its partner by memory. If you were to cut some potatoes into shape stamps (cut potato in half, pare away the outer edge of the flat side to leave required shape in relief), and fill a few saucers with paint, children will enjoy making the pairs of shape cards themselves.

● Number-bond Pelmanism. Use a normal pack of cards but only numbers up to, say, 7. Each of you flips over a card, trying to find two different cards that make 7. Say 'snap' when the two cards on show add up to 7. Play again with numbers up to 8, 9 or 10.

● Guess the Number. Fill some plastic sandwich bags with different numbers of buttons, coins, pasta pieces or whatever comes to hand. Ask your child to guess how many are inside, then see if they're right. Your child could reverse the game and fill the bags with amounts they've chosen and recorded and ask you to guess. Lots of opportunity for 'How many more would I need to have 20?' type questions.

● Fruity Fractions. Fruit is great for teaching fractions further up the school but, at this stage, have your child try to cut a banana in half (or to show you where they want you to cut it). They can test their accuracy by using digital weighing scales. Then you can try with quarters, etc.

● How Tall? Stick a height chart on the wall in your child's bedroom and mark their growth every couple of months. Top tip: use centimetres rather than inches; it creates the impression they're growing faster and lots of primary schools don't teach inches until further up the school.

● Kitchen Helpers. Kitchens are full of measuring tools: nests of measuring cups and spoons, measuring cylinders, weighing scales, thermometers, etc. All can be used by children in guessing and measuring games, such as 'Would five cups of water make this jug overflow?' and 'How many apples until the scale says 1 kilogram?' Ask your child to look at the remaining spaces in the muffin tray when you've filled a few and follow with the obvious 'How many more spaces am I going to fill before I run out of mixture?' question.

● Snakes and Ladders. Get your child to count the spaces aloud and call out the number of the square they've landed on. There's lots of opportunity for questions like 'How many squares ahead/behind am I?'

● Numbers and Dots. Make a set of twenty blank cards. Draw from one to twenty large dots on one set (use regular patterns: it's easier that way). Shuffle them. Get your child to count the dots on each card and write that number on a blank card. Now take one set of cards each, you the set with the dots on, your child the set with the numbers on, and play Snap. It'll be slow at first, but you soon get good at recognizing how many dots there are!

● Bingo. Need we elaborate? Create a board with a grid of spaces with a random selection of numbers between 1 and 20 in each. Make a few sets of cards that fit the grid spaces and number them 1 to 20. Get your child to pull these cards out of a hat, read out the number and place it on their grid if they have a space that corresponds. You will be racing your child to fill your grids. Whoever fills their grid first is the winner.

● Adding and subtracting. Once you start looking for opportunities to ask adding or subtracting questions, they come thick and fast. They arise in all the games above. Ask a machine-obsessed child (i.e. a boy) how many tractors you'd need to have 20 big tyres (counting in 2s), or a scooter user how many scooters, etc. For counting in 5s, ask how many fingers in this car, or this room, or this family.

● A good support book for any parent whose child is struggling with maths is *Maths Support Book – Plus 1*. This is the first in a series by www.powerof2.co.uk.

Science

Science teaching in Key Stage 1 is focused on getting children to look more closely at the natural and man-made world around them. No exciting explosions or bubbling vats of chemicals at this stage. Rather, children begin to ask their own questions and recognize scientific ways of answering them. A child needs first-hand experience even to begin to understand the world of plants and animals, or the idea that different materials behave in different ways, or how the seasons vary and why. They need to observe changes over a period of time, be encouraged to notice patterns, to group and classify things and carry out simple comparative tests. They need to get their hands dirty. They will use simple measurements and equipment, e.g. hand lenses, egg timers, to gather data, carry out simple tests and talk about what they have found out and how they found it out. They will also, of course, use books, photographs and videos for the things that can't be brought into the classroom and experienced directly.

The national curriculum organizes the science to be covered in Year 1 under the headings 'Plants', 'Animals (including humans)', 'Everyday materials' and 'Seasonal change'. There is no prescribed order, but for obvious reasons work on plants that involves the children actually growing them tends to be taken on in the summer term. Some teachers will include the science material in Topic, covering other subjects at the same time. For instance, a unit called 'Living and growing' might have a science focus but would involve asking children to write instructions for planting seeds and creating a piece of music that represents a growing plant. Even those primaries that teach science as a stand-alone subject may not allot more than one period a week to it. (For the 'Purpose of Study' and 'Aims' of the science curriculum, see p. 461.)

Plants

Your child will, we hope, be taken out of the classroom to have a look at plants in the local environment so they start to ask and answer questions about plants growing in their habitat. Ideally, they do this throughout the year, but the logistics can be tricky. Teachers will take any opportunity – a weekly trip to a sports facility or park, or an organized school trip – to point out seasonal changes in plants. They will ask children to bring samples for study into the classroom.

Where possible, your child will grow their own flowers and vegetables (sunflowers are always a favourite, cress is nice and fast, and broad beans have good roots to watch). Some lucky children in rural areas often get a whole vegetable patch in their school garden and compete over the quality of their produce. One way or another, your child will observe plant growth and take some rudimentary measurements.

They should become familiar with the common names of flowers, examples of deciduous and evergreen trees, and plant structures (including leaves, flowers, petals, fruit, roots, bulb, seed, trunk, branches and stem).

Your child might work scientifically by, among other things, observing closely, perhaps using magnifying glasses, and comparing and contrasting familiar plants. Or by describing how they were able to identify and group the plants and drawing diagrams showing the parts of different specimens (including trees). They might keep records of how plants have changed over time – the leaves falling off the trees and buds opening, for instance – and compare and contrast what they've found out about various plants.

Animals (including humans)

As far as humans are concerned, in Year 1 the national curriculum focuses exclusively on naming body parts. In particular: head, neck, arms, elbows, legs, knees, face, ears, eyes, hair, mouth and teeth. (No shoulders or toes, for some reason.)

This is likely to be done through a combination of games, actions, songs and rhymes. They will probably draw and label pictures of themselves or their friends or siblings and be encouraged to use body-part words in lots of contexts outside the science lesson. Very few Year 1 children won't already be familiar with these words.

As for animals, in Year 1 your child will learn to iden-tify and name a number of common animals, including fish, amphibians, reptiles, birds and mammals (leaving out invertebrates at this stage). They will learn to describe and compare the structure of these animals (fish have scales, mammals have fur, etc.) and are bound to discuss their pets in some detail. Some primary schools will let children bring their pets in (within reason) for everyone to have a look.

Your child should learn to use the terms 'carnivore', 'herbivore' and 'omnivore' (and give examples of each) and then be able to group animals according to what they eat.

When they are out of the classroom or school throughout the year, children will be encouraged to take the chance to find out about animals in their natural habitat.

Everyday materials

Before children can start thinking about materials, they need to be able to distinguish between an object and the material from which it's made. Then they learn to identify and name a variety of everyday materials, including wood, plastic, glass, metal, water and rock. By trying to answer questions such as 'How do you know that this spoon is plastic but this one is metal?', they learn the concept of 'properties of materials', although they're unlikely to use that phrase. The properties they'll become familiar with are hard/soft; stretchy/stiff; shiny/dull; rough/smooth; bendy/not bendy; waterproof/not waterproof; absorbent/non-absorbent; and opaque/transparent.

Your child will then learn to describe the simple physical properties of a number of everyday materials using these words, and to compare and group together a variety of such materials on the basis of these properties. For example, they'll put 'all the shiny things' in one pile and then sort them into metal and non-metal objects.

Your child will explore and experiment with a wide variety of materials, not only those listed above. These will include brick, paper, fabrics, elastic and foil.

They will do simple tests to explore questions such as

'What is the best material for an umbrella? . . . for lining a dog basket? . . . for curtains? . . . for a bookshelf? . . . for a gymnast's leotard?' and 'What makes it the best material for that thing?' Scope for cross-curricular work with DT (design and technology) here.

Seasonal change

The changes across the four seasons will be observed and recorded, with associated weather changes and the varying length of the day. In most Year 1 classes there are movable laminated pictures on display which illustrate the seasons and the many weather possibilities and one lucky child is chosen each day to put the appropriate ones in the correct position. Children will sometimes be asked to bring evidence of the changing seasons into school, such as berries, twigs or blossom. They will talk about the changes in their clothing and how dark it is in the mornings just before Christmas, for example.

The seasons and the weather provide lots of material for developing scientific skills beyond observation. Your child is likely to make tables and charts about the weather and displays of what happens in the world around them, including the length of the day as the seasons change. Scope for links with the work they're doing in geography here.

What can you do to help?

● Encourage your child to be observant. Point out changes in plants through the seasons or trees that have kept their leaves in the depths of winter when you're out and about. Learn plant names together. Play 'Pick me five daisies and two dandelions' when you're walking through a field or a park. Ask which are your child's favourite dogs and tell them the name of the breed. Talk about why some animals are good pets and some aren't.

● Most children like animals. Many become passionate about one type or another and, if encouraged, can become a mine of information about them. There are lots of animal and nature programmes for children on television that will equip them better for school than screen games, so watch them.

● Collect leaves, or seeds, or berries, or bark, and make seasonal displays. An early ability to name different trees from their leaves is the start of a lifetime of pleasure noticing which trees grow where. If you don't know them, look them up.

● Grow plants. Or, rather, get your child to grow plants. If you have no success using seeds, buy seedlings from garden centres. Growing food is really exciting. Not just the fast ones like cress, but tomatoes in a growbag, or peppers, and carrots if you have even a small outside space.

● Bathtime fun. Encourage your child to explore which things float and which sink. Talk about the difference between them. Let them use small containers to fill big ones, but try to encourage a more observant approach than they would take alone. Ask them to guess how many small cups will fill each bigger one.

● Fill an old plastic bottle with different oils and liquids, e.g. honey, karo syrup (a light corn syrup), Fairy Liquid, water, vegetable oil, rubbing alcohol and lamp oil. Because they all have different densities, they'll separate, leaving them in layers on top of one another.

Shake the bottle so they get mixed up, then watch as they separate again.

● Make a weather vane. Use a plastic straw as the horizontal, with a cardboard triangle pointer on one end and a cardboard 'tail' on the other. Stick a pencil, point down, vertically in the ground. Stick a pin through the straw at its balance point and into the rubber on the pencil. The pointer should indicate the direction the wind is blowing.

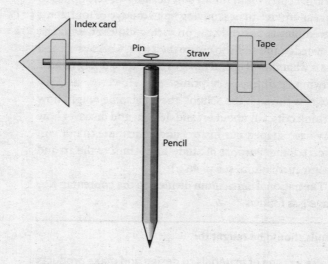

Art and Design

According to the national curriculum, art and design is a wholly separate subject from design and technology (DT) and in most schools it's simply referred to as 'art'. Having said that, the amount of time primaries devote to each of these subjects – and how carefully they differentiate between the two – will vary. The majority of primaries will not set aside more than one period a week in which to study art and DT, sometimes running them together as 'art/DT', sometimes switching them every half-term. Alternatively, they might spend a week every term doing both and call it 'Art Week'. Some schools that are keen on these 'creative' subjects may do all three, i.e. allot a period a week to art, a period a week to DT and have an Art Week. But that's rare.

If you read the 'Purpose of Study' section in the national curriculum for art and design (which applies to what children will be studying up to the age of fourteen), the emphasis is firmly on providing children with the knowledge and skills to create their own works of art and that's what they'll spend most of their time doing in art – drawing, painting, sculpting, etc. However, as they progress through the school, they'll also be taught how to think critically about art and design, and discover how they have shaped our history and contribute to our culture. (For the 'Purpose of Study' and 'Aims' of the art and design curriculum, see p. 462.)

The national curriculum divides up the content in Key Stage 1 as follows.

Pupils should be taught to:

- use a range of materials to design and make products

- use drawing, painting and sculpture to develop and share ideas

- develop a range of art and design techniques, using colour, patterns, texture, line, shape, form and space

- learn about the work of various artists, craft makers and designers, describing the differences and similarities between the separate disciplines, and making links to their own work.

Expect your child to do a lot of scrunching, tearing and plaiting in Year 1 – and not just of their classmates' hair. In addition to fabric work, they'll explore a number of different tools and techniques for making art, including charcoal, pastels, watercolours, printing blocks, papier mâché and stencils. Schools love to immerse children in different artistic *processes*, including changing the colour of different fabrics by using natural dyes such as beetroot, red-onion skins and blackberries. That's one activity we suggest you *don't* do at home, particularly if you have a wooden kitchen table.

Much of your child's work in Year 1 will consist of 'cutting and sticking' – an activity they will already be familiar with from nursery and Reception. Collages are a particular favourite, often handed to you by your child when you pick them up from school. On the way to the car you'll find yourself constantly bending down to pick up the buttons/bottle tops/bits of cellophane that keep falling off. (Can't they use stronger glue?) Try not to leave them in the footwell of your car when you get home.

Your child will also do a fair amount of colour mixing and modelling. You'll know when your child has been painting or making sculptures (usually with salt dough rather than clay) because they'll come home looking like they've spent the afternoon playing paintball with the Teenage Mutant Ninja Turtles. It's at times like these that you'll make a mental note to buy their school uniform from Asda next time and not from a specialist supplier.

The artists, craft makers and designers the children learn about in Key Stage 1 are usually those whose work they can reproduce in the classroom, e.g. Andy Warhol so they can make a version of the *Marilyn Diptych* using photographs of themselves, and Georges Seurat's *Bathers at Asnières* so they can try their hand at pointillism.

What can you do to help?

● There's a brilliant website called Art UK (artuk.org) which aims to show the entire United Kingdom national collection of oil paintings, as well as the stories behind them and where to see them for real. Use it to show your child some of your favourite paintings and, if they're not being kept too far away, arrange to visit some of the ones your child picks out.

● There is a range of art storybooks for children that is designed to introduce them to the work of particular artists, e.g. *Degas and the Little Dancer* by Laurence Anholt and *Katie Meets the Impressionists* by James Mayhew.

● If you're on a bucket-and-spade holiday, spend a few hours on the beach making a mosaic using different-coloured pebbles. Even if your child can't summon up much interest in the mosaic itself, they will enjoy being sent off with a bucket to find pebbles of a particular shade and colour.

● Cut some squares, rectangles, etc., out of coloured plastic and get your child to make a Matisse cut-out by sticking them on a sheet of white A4 card.

● Play-Doh is expensive and your child will probably ruin it by (a) mixing up the colours and (b) leaving it out overnight. So why not make your own? There are hundreds of websites containing homemade playdough recipes, from salt playdough to Kool-Aid playdough.

(Alternatively, make your own Moon Sand: Four cups of sand, two cups of cornflour and one cup of water.)

● Find a large, flat stone and get your child to paint a picture on it, using acrylic paints. You can then varnish it and use it as a paperweight.

● There's a good website called Art for Small Hands (www.artforsmallhands.com), where teachers post pictures of art which their pupils have made. Some of the posts contain directions about how to make the same things with your child.

Computing

The Royal Society produced a report in 2012 recommending that information and communication technology (ICT) be replaced by something more intellectually rigorous and according to Michael Gove the new computing curriculum is 'world class' and will create 'a generation of young people able to work at the forefront of technological change'. The boffins at Facebook and Google were impressed, but teachers were a little nervous to begin with and some will still feel a bit insecure about teaching it. That's not just because it replaced an old subject with something new, thereby plunging them into uncharted territory. It's also because it's a lot harder than ICT.

For instance, one of the exercises recommended for Year 1 children in ICT under the old curriculum was typing their name into a computer:

Explain to the children that they are going to type their name into the computer, using the keyboard. Show the children how to press a key, with a light but firm press, and not hold down their finger. Demonstrate how to use the delete/backspace key if they have mistyped or repeated a letter. Print their names and ask them to add a picture of themselves.

Contrast this with the 'Aims' of the new curriculum for computing, whereby all pupils should be able to:

- understand and apply the fundamental principles and concepts of computer science, including abstraction, logic, algorithms and data representation

- analyse problems in computational terms and have repeated practical experience of writing computer programs in order to solve such problems

- evaluate and apply information technology analytically to solve problems, including new or unfamiliar technologies

- be responsible, competent, confident and creative users of information and communication technology.

Admittedly, these 'Aims' are what children should be able to do by the time they're sixteen, but your child will still be expected to know a good deal of this by the end of Key Stage 2. In light of this, most primaries will eventually teach computing as a stand-alone subject.

One way of looking at the new computing curriculum in Key Stage 1 is to distinguish between those components that involve teaching children 'computer science' (the first three bullet points below) and those aimed at teaching children 'digital literacy' (the next three). Broadly speaking, the digital literacy components are quite similar to what children used to study in ICT under the old curriculum and some of the units schools have taught before will crop up again. It's the computer science stuff that's new, so harder to predict how that will be taught – and the current curriculum deliberately leaves room for teachers to approach it in different ways. For all its challenges, though, we think this a very exciting part of the new curriculum and regret that not all our children have been taught it. (For the 'Purpose of Study' and 'Aims' of the computing curriculum, see p. 463.)

The national curriculum divides up the content in Key Stage 1 as follows.

Pupils should be taught to:

- understand what algorithms are and how they're implemented as programs on digital devices

- create and debug simple programs

- use logical reasoning to predict the behaviour of simple programs

- use technology to create, organize, store, manipulate and retrieve digital content

- recognize common uses of information technology beyond school

- use technology safely and respectfully, keeping personal information private, and identify where to go for help when worried about content on the internet or other online technologies.

Computer science

An algorithm is a precisely defined procedure – a set of rules or instructions – for performing a specific task.

Programming a computer to do something involves turning an algorithm into code by using a programming language and, at present, the most popular programming languages in primary schools are Scratch, Logo and Kodu. Which isn't to say that all schools will use programming languages – at least, not yet. Most Year 1 teachers will begin by asking your child to come up with a simple algorithm, e.g. instructions for making a sandwich.

Getting your child to start writing computer programs in Year 1 isn't as ambitious as it sounds. If your child's school uses Scratch, for instance, they can use on-screen program-building blocks to create a simple program. Here's an example of a Scratch program for a maths quiz:

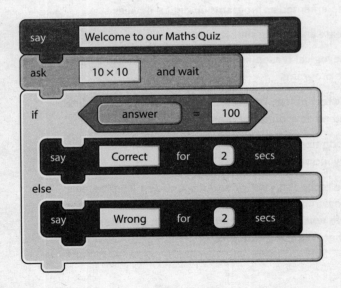

In all likelihood, your child's first program won't work as it's supposed to, but will make various mistakes. Finding and fixing these mistakes – or bugs – is known as 'debugging'. There's a lot of scope for collaboration in these sorts of exercises, so your child is unlikely to be writing or debugging a program by themselves. The school will also have some programmable toys which your child can experiment with, such as Bee-Bots, Roamers and Pro-Bots.

Computers are very predictable, in that their behaviour is completely determined. This means that once you've understood the program a particular computer is running you should be able to predict what it's going to do next. Your child's Year 1 teacher is likely to ask what their program will do before your child clicks the start button and ask them to explain why it's going to behave in this way and not another.

Digital literacy

Digital content can mean anything from word-processing to creating animated characters, so it's hard to know what your child will be asked to do in Year 1. The teacher may ask the whole class to 'create' a blog, with different children writing posts, uploading photographs, embedding video clips, etc. (This is probably all done via teacher and parents at this stage.) 'Organizing' digital content may involve organizing files in a documents directory or tagging photos and posts online; 'storing' involves understanding how size is measured digitally – kilobytes, megabytes, gigabytes, etc. – and learning the difference between a hard disk, USB sticks and the school's network server; 'manipulating' is likely to mean word-processing and/or using image- or video-editing software; 'retrieving' will involve searching for files, both on a computer's hard drive and on the World Wide Web, using a search engine such as Google.

When it comes to recognizing 'common uses of information technology' beyond school, it's hard to know where to begin because information technology touches almost every aspect of our daily lives, from the smartphone in our pocket to the microwave in our kitchen. One possibility is that the teacher will ask children to photograph common uses of technology outside the school, then, when they're back in class, 'model' one or other of them by pretending to be circuits and signals.

The last bullet point above is the e-safety bit. Your child will be told to treat other online users with courtesy and respect and advised not to share private information, but they are unlikely to be at risk of accessing inappropriate content on any of the school's computers – unless they've worked out how to 'hack' the school's security system. At the primary school attended by some of our children, the online security system is so draconian that the school's own website is blocked. Schools may organize a 'Safer Internet Day' or arrange visits from police community support officers to get these messages across.

What can you do to help?

The purpose of computing isn't simply to teach children how to use computers, but to understand how they work and, at its most challenging, *change* how they work. Quite ambitious, in other words, so the more you can do at home to complement what your child is learning in school, the better.

Many of the games and activities we've suggested assume that your child will have access to smartphones, tablets and computers at home, but not every child will. If yours doesn't, it's worth bringing this to the attention of your child's teacher. Most schools offer lunchtime or after-school computer clubs and some will lend or give away old computers to families that cannot afford to buy them.

● If your child is having difficulty grasping what an algorithm is, you could pretend to be a robot and ask them to write some instructions for you to get from the kitchen to the bedroom. Tell them that the instructions can include only the following commands: 'Right', 'Left', 'Forward', 'Back', 'Rotate left 90 degrees' and 'Rotate right 90 degrees'. After the child has written them down, try them out and see what room you end up in. If it's not the bedroom, they'll have to 'debug' the program, i.e. rewrite the instructions so that you do end up in the bedroom. Alternatively, if you have two children, get them to write teeth-brushing programs for each other and see if they work. (We're indebted to Phil Bagge, a primary school teacher, for these ideas, as well as the image of the Scratch program. You can find lots of good ideas about how to complement the computing curriculum at his website www.code-it.co.uk.)

● Your child will constantly pester you to use your computer/smartphone/tablet so they can play games (assuming they don't have one of their own) and you'll find it hard to resist. However, if you want them to start coding, try and keep one device – a laptop or a desktop – for educational use only. Sometimes, when they ask to play on a computer, tell them they can only use this one and then sit down beside them and make sure they're using it to learn something.

● Find out what programming language your school is using in Year 1 (if any) and download the relevant application so your child can play around with it. If your child gets stuck, don't worry if you don't know anything about programming. There are plenty of free online courses aimed at young children on how to use different programming languages, and some of them – Scratch and Kodu, for instance – have online user communities with forums where children can ask questions and share their work.

● Have your child join an after-school coding club. Some of these, such as Code Club (www.codeclub.org.uk), are aimed at older children, but others, such as CoderDojo (coderdojo.com) welcome children from the age of five. To find your nearest CoderDojo, go to the website and type in your postcode. It's free and open to all, but your child will need their own laptop and parents are asked to stick around and supervise, so don't expect to drop and shop.

● There are numerous apps and games designed to teach young children basic programming skills. The Swedish company Toca Boca (literally, 'touch the mouth' in Spanish) produces a range of games that children can help to design. Other apps designed to introduce children to programming include Move the Turtle, Kodable, Build a Car, Create a Car, Daisy the Dinosaur, Bee-Bot and A.L.E.X.

Design and Technology

The authors of the national curriculum have high hopes for this subject, in spite of it only taking up one period a week (at most). 'Pupils learn how to take risks, becoming resourceful, innovative, enterprising and capable citizens,' it says under 'Purpose of Study' (intended to apply to everything children learn up to the age of fourteen). That's quite a list, given that most children's exposure to DT in Key Stage 1 won't extend much beyond sticking glitter on photo frames and Sellotaping empty cereal packets together (junk modelling). (For the 'Purpose of Study' and 'Aims' of the design and technology curriculum, see p. 465.)

The national curriculum divides up the content in Key Stage 1 as follows.

Pupils should be taught to:

- design useful, appealing products, communicating ideas through talking, drawing, templates, mock-ups and, where appropriate, information and communication technology

- use an assortment of tools to perform practical tasks like cutting, shaping, joining and finishing, choosing from a range of different materials

- build structures, exploring how they can be made stronger and more stable, and use mechanisms such as levers, sliders, wheels and axles

- understand where food comes from and use the basic principles of a healthy diet to prepare dishes.

Given that most children struggle to hold a pencil at this age, don't expect them to be competing with Kevin McCloud in Year 1. They may be asked to create replicas of their school buildings and/or the school playground. Alternatively, they might be asked to create containers for different products. In all likelihood, the tools they'll be using will be our old friends scissors, glue and Sellotape.

In the past, Year 1 children have often been asked to create cards with moving parts in DT, such as figures with legs that open and close and arms that windmill up and down. More ambitious teachers may ask your child to create a moving picture book based on a fairy tale or nursery rhyme.

Most Year 1 children will be taken on a school trip to a nearby farm – a city farm if the school's in an urban area – where they'll be introduced to the rudiments of food production. Some schools will have gardens where the children can grow vegetables. Your child might also be asked to make a 'healthy' snack, e.g. a honey sandwich (don't ask).

What can you do to help?

● Did you know that Plasticine was invented by an art teacher? It was created in 1897 by William Harbutt, a teacher at a school in Bath, because he wanted his pupils to be able to use a modelling clay that didn't dry out. It's generally used by children to make human and animal figures, but why not get your child to create a prototype for a new consumer product out of Plasticine? Some ideas: a smartphone, a miniature tablet, a hand-held video-game console.

• Set aside a patch of garden or a window box for your child and get them to grow their own vegetables, such as tomatoes or runner beans. Then, when the vegetables are ready to harvest, set your child the challenge of creating a dish using their home-grown produce.

• Children love cooking and your child will be happy to help with measuring, kneading, mixing, etc. However, instead of just making chocolatey stuff, why not try making something together that is as unfamiliar to you as it is to them? That way, you can both learn at the same time. If you haven't made bread before, try that. Sit down with your child beforehand and discuss ways in which you can make it as healthy as possible.

• Challenge your child to make something out of empty cereal packets, yoghurt pots, etc. Get them to design it first instead of going straight to the building phase, sketching out what it's supposed to look like at various stages of construction. When they've finished, ask them if there's anything they could do better next time?

• Get your child to make a miniature bow from a lollipop stick and dental floss and fire cotton-bud arrows. They go surprisingly far. Not recommended if you have a cat or a dog.

Geography

The geography national curriculum caused a certain amount of controversy when it was unveiled because, unlike the old one, it didn't contain any references to 'environmental change' or 'sustainable development'. In the current curriculum, the emphasis is on teaching children more traditional geographical knowledge, such as the names of the seven continents, the difference between latitude and longitude, how to find places by using globes, atlases and maps, etc.

In spite of this, the manner in which geography is taught hasn't changed very much. Rather than appearing in the timetable as a stand-alone subject, geography is usually taught alongside history under the general heading of Topic (or Humanities), which is how it was taught under the old curriculum. Two periods a week are usually devoted to Topic, so one of these can be set aside for geography and another for history – and that happens in some schools. However, most schools continue to teach the two subjects in Topic for the time being. All of the units your child studies in Topic will lend themselves to cross-curricular work to a greater or lesser degree, but the bulk of the subject matter in each unit will usually be either geographical or historical. (For the 'Purpose of Study' and 'Aims' of the geography curriculum, see p. 466.)

The national curriculum divides up the content in Key Stage 1 as follows.

Pupils should be taught to:

- name and locate the world's seven continents and five oceans, as well as the four countries that make up the United Kingdom and their capital cities

- understand geographical similarities and differences through studying a small area of the United Kingdom and a small area in a contrasting non-European country

- identify seasonal and daily weather patterns in the United Kingdom and the location of hot and cold areas of the world in relation to the equator and the North and South Poles; use geographical vocabulary to refer to key physical features, including beach, cliff, coast, forest, hill, mountain, sea, ocean, river, soil, valley, vegetation, season and weather; and key human features, including city, town, village, factory, farm, house, office, port, harbour and shop

- use maps, atlases and globes to identify the United Kingdom and its countries; use simple compass directions (North, South, East and West) and locational and directional language to describe features and routes on a map; use aerial photographs to recognize landmarks and basic human and physical features; draw a simple map, including a key; and use fieldwork and observational skills to study the geography of the school and the key human and physical features of its surrounding environment.

Before your child starts learning the seven continents, the five oceans, etc., it would be a good idea to make sure you know these facts yourself. In school your child will probably study a variety of geographical information sources – globes, maps, atlases, aerial photographs, satellite images, etc. – and to complement this at home you should buy a globe, at the very least. Your child is unlikely to retain this knowledge without plenty of repetition, so don't be afraid to go over these facts again and again. (For some useful mnemonics, see p. 100.)

The second bullet point is a departure from the old curriculum, which required children to study their local area and compare it to a contrasting area either at home or abroad. Under the current curriculum, it needn't necessarily be their local area and it must be contrasted with somewhere overseas. Nevertheless, teachers still do a unit called 'Where in the world is Barnaby Bear?' This involves anointing a teddy bear as the class mascot (sometimes created at a local branch of Build-a-Bear Workshop), then letting children take it in turns to take the teddy with them when they go away for the weekend or on holiday and taking photographs of Barnaby in different poses – on the plane, sightseeing, relaxing by the pool, etc. This is designed to help children understand that other places may be different from their locality. Be warned: if your child loses Barnaby Bear when they are acting as his custodian, it can cause lasting trauma. We speak from experience.

The stuff about climate is quite specific – and some of it is new – so Key Stage 1 teachers have had to think carefully about how to teach it. Seasonal and daily weather patterns in the United Kingdom may be covered through a daily 'calendar maths' session in which the children agree on the weather outside and perhaps record this on a bar chart. Your child will probably be introduced to the equator and the North and South Poles – another reason to have a globe handy. These will often be introduced within the context of a story that children are familiar with, such as *Father Christmas Goes on Holiday* by Raymond Briggs. Getting children to use geographical vocabulary such as 'mountain', 'ocean', 'valley', etc. pre-dates the 2014 curriculum, so teachers will have worksheets to hand, as well as other teaching materials, such as felt boards.

When it comes to map-reading, using a compass and so on, the focus will be on your child's school in Year 1, and they'll be given a plan of the school showing where their classroom is, where the playground is, etc. Teachers often use the same materials they used to teach an old national curriculum unit called 'Around our school – the local area'.

What can you do to help?

● There is a series of books by Rachel Bell whose titles begin A Visit to . . . , designed to help children of this age understand what it's like to be a child in another country and which serves as a good introduction to geography. The books include fact files, maps, photos, illustrations and some basic words in the local language. There's another series called The Passport to the World, which is similar, and Miroslav Šašek's This is . . . series (This is San Francisco, This is New York, This is London, etc.) has a certain old-fashioned charm. Finally, there's the Katie . . . series by James Mayhew. One of our children did Katie in London as his Year 2 class assembly.

● Encourage your child to start collecting plastic animals and each time they get a new one ask them to identify what country it's from on a map of the world. If the map is large enough, they can put the animal on the country. Get them to put all their animals in the right countries.

● To help your child distinguish between the different countries in the United Kingdom, get three bits of tracing paper and draw a rectangle on each one, making sure they're all the same size. Then, find some pictures of the St George's Cross, St Andrew's Cross and St Patrick's Cross, making sure that their dimensions are the same as your rectangles. Ask your child to trace all three flags and then lay them on top of each other to create the Union flag.

● There's a good app called Stack the Countries in which children have to answer geography questions in order to make progress. If they get a question about a particular country right, they 'win' that country and it appears at the bottom of the screen in their 'stack'. One of the good things about the game is that the countries are the correct size relative to each other, though discovering how tiny the United Kingdom is can be a shock.

MNEMONICS AND MEMORY AIDS

● To help your child learn the different points of the compass, you can use the acronym 'NEWS': North at the top; East on the right; West on the left; South at the bottom. Alternatively, if you start at the top and proceed in a clockwise direction, the first letters of each word in 'Never Eat Shredded Wheat' correspond to the first letters of the points of the compass. (Alternatives: 'Never Eat Slimy Worms', 'Never Eat Soggy Waffles', 'Naughty Elephants Squirt Water' and 'Never Enter Santa's Workshop'.)

● To remember the names of the seven continents – Europe, Asia, Africa, Australia, Antarctica, North America and South America – the following phrases might be helpful: 'Eat An Aspirin After A Nasty Sandwich', 'Eat An Apple As A Nice Snack'.

● A good way to remember the names of the Earth's five great oceans is to use this phrase: 'I Am An Amazing Person.' The first letter of each word corresponds to the first letter of each of the big oceans: Indian, Atlantic, Antarctic, Arctic and Pacific.

History

In the 'Aims' section at the beginning of the history national curriculum, which is intended to apply to everything children learn in the subject up to the age of fourteen, the first bullet point says that all children should 'know and understand the history of these islands as a coherent, chronological narrative, from the earliest times to the present day'.

Some people mistakenly believe this to be a departure from the old national curriculum but, in fact, that too asked children to 'place events and objects in chronological order'. However, the reality was that under the old curriculum children would usually flit back and forth between different historical figures and periods, studying Mary Seacole in Year 2, the Tudors in Year 3, the Second World War in Year 4 and the Victorians in Year 5. In the post-2014 curriculum, it doesn't explicitly say children have to study the different units in chronological order – that was in an earlier draft, but was taken out – but that's largely beginning to happen in most schools. We should caveat this by saying we've seen a good deal of variation of which units are taught in which year groups.

As with geography, history continues to be studied in lessons called Topic (or Humanities) – and teachers have carried on teaching some of the history units they taught under the old curriculum, such as 'The Vikings' and 'Ancient Egypt'. However, with the introduction of the new curriculum, the units taught in Topic are more likely to be presented in the correct chronological sequence. At least, that's the case in Key Stage 2. In Key Stage 1 your child's teacher is likely to introduce them to the concepts they'll need to make sense of history as a subject. Thus, your child will be introduced to the idea of placing events in chronological order; using common words and phrases relating to the passing of time, such as 'before', 'after', 'present' and 'past'; and identifying the many different sources of historical knowledge, such as official records, eyewitness accounts, artefacts and museums.

In addition, your child will be introduced to the historical periods they'll study in greater depth in Key Stage 2 and Key Stage 3 – the Stone Age, the Iron Age, the Roman Empire, Anglo-Saxons, Vikings, etc. – but only fleetingly and possibly not in the right order. (For the 'Purpose of Study' and 'Aims' of the history curriculum, see p. 468.)

The national curriculum divides up the content in Key Stage 1 under the following headings:

- Changes within living memory, particularly those that reveal significant changes in our national life

- Events beyond living memory that are significant nationally or globally

- The lives of significant individuals in the past who've contributed to national and international achievements

- Significant historical events, people and places in your local area

---

When it comes to 'changes within living memory', most Year 1 teachers will stick to the history units they're already familiar with, namely 'How are our toys different from those in the past?' and 'What were homes like a long time ago?' This is in keeping with the child-centred approach that has become increasingly dominant in the primary national curriculum since it was first introduced in 1989. The idea is that the best way to interest a child in a subject such as history is to start with what they already know – their toys, their home, their local area – and work outwards from there.

Year 1 teachers don't have a huge range of 'changes' to choose from if they've got to be 'within living memory' of five- to six-year-olds (though presumably that's not what it means), but the more imaginative ones will come up with some units of their own. (As we said in the Introduction, one of the virtues of the current national curriculum is that it leaves more room for teachers to devise their own programmes of study.) They might choose 'The Olympic Games', for instance, starting with London 2012 and going back through time to Ancient Greece. If your child's primary is in or near London, the teacher might even organize a school trip to the Olympic Park in Stratford.

With respect to 'events beyond living memory', the authors of the national curriculum have diplomatically added the words 'nationally or globally' to avoid accusations of Little Englandism and included some suggestions: the Great Fire of London, the first aeroplane flight and events commemorated through festivals or anniversaries.

We wouldn't expect children to do the Great Fire of London in Year 1 – it's been a standard Year 2 unit taught in Topic for some time – but teachers have been taking up the other two suggestions. In our experience, most teachers are keen on festivals and anniversaries. In the run-up to 2018, there will be plenty of events commemorating significant moments in the First World War.

The range of historical figures schools can choose from is so vast you'd imagine it would be impossible to predict who your child will study, but the national curriculum helpfully includes some (non-statutory) suggestions for Key Stage 1: Elizabeth I and Queen Victoria, Christopher Columbus and Neil Armstrong, William Caxton and Tim Berners-Lee, Pieter Bruegel the Elder and L. S. Lowry, Rosa Parks and Emily Davison, Mary Seacole and/or Florence Nightingale and Edith Cavell.

Your child is unlikely to be introduced to Queen Victoria, Christopher Columbus or Florence Nightingale in Year 1, but Neil Armstrong is a possibility, particularly with the fiftieth anniversary of the moon landing coming up. Most Year 1 teachers taught the moon landing under the old curriculum.

What your child's teacher does about the history of the local area will vary according to where you live, but expect your child's Year 1 teacher to organize plenty of trips to local museums, monuments, historical land-marks, etc.

What can you do to help?

● A fantastic app, Streetmuseum, has been developed by the Museum of London which, effectively, turns your smartphone into a time machine. Go to a location identified on a map of London, hold your phone up as if to take a picture, and an image of the same streetscape, but in the nineteenth or early twentieth century, appears in your viewfinder. This is a great way of bringing history alive for your child, the next best thing to being able to travel back in time.

● Make a family tree with your child, tracing your family back as far as you can. Create a scrapbook with old family photos and mementos to go with it, something your child can take into school for Show and Tell.

● If your child is studying 'The first aeroplane flight' in Topic in Year 1 you should think about a trip to the Science Museum in London, which devotes an entire floor to the history of flight, beginning with Leonardo da Vinci's helicopter sketches and ending with a Eurofighter. The Wright Brothers' historic flight at Kill Devil Hills in 1903 is well documented, with a series of scale models in glass cabinets.

● *Horrible Histories* aren't to everyone's taste and the books are often light on historical facts, but lots of children enjoy the irreverent approach. The CBBC TV series dates back only to 2009, while the first books in the series – *Awesome Egyptians* and *Terrible Tudors* – were published in 1993. Check the website of the Birmingham Stage Company to see if there's a *Horrible Histories* stage production touring in your area.

● Usborne cut-out models are quite fun and titles in the series include *Greek Temple*, *Roman Fort*, *Viking Settlement* and *Crusader Castle*. All your child will need is a pair of scissors and some glue (and a little help from you).

MNEMONICS AND MEMORY AIDS

To help your child remember why we celebrate bonfire night – and the date – the following rhyme may be useful: 'Remember, remember, the fifth of November/ Gunpowder, treason and plot.'

Music

Under 'Purpose of Study' for the music national curriculum it says that children 'should develop a critical engagement with music, allowing them to compose, and to listen with discrimination to the best in the musical canon'. Phrases like 'the best in the musical canon' illustrate the main difference between the current curriculum and the old one, which expected children to relate to music in a more touchy-feely way, e.g. 'Explore and express their ideas and feelings about music by using movement, dance and expressive and musical language.' (For the 'Purpose of Study' and 'Aims' of the music curriculum, see p. 470.)

The national curriculum divides up the content in Key Stage 1 as follows.

Pupils should be taught to:

- use their voices expressively and creatively by singing songs and speaking chants and rhymes

- play tuned and untuned instruments musically

- listen with concentration and understanding to a range of high-quality live and recorded music

- experiment with, create, select and combine sounds, using the interrelated dimensions of music.

The majority of your child's musical education in Key Stage 1 – which will probably only take up a single period a week – will consist of singing. Popular songs include 'Old MacDonald Had a Farm', in which your child will have the opportunity to make all the different animal noises; 'Head, Shoulders, Knees and Toes', in which your child may be asked to speed up or slow down, introducing them to the idea of tempo; and 'If You're Happy and You Know It', where clapping will help all the children stay synchronized.

In Key Stage 1 the 'tuned instruments' your child is likely to be playing are percussion instruments such as the xylophone, vibraphone, glockenspiel and chimes. 'Untuned instruments' means percussion instruments that don't produce a definite pitch, such as drums (snare, bass, drum set, etc.) and instruments generally used for special effects (triangle, gong, castanets, rattle, cowbell, tambourine, maracas, etc.).

Some schools will have a dedicated music teacher, but small schools either bring in peripatetic help or get by using the teachers' skills. If they can play the piano, and if there is one to hand, teachers often play children piano pieces and ask what sort of mood or animal they have conjured up. The curriculum also asks them to get children listening to 'a range of high-quality live and recorded music' as well. Easy enough to introduce the children to different genres and styles of music via recordings, but going to see orchestras and bands performing locally may prove difficult logistically. Most schools will invite some performers in at least once a year.

Asking children to make music in class isn't new. What teachers in Key Stage 1 generally do is ask the class to sit in a circle, place a large pile of instruments in the middle and invite the children to take it in turns to choose one and then play it – or, at any rate, use it to make a sound. Then, when everyone's got an instrument, the real fun can begin.

What can you do to help?

- Obviously, the best thing you can do is encourage your child to learn an instrument. Many children start with the recorder, not least because you can get one for only a few pounds. Most schools have a piano and can provide lessons, although they are expensive and getting your child to practise every day is a chore – as much for you as for them. It's worth persevering because the rewards are huge. Not only will your child learn how to play, and discover an enormous amount about music in the process, they'll also learn about the link between commitment, hard work, patience and achievement. Some children find working upwards through the different musical grades motivating, but others hate the pressure (which can be enough to stop them playing at all, so be careful!).

- Pianos are expensive and take up a lot of space. Electric keyboards take up less room, don't need tuning, can be played with headphones on (a blessing, for obvious reasons) and can be bought for as little as £25 on eBay.

- Children are never too young to start learning an instrument. Piano (or keyboard) lessons for the under-fives generally involve listening to the teacher play a tune and then clapping out the rhythm and singing in time.

- For families on low incomes, there are various grants and loans available to help with the cost of learning instruments, such as the Take It Away scheme (www.takeitaway.org.uk), supported by Arts Council England, which offers interest-free loans to purchase musical instruments. Some local councils also provide help.

Special Educational Needs (SEN)

Not all children have the same facility to learn to read, write and spell or do maths. When we started writing this book, we found ourselves constantly having to make caveats to allow for the fact that children with SEN (Special Educational Needs) may not make as much progress as others – or, in rare cases, may progress faster in some areas. We quickly found this becoming repetitive, so we decided to say everything we have to say on the subject here instead.

When we say something like 'By now your child should be reading fluently . . .', please don't think we believe that will be the case for *all* children, or that we think the fault lies with your child or the school – or you – if your child isn't. The national curriculum is designed to be accessible to children of all abilities, but there will be children who struggle to make the expected progress within each year.

Some children have SEN, while others are less 'school ready' when they start Reception, and that can have a knock-on effect in later years. Some 'summer babies' struggle to keep up with their peers born earlier in the school year, and much has been written about the advantages and disadvantages of children starting their formal education a few years later than they do in the United Kingdom, as in some Nordic countries. We haven't addressed any of those issues in this book. We've just tried to describe how the national curriculum is taught to ordinary children in a typical primary school and what you can do to help.

Your primary school will have a member of staff with responsibility for children with SEN, usually called a 'SENCO' (Special Educational Needs Coordinator). If you have concerns, you must talk to your child's class teacher and take it from there.

The 2015 Special Educational Needs and Disability code of practice

A child or young person has SEN if they have a learning difficulty or disability which calls for special educational provision to be made for them. A child of compulsory school age or a young person has a learning difficulty or disability if they:

(a) have a significantly greater difficulty in learning than the majority of others of the same age; or
(b) have a disability which prevents or hinders them from making use of educational facilities of a kind generally provided for others of the same age in mainstream schools.

Department for Education

Teachers are trained to identify a range of special needs early on and will have tried-and-tested methods for dealing with them. If you are worried that your child may have needs that haven't been noticed or addressed, then talk to the teacher and the head teacher at the school and if you feel you're still not being heard contact the Children's Services Department of your local council.

The SEN code of practice says that where a SEN is identified schools should put 'appropriate evidence-based interventions' in place. (Examples might be one-to-one support in class or individually targeted worksheets and homework.) There should be regular reviews of the progress made and the support provided may be adapted as required. According to the code of practice, 'Plans for the use of support should relate to a clear set of expected outcomes, which should include stretching and relevant academic and developmental targets. Progress towards these outcomes should be tracked and reviewed regularly, at least termly.' You will be consulted before special provision is made for your child, and you will be invited to take part in the termly reviews and setting of targets.

The SEN code of practice gives guidance to schools on taking a graduated approach to identifying and supporting pupils and students with SEN. Those with more complex needs will be subject to an individually constructed Education, Health and Care Plan (EHC Plan), which replaces what used to be called a 'Statement'. If your child falls into the 'EHC' category they can get various forms of support, including teaching support, paid for by the local authority. In the past getting a statement was a laborious process involving more than one clinical assessment and many parents of children with severe SEN found it quite soul-destroying. However, under the current code of practice the process should be less arduous. (Should be, but may not be.) If you think your child might be eligible for an EHC Plan you should discuss this with their class teacher. They can advise you whether it's worth pursuing.

The Department for Education's code of practice for SEN can be found here: www.gov.uk/government/uploads/system/uploads/attachment_data/file/398815/SEND_Code_of_Practice_January_2015.pdf

Different Types of SEN

Some common conditions that may result in a child having SEN are dyslexia, dysgraphia, dyscalculia, dyspraxia and ADHD (Attention Deficit Hyperactivity Disorder). We've described some of the symptoms of these conditions below, but please don't jump to the conclusion that your child is suffering from any of them simply because they present with some of these symptoms. If you have any concerns we strongly advise you to raise them with your child's teacher as a first port of call.

Dyslexia

The British Dyslexia Association (www.bdadyslexia.org.uk) lists, among others, the following indicators for a child of primary school age:

- has particular difficulty with reading and spelling

- puts letters and figures the wrong way round

- has difficulty remembering times tables, alphabet, formulae, etc.

- leaves letters out of words or puts them in the wrong order

- occasionally confuses 'b' and 'd', and words such as 'no' and 'on'

- poor concentration

- has problems understanding what they have read

- has problems processing language at speed

  Primary-school-age non-language indicators:

- has difficulty tying shoelaces and ties, or dressing in general

- has difficulty telling left from right, order of days of the week, months of the year, etc.

- surprises you with their inability to 'get' some things, because in other ways they are bright and alert

- has a poor sense of direction

Plenty of children presenting the above symptoms may well not be dyslexic. Under 'Helping your child at home' on the British Dyslexia Association's website, there are lots of resources and tips that may help.

USEFUL WEBSITES

Dyslexia A2Z (www.dyslexiaa2z.com)
Dyslexia Action (www.dyslexiaaction.org.uk)
The Dyslexia Association (www.dyslexia.uk.net)

Dysgraphia

Dysgraphia is commonly referred to as 'the handwriting disability'. It's a learning disability resulting from a processing disorder that makes the act of writing difficult for a child. Normally, the brain takes in information, processes it and then sends signals to the hand to turn that information into written expression. The dysgraphic hand fails to understand those brain signals, which often results in frustration, misspelt words, incorrectly formed lines and shapes and even hand cramps. It can lead to problems with spelling, poor handwriting and an inability to put thoughts down on paper. Children with dysgraphia can have trouble organizing letters, numbers and words on a line or a page. This can result partly from:

- visual-spatial difficulties: trouble processing what the eye sees

- language-processing difficulties: trouble processing and making sense of what the ear hears.

Just having bad handwriting doesn't mean a child has dysgraphia, so we would recommend talking to your child's teacher before diagnosing your child yourself.

SOME WAYS YOU CAN HELP AT HOME

- Be patient and positive, encourage practice and praise effort. Becoming a good writer takes time and practice.

- Get your child to use paper with raised lines as a sensory guide to staying within the lines.

- Try different pens and pencils to find one that's the most comfortable for your child.

- Have your child practise writing letters and numbers in the air with big arm movements to improve motor memory of these important shapes (see the Appendix 'How to Form the Letters of the Alphabet' on p. 473). In addition, practise letters and numbers with smaller hand or finger motions.

- Encourage proper grip, posture and paper positioning for writing. It's important to reinforce this early, as it's difficult for students to unlearn bad habits later on.

- Use multisensory techniques for learning letters, shapes and numbers. For example, to write the letter 'b', make the shape of a big stick going down and then circle away from your body.

- Introduce your child to word-processing at quite an early stage in their education, say Year 3, but don't eliminate handwriting altogether. While typing can make it easier to write by alleviating the frustration of forming letters, handwriting is a skill your child won't be able to do without in adulthood.

USEFUL WEBSITES

Dysgraphia is considered a form of dyslexia and dyslexia websites have lots of helpful information.

Dyslexia A2Z (www.dyslexiaa2z.com)
British Dyslexia Association (www.bdadyslexia.org.uk)

Dyscalculia

Dyscalculia is a condition that affects a child's ability to acquire arithmetical skills. Sufferers may have difficulty understanding simple number concepts, lack an intuitive grasp of numbers and have problems learning number facts and procedures. Even if they produce a correct answer or use a correct method, they may do so mechanically and without confidence.

Dyscalculia is a bit like dyslexia (and is often considered a form of dyslexia) but very little is known about its prevalence, causes or treatment. Current thinking suggests that it is a congenital condition, caused by the abnormal functioning of a specific area of the brain. People with dyscalculia experience great difficulty with the most basic aspects of numbers and arithmetic.

Best estimates indicate that somewhere between 3 and 6 per cent of the school-age population are affected. These statistics refer to children who are 'purely' dyscalculic, i.e. they have difficulties only with maths and are good or even excellent performers in other areas of learning.

USEFUL WEBSITES

Dyscalculia, as well as dysgraphia, is considered a form of dyslexia, so dyslexia websites have lots of helpful information.

The Dyscalculia Centre (www.dyscalculia.me.uk/ parent.html)
Dyslexia A2Z (www.dyslexiaa2z.com)
British Dyslexia Association (www.bdadyslexia.org.uk)

Dyspraxia

Dyspraxia is a common disorder affecting fine motor coordination in children and adults. Children with dyspraxia may have difficulties with self-care, writing, typing, riding a bike and playing, as well as other educational and recreational activities. In addition, children with dyspraxia have problems planning, organizing and carrying out movements in the right order in everyday situations. Dyspraxia can also affect articulation and speech, perception and thought.

USEFUL WEBSITES

The Dyspraxia Foundation (www.dyspraxiafoundation.
    org.uk)
NHS Choices (www.nhs.uk/Conditions/Dyspraxia-
    (childhood)/Pages/Introduction.aspx)

ADHD

ADHD (Attention Deficit Hyperactivity Disorder) is
thought to be caused by a chemical imbalance in the
brain that affects attention, concentration and impul-
siveness. Studies show that ADHD may affect certain
areas of the brain that allow us to solve problems, plan
ahead, understand the actions of others and control our
impulses. ADHD begins in childhood and can continue
through adolescence and into adulthood.

Someone with ADHD might have difficulty concentrating, appear restless, fidgety, overactive and impulsive.
They may act without thinking and often speak before
thinking, blurting out and interrupting others. Symptoms
include:

- overactive and/or impulsive behaviour

- inattention to detail that leads to careless mistakes

- trouble finishing work

- difficulty in paying attention

- easily distracted

- always 'on the go'

- impatient

USEFUL WEBSITES

Living with ADHD (www.livingwithadhd.co.uk)
The Mental Health Foundation (www.mentalhealth.
  org.uk)
The National Autistic Society (www.autism.org.uk)

Year 2

Introduction

The end of Year 2 is the end of Key Stage 1, and your child will do official tasks and tests (often still referred to as SATs) in reading, grammar, punctuation and spelling and maths. They will also be assessed by their teacher (known as the teacher assessment) on speaking and listening, on writing and in science.

That means the foundation subjects will play second fiddle to the core subjects in Year 2 and your child's teacher will put even more emphasis on cross-curricular links with English, maths and science.

(For more detail on the tasks and tests children do in Year 2, see 'Reports and Assessment' on p. 52.)

English

A class of Year 2 children will start (and end) the year with a range of levels in reading and writing, but they should all arrive able to read lots of common words, such as 'shout', 'hand', 'stop' and 'dream', without having to blend the sounds out loud first. Your child should be able to read all the common graphemes ('ay', 'sh', 'ck', 'wh', 'ow', etc.) so well that they can read unfamiliar words containing them accurately and quickly by sounding them out. In addition, they should be able to read the most common tricky words (also called 'exception words'), such as 'you', 'could', 'many' and 'people'. And they should have become pretty good at retelling stories, both old favourites they know off by heart and new ones they've heard that week.

During Year 2 your child's teacher will continue to focus on getting them reading many more words accurately and speedily. The teacher will read and discuss a wide range of stories, poems, plays and information books. The sooner your child can read well, the better, because it will enable them to access the rest of the primary curriculum.

When it comes to writing, your child should arrive in Year 2 able to compose individual sentences orally and then write them down. (This skill – to retain what they have composed for long enough to get it on paper – is surprisingly difficult for young children.) They should be able to spell lots of words learnt in Year 1. They should also be able to make phonically plausible attempts to spell words they haven't yet learnt. Finally, they should be able to form individual letters correctly. That means establishing good handwriting habits from the beginning.

This is the year when your child will begin to meet extra challenges in terms of spelling. Increasingly, they will see that there is not always an obvious connection between the way a word is said and the way it's spelt. Variations include different ways of spelling the same sound, the use of so-called 'silent' letters and groups of letters in some words and, occasionally, spelling that has become separated from the way that words are now pronounced, such as the 'le' ending in 'table'. Some children, more often boys, still won't have developed the motor skills needed to write as accurately or as fast as they'd like and this can be frustrating. Remember, writing is intrinsically harder than reading: children will be able to read and understand more complicated bits of writing than they're capable of producing themselves.

As in Year 1, the English curriculum is divided into reading and writing. Reading is further subdivided into word reading (what we think of as reading) and comprehension (understanding what you've read). Writing is subdivided into transcription (spelling and handwriting), composition and, finally, vocabulary, grammar and punctuation.

To summarize:

- Reading = word reading; comprehension

- Writing = transcription (spelling and handwriting); composition; vocabulary, grammar and punctuation

We will tackle each of these subdivisions below, explain what sort of thing your child will be doing and how you can help, with the exception of the last, which we've dealt with in 'Grammar and Punctuation' on p. 375. (For the 'Purpose of Study' and 'Aims' of the English curriculum, see p. 458.)

Reading

WORD READING

In Year 2 children will continue to apply phonic knowledge and skills as the route to decode words until automatic decoding has become second nature and

> reading is fluent. They will learn to read most words quickly and accurately, without overt sounding and blending, when they have been frequently encountered.

Your child's reading will probably progress in leaps and bounds this year. In the phonics lesson at the beginning of each day they will revise and consolidate what they learnt in Year 1 and be introduced to a wider variety of words. They will learn how to read suffixes, e.g. '-ment', '-ness'. They will be taught how to read longer words, by being shown syllable boundaries and how to read each syllable separately before combining them to make a word. They will often chant words of more than one syllable by clapping each syllable. They'll learn how to read many more tricky words. They will read books aloud, matched to their improving ability, sounding out unfamiliar words accurately, automatically and speedily. And they will then reread them to build up their fluency and confidence.

Even fluent readers benefit enormously from reading aloud, so every child will still read on a one-to-one basis with a teacher, teaching assistant or volunteer. They will also read to each other.

What can you do to help?

● Everything in the 'What can you do to help?' section in Year 1 (p. 60) still applies. The more you can read with your child, the better. The daily chore of having to read the book they bring home in their book bag remains vital, but this should not be the only book you read. Read a story with more advanced text than they are comfortable with and ask your child to try sentences, pages or chapters themselves. Some parents manage to persuade children to read alternate chapters of a book the child is gripped by, such as *Charlotte's Web* by E. B. White. (See the Reading List at the end of Year 6 on p. 455.)

● In addition, word games are a good way to make decoding words fun. Scrabble is probably a bit too demanding at this age, but Boggle should work.

COMPREHENSION

Children will continue to develop pleasure in reading, as well as their vocabulary and understanding, by listening to, discussing and expressing views about a wide range of contemporary and classic poetry, stories and non-fiction.

They will continue to check that the text makes sense to them as they read and correct inaccurate reading. They will be asked to make inferences on the basis of what is being said and done, to predict what might happen next, to participate in discussion about books, poems and other works that are read to them or that they're reading themselves, to take turns and listen to what others say, and to explain and discuss their understanding of texts.

In Year 2 your child will become increasingly adept at understanding what they're reading. This is achieved with practice, not surprisingly, and with structured questions about the text. Your child should become familiar with and good at retelling an ever-wider selection of stories and they'll be introduced to non-fiction books that are structured in different ways. They will start recognizing simple recurring literary language in stories and poetry, discussing and clarifying the meanings of words, linking new meanings to known vocabulary, talking about their favourite words and phrases and continuing to build up a repertoire of poems learnt by heart.

Deliberate steps will be taken to increase your child's vocabulary and their awareness of grammar so that they continue to understand the differences between spoken and written language. The meaning of new words will be explained to them within the context of what they're reading. They will learn about cause and effect in both fiction and non-fiction, e.g. what has prompted a character's behaviour in a story, or why certain dates are commemorated annually.

They will be guided to participate in discussions and asked to consider the opinions of others. Role play and other drama techniques are often used to help your child explore different characters. In these ways, your child will extend their understanding of what they're reading and have opportunities to try out the new vocabulary they've learnt.

What can you do to help?

● When reading with or to your child you can develop their comprehension skills by talking about what you've read. Thinking aloud when reading to your child may help them understand what skilled readers do. By this, we mean pausing and making comments like 'Doesn't she sound grumpy!' or asking questions: 'Why do you think he said that?'

● Following recipes is a great stimulus ('What do we have to do next?') and it helps to have the reward of being able to eat something chocolatey and delicious if you follow the recipe correctly.

● Encourage your child to follow written instructions when building models or playing a new board game – even if you are the one doing the reading.

● Create simple treasure hunts using legible clues in words they can read. If you have terrible handwriting, type them instead.

● Write letters from the tooth fairy or other imaginary correspondents.

● Ask your child to learn poems by heart. There are helpful apps for this. Try iF Poems (set up by the actress and writer Allie Esiri and former *Times* journalist Rachel Kelly), which allows you to read, listen to, record and share your favourite poems from a collection of more than two hundred classics.

Writing

TRANSCRIPTION

a) Spelling

In Year 2 children will learn to spell many new words, both those that follow phonetic rules and those that don't. They'll learn some homophones ('bare', 'bear') and how to spell words with contracted forms ('can't', 'didn't', 'hasn't'). They'll learn about the possessive apostrophe ('John's', 'Emma's') and to add suffixes to spell longer words, including '-ment', '-ness', '-ful', '-less', '-ly'. They'll learn lots of spelling rules, such as 'y' changes to 'i' before 'es' is added ('babies', 'carries'), or that the letter 'x' is never doubled ('mixing', 'boxer').

The process of spelling will be emphasized: that is, that spelling involves segmenting spoken words into phonemes and then representing all the phonemes by graphemes in the right order. Your child should already know this for one-syllable words, but now it's extended to multi-syllabic words.

What can you do to help?

- Most schools send weekly spellings home in book bags which your child will be expected to learn. It really helps the teacher and, more importantly, your child if you make sure your child learns these. Children are taught a method: look, cover, write, check. It's a good technique and worth reinforcing at home. Some children find spelling easy, but some will struggle. For the strugglers, it's a kindness to them to go over their spellings 'just one more time' before they get to school (where they'll be tested on them), but counter-productive to make them spell the words on the list over and over again. As with most things in life, positive encouragement ('Oh, so nearly right!') rather than negative ('Duh!') tends to work better. Mnemonics often help – the sillier, the better, e.g. 'People' = People Eating Orange Pants Love Elephants.

b) Handwriting

In Year 2 children will be taught to form lower-case letters of the correct size relative to one another. They will start using some of the diagonal and horizontal strokes needed to join letters and understand which letters, when adjacent to one another, are best left unjoined. They will write capital letters and digits of the correct size, orientation and relationship to one another and to lower-case letters. They will use spacing between words which reflects the size of the letters.

In school, your child will revise and practise correct letter formation frequently. They should be taught to write in a joined-up style as soon as they can form letters securely with the correct orientation – and this tends to be in Year 2.

What can you do to help?

> ● If you are aware of how your child has been taught to draw each letter, it's easier to be helpful (see the Appendix 'How to Form the Letters of the Alphabet' on p. 473). As always, there's a fine line between positive encouragement and nagging. At this stage it's probably better not to stifle your child's creative urges by constantly going on about handwriting, but for special occasions (birthday cards to grandparents, for example) you should ask for their neatest efforts.

COMPOSITION

Teachers will employ various methods to build up children's stamina for writing and to develop a positive attitude in them towards it. Children will write narratives about their own experiences, as well as fictional stories. Alternatively, they might be asked to write their own version of a story they're already familiar with, such as 'Little Red Riding Hood'. They will write poetry and about real events. They will plan out loud and write down key words or new vocabulary before they start. They will start proofreading to check for errors and that their writing makes

sense. And they will read their work out loud, using varied intonation to make the meaning clear.

Reading and listening to whole books, not simply extracts, will help your child increase their vocabulary and grammatical knowledge, including that of Standard English, which may not be the way they talk. In this way, they start to understand how different types of writing, including narratives, are structured. All these can be drawn on for their own writing.

Your child will learn through example the skills and processes essential to writing: that is, thinking aloud as they collect ideas, and drafting and rereading to check their meaning is clear.

Drama and role play are often used in Year 2 because to play different roles and improvise scenes in various settings helps children order their ideas – and because it's fun.

A visit to a good Year 2 classroom will show an excit-ing breadth of creative writing, which should be fluent and energetic. You will see that great efforts are made to use exciting vocabulary and to make your child's prose more interesting by the use of more connectives (such as 'although', 'because' and 'despite').

What can you do to help?

● Most of the advice given in this section in Year 1 still applies, and your child should have more stamina for writing by now. Some schools will set homework involving some story writing at this stage, or writing a piece of news after a holiday. Encourage your child to use more interesting vocabulary where you can and remind them that full stops and capital letters do make a difference.

Maths

The national curriculum sets out what your child should learn in Year 2 under the various headings below. (For the 'Purpose of Study' and 'Aims' of the maths curriculum, see p. 459.)

Number and place value

Your child should learn to count in steps of two, three and five from 0, and in tens (forwards and backwards, beginning with any given number) and to read and write numbers to at least 100 in numerals and in words. They should learn to understand that in a two-digit number a digit's value depends on its place (whether it's in the units column, or the tens column).

They will learn to compare and order numbers from 0 up to 100, and how to use the symbols for less than (<), more than (>) and equals (=). They'll be taught how to use place value and number facts to solve problems. (An example of a number fact is $11 + 2 = 13$ or $15 - 4 = 11$.)

Using materials and a range of representations such as counters, number lines or number charts, your child should practise counting, reading, writing and comparing numbers to at least 100 and solving a variety of related problems to develop fluency. They will probably count in multiples of three to help later understanding of the fraction a third.

As they become more confident with numbers up to 100, your child is likely to be introduced to larger numbers to give them a better feel for the patterns within our number system.

They'll probably be asked to partition numbers in

different ways, e.g. 23 = 20 + 3 and 23 = 10 + 13, because this will help them subtract. They should become fluent enough with these numbers to reason with, discuss and solve problems that emphasize the value of each digit in two-digit numbers. They will also begin to understand 0 as a place holder – that a 0 in the unit column means no units. Seems obvious to us, but it isn't always to children.

Addition and subtraction

By the end of Year 2 your child should be able to recall and use addition and subtraction facts up to 20 fluently, e.g. 7 + 3 = 10 or 20 − 5 = 15, and derive and use related facts up to 100, e.g. 6 + 3 + 5 = 14, or 84 − 7 = 77, or 35 + 10 = 45, or 61 + 13 = 74, in ascending order of complexity.

Your child will be taught an important rule: that addition is commutative (the addition of two numbers can be done in any order) but the subtraction of one number from another is not.

They should realize that the relationship between addition and subtraction is inverse (if 2 + 6 = 8 then 8 − 6 = 2) and use this to check calculations and solve missing-number problems.

They should learn to use the terms 'sum', 'difference', 'addition' and 'subtraction'. While 'sum' and 'addition' are synonyms, finding the difference between two numbers is not the same operation as subtracting one number from another.

Your child will probably practise addition and subtraction to twenty repeatedly to become increasingly fluent in deriving facts. For instance, they will use such facts as 3 + 7 = 10, 10 − 7 = 3 and 7 = 10 − 3 to calculate 30 + 70 = 100,

$100 - 70 = 30$ and $70 = 100 - 30$. They will learn to check their calculations, including using addition to check subtraction and adding numbers in a different order to check addition, e.g. $5 + 2 + 1 = 1 + 5 + 2 = 1 + 2 + 5$.

They should start writing their sums in columns, with tens above tens and units above units. This emphasizes the importance of place value and prepares your child for formal written methods with larger numbers. However, at this stage, they won't be 'carrying' digits from column to column.

Multiplication and division

This is the year when multiplication tables rear their head for the first time, but by no means the last. (See 'Times Tables' on p. 163.) In Year 2 your child should 'do' their 2, 5 and 10 times tables, as these are the easiest ones. Counting in steps of two, five and ten is pretty straightforward. The challenge is to learn the 'facts'. Saying 'Two, four, six, eight, ten' is one thing. Knowing (without counting) that $2 \times 6 = 12$ is another. Understanding that 2×7 means seven piles of two is very important.

Learning the 2 times table provides the perfect opportunity to learn what odd and even numbers are.

Your child should come to see that multiplication is repeated addition, and they'll learn how to work out multiplication and division facts (such as $6 \times 2 = 12$) and write them, using the multiplication ($\times$), division ($\div$) and equals ($=$) signs.

They will be able, then, to show that the multiplication of two numbers can be done in any order (commutative) and that the division of one number by another cannot. This is quite hard to understand. That seven piles of two will come to the same number as two piles of seven is not obvious.

They'll solve problems involving multiplication and division, using various methods: arrays, repeated addition, mental methods. An array is a number of counters set out in lines to show a multiplication fact, e.g. twelve counters set out in two rows of six, to show that $6 \times 2 = 12$ and, importantly, $2 \times 6 = 12$; or in four rows of three to show that $3 \times 4 = 12$ and $4 \times 3 = 12$.

Your child will probably connect the ten times table to place value, and the five times table to the divisions on the clock face.

They'll work with a range of three-dimensional materials in different contexts in which multiplication and division relate to grouping and sharing. They will begin to relate their understanding of multiplication to fractions and measures, e.g. $40 \div 2 = 20$; 20 is half of 40. They will use commutativity and inverse relations to develop multiplicative reasoning, e.g. $4 \times 5 = 20$ and $20 \div 5 = 4$.

Fractions

In Year 1 your child will have learnt 'half' and 'quarter'. In Year 2 they should move on to a third, a quarter, two quarters and three quarters (⅓, ¼, ²⁄₄ and ¾). They'll be taught to recognize, find, name and write these as fractions of a length, a shape or a quantity. They should be able to write things like '½ of 6 = 3' and recognize the equivalence of and a ½.

After all this, your child should be able to count in fractions up to ten, starting from any number, e.g. 1¼, 1²⁄₄ (or 1½), 1¾, 2. This reinforces the concept of fractions as numbers and that fractions can add up to more than one.

Measurement

An understanding of measurement and scale underpins lots of science, and it is in Year 2 maths lessons that your child will first start using what are called 'standard units' and – more importantly – be able to estimate measurements in these units. Standard units are represented by recognized symbols: metres (m) or centimetres (cm) for length; kilogram (kg) or gram (g) for mass (in everyday speech the words 'mass' and 'weight' are used interchangeably, which is not the case in science); degrees Celsius (°C) for temperature; and litres (l) or millilitres (ml) for capacity and volume. (Later, volume is measured in centimetres cubed, but not in Year 2.)

Using rulers, scales, thermometers and measuring vessels, your child should learn to take measurements in the right units and to make comparisons of measurements they've made using >, < and = symbols. Comparing measures will include simple multiples such as 'half as high' and 'twice as wide'.

Money comes under this section: children will probably find different combinations of coins that equal the same amounts of money and learn about pounds (£) and pence (p). They may play 'shops' and work out how to give the right amount of change (keeping it fairly simple at this stage).

In Year 2 time-telling skills improve. Your child will probably be taught to tell and write the time to five minutes, including quarter past or to the hour, and will draw the hands on a clock face to show these times. They may, in fact, become fluent in telling the time on analogue clocks, though they're not required to tell the time to the nearest minute until Year 3.

Geometry

Your child should get to handle and name a wide variety of common 2D and 3D shapes, including quadrilaterals and polygons, and cuboids, prisms and cones, and be able to identify the properties of each shape, e.g. number of sides and faces. They'll identify, compare and sort shapes on the basis of their properties and use vocabulary precisely, such as 'sides', 'edges', 'vertices' and 'faces'.

They'll draw lines and shapes with a ruler – a fine motor skill some will find tricky to master.

They'll be introduced to the term 'right angle' and how to use it for quarter, half and three-quarter turns (clockwise and anticlockwise). They are likely to play lots of games involving pretending to be robots and giving each other movement instructions, or to play Simon Says, using vocabulary, such as 'Turn 90 degrees clockwise' or 'Turn a quarter anticlockwise' to help embed the message.

Statistics

It sounds rather grand to include the term 'statistics' when talking about a Year 2 class. But this is where it starts. Your child should learn to interpret and construct basic pictograms, tally charts, block diagrams and simple tables, and to ask and answer questions about totalling and comparing data sorted by category.

What can you do to help?

Maths needs to be practised repeatedly. Leave the school to do the teaching, but anything you can do at home to reinforce the concepts they've learnt at school will help your child's maths fluency. The main thing that stops children enjoying maths is an anxiety that can come from feeling that they are bad at it, so avoid that happening by giving your child opportunities to practise. It will help your child if you have some understanding of the techniques used by the teacher. A key piece of equipment is a laminated number square:

1	2	3	4	5	6	7	8	9	10
11	12	13	14	15	16	17	18	19	20
21	22	23	24	25	26	27	28	29	30
31	32	33	34	35	36	37	38	39	40
41	42	43	44	45	46	47	48	49	50
51	52	53	54	55	56	57	58	59	60
61	62	63	64	65	66	67	68	69	70
71	72	73	74	75	76	77	78	79	80
81	82	83	84	85	86	87	88	89	90
91	92	93	94	95	96	97	98	99	100

This will be used for addition: to add, for example, 31 + 27, children will place a marker on 31, recognize that 27 is the same as one 20 and one 7, move vertically down two squares to add the 20, then horizontally along seven squares to add the 7, arriving at 58. This also visually emphasizes the place value of the digit 2 in the number 27.

The same number square is used for subtraction.

We explained what a number line is in the Year 1 maths section. Number lines continue to be used in

Year 2, and children will make their own, starting at the number they need for help with addition or subtraction.

There is never enough time in school for children to talk about numbers and mathematics as much as teachers would like. This is where you can really help. Children take time to absorb the ideas around the manipulation of numbers, so talking about them is of great benefit. Ask questions such as 'How do you work out what 24 plus 8 is?' Thinking about how they do it will help reinforce the method in your child.

ACTIVITIES

With a bit of imagination, you will find countless (ha ha) ways to bring mathematics into your child's conversation and play. Here are some ideas:

- Numbers up to 100. Open a book (with about a hundred pages) at a random page and ask them to tell you the number of the next or previous page.

- Make the same number. How many ways can you make 6? Take it in turns when you are in the car or walking to school. You go first with 4 and 2 makes 6 (then use language like '4 plus 2 equals 6' once they've really understood that it's the same), and then it's their turn. This can get as hard as either of you like and, when you try it with increasingly big numbers, your child may start to see patterns in how to get all the possibilities with a logical approach.

- Play Shops using real coins. Even better, start actually shopping together and reward addition and subtraction attempts with a treat. (If I give you 50 pence how much change will you get when you buy a Curly Wurly?)

● Ask your child to sort out the coins in your purse, guess how much they will add up to and then check. You could guess, too, and then there's an element of competition.

● Buy a teaching clock, which has words saying things like 'twenty to' or 'ten past' under the numerals. Practise. Tell your child they can go to bed ten minutes later if they can tell the time now and say what it will be in ten minutes. Your child may become good at telling the time and then, a month later, you could find they've completely forgotten. They may be reluctant to relearn, but persevere. Like most things mathematical, it takes practice. Owning their own (analogue) watch is a good incentive.

● Multiplication. (See 'Times Tables' on p. 163.) Once your child has learnt a times table, try to find opportunities to use those 'facts', e.g. spot an articulated lorry, ask your child to count how many sets of wheels it has and then to tell you how many wheels there are in total.

● There are lots of resources for doing mathematics in the home that you can buy or make, such as flashcards, number squares, posters with fractions or times tables on. There are board games for all ages that help embed the ideas your child has learnt. And there are computer games and apps galore. Two good apps for learning to tell the time are Jungle Time and Tick Tock.

● Try Bond Assessment papers. These are old-fashioned tests designed to prepare children for the 11+. There are different tests for children of different ages, starting with five-year-olds. Lots of children really enjoy the sense of achievement they get from completing them, but some will see them as an extension of the school day. Worth a try.

● Try this game, which was included in an article by Marilyn Burns in which she describes nine ways to help your child catch up in maths:

72	36	49	88	54
84	77	96	132	56
63	81	48	108	121
(66)	99	144	64	42

6   7   8   9   11   12

Player 1 chooses two numbers from those listed (in the game shown here, 6 and 11) and circles the product of those two numbers on the board with his or her colour of marker.

Player 2 changes just one of the numbers to another from the list (for example, 6 to 9, so the factors are now 9 and 11) and circles the product with a second colour.

Player 1 might now change the 11 to another 9 and circle 81 on the board.

Play continues until one player has completed a continuous pathway from one side to the other by circling boxes that share a common side or corner.

Science

The national curriculum organizes the science to be covered in Year 2 under the headings 'Plants', 'Animals (including humans)', 'Use of everyday materials' and 'Living things and their habitats'. In most primaries the teachers will use different topic names and won't necessarily group what is taught in the following way, but all this material will be covered at some point during the year. (For the 'Purpose of Study' and 'Aims' of the science curriculum, see p. 461.)

Plants

Your child is likely to be encouraged to observe how different plants grow in the local environment throughout the year. They'll learn what plants need for germination, growth and survival: that seeds and bulbs need water to grow, that most do not need light at first, but that light is needed for the plant to mature and stay healthy. They'll also learn that seeds and bulbs have a store of food inside them. They'll probably grow some plants from seed, observing and recording, with some accuracy, the growth of a variety of specimens as they change over time from a seed or bulb, or observing similar plants at different stages of growth. A standard Year 2 activity will be to set up comparative tests to show that plants need light and water to stay healthy.

Animals (including humans)

Your child should be introduced to the basic needs of animals for survival (water, food and air), as well as the importance of exercise and eating the right amounts of different types of food for humans. They will also consider the notion of reproduction and growth in animals. The focus at this stage will be on questions that help children to recognize growth; they will not be expected to understand how reproduction occurs.

The following examples might be used: egg, chick,

chicken; egg, caterpillar, pupa, butterfly; spawn, tadpole, frog; lamb, sheep. Humans growing into adults will include references to baby, toddler, child, teenager and adult.

Some lucky children may get the chance to incubate eggs and watch chicks emerge. Some may be taken on farm trips during lambing season. One way or another, they will observe through video or at first hand how different animals, including humans, grow. They may take height measurements of themselves or their families, and be asked to bring in photographs of themselves at different ages.

Use of everyday materials

Your child is likely to identify and discuss the uses of different everyday materials so that they become familiar with how some materials are used for more than one thing (metal can be used for coins, cans, cars and table legs; wood can be used for matches, floors and telegraph poles). Or how different materials are used for the same thing (spoons can be made from plastic, wood or metal, but not normally from glass). They will find out how the shapes of solid objects made from some materials can be changed by squashing, bending, twisting and stretching. They should think about the properties of materials which make them suitable or unsuitable for particular purposes and they should be encouraged to think about unusual and creative uses for everyday materials. Your child might find out about people who have developed useful new materials, e.g. John Dunlop, Charles Macintosh and John McAdam.

They might compare the uses of everyday materials in and around the school with materials found in other places (at home, on the journey to school, on visits, and in stories, rhymes and songs). Scope for cross-curricular links with DT here.

Living things and their habitats

Your child will be asked to think about how to decide if something is living, dead or has never been alive, by looking at the differences between these conditions. They should be taught that all living things have certain characteristics that are essential to keep them alive and healthy, such as needing water, warmth and air. They are likely to do some sorting and classifying activities, answering such questions as 'Is a flame alive?' 'Is a deciduous tree dead in winter?'

They will be introduced to the terms 'habitat' (a natural environment or home of a variety of plants and animals) and 'micro-habitat' (a very small habitat, e.g. for woodlice under stones, logs or leaf litter). They should raise and answer questions about the local environment that help them to identify and study a variety of plants and animals within their habitat and observe how living things depend on each other, e.g. plants serving as a source of food and shelter for animals. They will see that most living things live in habitats to which they are especially suited and describe how different habitats provide for the basic needs of different kinds of animals and plants, and how they depend on each other. They will probably compare animals in familiar habitats with animals found in less familiar habitats, e.g. on the seashore, in woodland, in the ocean and in the rainforest.

They will learn how animals obtain their food from plants and other animals, using the idea of a simple food chain, and identify and name various sources of food.

They are likely to construct a simple food chain that includes humans, e.g. grass, cow, human. They may well be taken out of the classroom to observe for themselves some local habitats so they can describe the conditions in different habitats and micro-habitats (under log, on stony path, under bushes, etc.) and find out how the conditions affect the number and types of plants and animals that live there.

What can you do to help?

● Learn the names of the plants, including trees, in your local environment. Take a pocketbook of plants and trees with you when you go out and identify the ones you see with your child.

● Let your child have an ant farm and discuss what the ants need and why the right habitat is important.

● Go to the zoo and focus on the habitats and environments as well as the animals.

● Talk about what things in your home are made of and ask why.

● Follow recipes. Following instructions, measuring and observing are all important skills for science and they all come into cooking.

● Do all the science activities suggested for Year 1 again!

Art and Design

Expect your child's Year 2 teacher to stress cross-curricular links with English, maths and science when teaching the foundation subjects, because they're required by law to assess them in those three core subjects. In art and design that means your child may be asked to study paintings that tell stories, e.g. *Saint George and the Dragon* by Paolo Uccello, to tie in with the work they're doing on narrative in English, create 2D and 3D shapes (cubes, cones, cylinders) to tie in with the shapes they're learning about in maths and do some leaf rubbing to tie in with the work they're doing on plants and trees in science. (For the 'Purpose of Study' and 'Aims' of the art and design curriculum, see p. 462.)

The national curriculum divides up the content in Key Stage 1 as follows.

Pupils should be taught to:

- use a range of materials to design and make products

- use drawing, painting and sculpture to develop and share ideas

- develop a range of art and design techniques, using colour, patterns, texture, line, shape, form and space

- understand the work of various artists, craft makers and designers, describing the differences and similarities between the separate disciplines, and making links to their own work.

In Year 2 your child will graduate from personalizing small, decorative objects (photo frames, jewellery boxes, paperweights) to making them. These often take the form of Mother's Day gifts (friendship bracelet, necklace) or Father's Day gifts (cufflink box, mug), depending on the time of year. Again, try not to leave them in the footwell of your car.

One of the suggested units in the old art and design curriculum was called 'Sculpture' and in some schools that's still being taught in Year 2. It involves taking the children on a school trip to a nearby park, forest or beach and telling them to look for 'natural' sculptures, e.g. plant, earth or rock formations. The teacher will then ask them to make sketches and notes, thinking about the different materials that make up this formation and the effect the weather has had on it. Finally, they'll be asked to collect materials with a view to making a collage or sculpture back in the classroom.

In Key Stage 1 many primaries make costumes for various religious festivals and rituals in art and design, such as a decorative bonnet at Easter and a candleholder for Diwali.

In addition to the narrative art mentioned above, your child is likely to be introduced to illuminated manuscripts (The Lindisfarne Gospels), murals (The Last Supper) and tapestries (The Bayeux Tapestry), as well as the treasures of Sutton Hoo.

What can you do to help?

- Buy a jigsaw puzzle of a famous painting and ask your child to help you do it. Don't plump for an easy one because you'll manage it too quickly. Get a hundred-piece jigsaw that will take a while to finish. Your child will be forced to really look at the painting and think about how the different parts of the picture fit together. If your child has been shown a particular painting in class, such as van Gogh's Sunflowers, choose a jigsaw of that.

- The Tate Gallery has a website called Tate Create that describes a number of arts and crafts activities children can do at home, e.g. making a small sculpture out of a bar of soap, creating a pop-art hat and turning a room in your house into an 'installation' using nothing but string. All the activities have been tried and tested by children who've visited one of the Tate galleries (www.kids.tate.org.uk).

● Give your child a digital camera and tell them to go on a 'colour hunt', i.e. photograph fifty things of just one colour. If you have a digital printer, you can print the photos, cut them out and stick them on a display board.

● Make your own sea glass by taking a large piece of broken glass – from a milk bottle or a jug, say – and placing it in a jar with sand. Close the lid and shake.

Computing

By the end of Key Stage 1, your child will be expected to write some elementary programs, if they haven't already, but don't be alarmed by this. Most primaries will have programmable toys (Bee-Bots, Roamers and Pro-Bots) which are simple to operate and, when it comes to computers, will use one of the programming languages (Scratch, Logo, Kodu) that are designed for young children. These sorts of activities fall under the general heading of 'computer science' (the first three bullet points below), but your child will also learn 'digital literacy' (the second three bullet points). (For the 'Purpose of Study' and 'Aims' of the computing curriculum, see p. 463.)

The national curriculum divides up the content in Key Stage 1 as follows.

Pupils should be taught to:

- understand what algorithms are and how they're implemented as programs on digital devices

- create and debug simple programs

- use logical reasoning to predict the behaviour of simple programs

- use technology to create, organize, store, manipulate and retrieve digital content

- recognize common uses of information technology beyond school

- use technology safely and respectfully, keeping personal information private, and identify where to go for help when worried about content on the internet or other online technologies.

Computer science

As we said in Year 1, an algorithm is a set of rules or instructions that describes precisely how to perform a specific task. When you program a computer to do something, you have to turn an algorithm into code using a programming language. In Year 2 your child is likely to be asked to write algorithms for some tasks that they (or you) perform every day, e.g. instructions for walking to school. This will help teach your child to think *algorithmically*, an essential programming skill.

Unless you have the patience of a saint – or don't own a smartphone or tablet – your child is likely to be pretty familiar with video games by the time they enter Year 2. (A recent survey of 2,000 parents in the United Kingdom found that 75 per cent share their smartphones with their children.) Their teacher may use this knowledge and ask your child to create and debug a program for a simple game using one of the programming languages designed for young children. Debugging a program can be quite time-consuming, so there's plenty of scope for collaborative work. Alternatively, your child might be asked to create simple action programs whereby key or mouse inputs result in a cursor moving ten places or a sound being played.

Again as we said in Year 1, computers are predictable in that their behaviour is entirely dictated by programs. This means that once you've understood the program a particular computer is running you can predict what it's going to do next. In Year 2 your child will be asked to use logical reasoning to explain why a programmable toy like a Bee-Bot – or its digital counterpart – is going to behave in a particular way, i.e. they'll have to refer to the algorithm encoded in the relevant program. Your child's teacher will also be looking to see if your child understands the rules governing the movements of a programmable toy. For instance, a Bee-Bot can turn only right or left by 90 degrees so if your child thinks it can move diagonally or go upstairs, they haven't understood the logical constraints of the device.

Digital literacy

In Year 2 your child may be asked to create a simple PowerPoint presentation on a unit they're studying in another subject, particularly in English, maths or science, e.g. 'Animals and their habitats'. This will enable them to develop all the digital literacy skills referred to in the fourth bullet point: they will 'organize' digital content by tagging photos and posts; work out how much information they can fit on the memory stick their presentation is 'stored' on; 'manipulate' the information they're presenting using word-processing and image- or video-editing software; and 'retrieve' the content used in their presentation from the Web, utilizing a search engine.

When it comes to recognizing 'common uses of information technology beyond school', your child may be taken on a school trip to a local factory or warehouse so they can see how computers are used by commercial businesses, and then be asked to 'model' these systems back in the classroom.

At this point, your child is likely to have had the school's e-safety drummed into them so their Year 2 teacher may consider them ready to start using a simple form of communication such as email or SMS. (There's a kids' email app called Maily.) You'll soon know if they're beginning to do this at school because you'll start receiving messages containing endless rows of emoticons.

What can you do to help?

● As we've said already, the purpose of this national curriculum subject isn't simply to turn your child into an efficient user of computers, but to furnish them with the skills to change how computers work – to turn children into budding coders (whom the singer Will.i.am has described as 'the new rock stars'). So the more you can do at home, the better.

● If your child is still having difficulty grasping the concept of an algorithm, you could pretend to be a sandwich robot. To do this, you'll need two pieces of bread, some butter, some jam and a knife. Place them on the kitchen table, then ask your child to give you a set of simple instructions for making a sandwich. If the program doesn't work, i.e. if the instructions don't enable you to make a sandwich, you can ask your child to 'debug' it by revising the instructions.

● Download some free computer animation software, e.g. Pivot, Animator, and get your child to create simple animated stories using stick figures and the like.

● Assuming you've already downloaded the programming language your child is using at school, ask them to stretch their legs a little. If they're creating video games, get them to introduce trapdoors and short cuts. Show them how to use Google so they can search YouTube for instructional videos. Encourage them to explore the online user communities linked to the programming language in question and make friends with other children of their own age. If you want your child to become a computer geek, they need to meet and hang out with other computer geeks.

● If your child doesn't like the school's programming language – or still finds it too difficult – you can download an alternative, such as 2Do It Yourself. They can use this to create their own platform games, design on-screen jigsaw puzzles and devise quizzes. You can give your child no end of amusement by allowing yourself to be defeated by the digital tests they come up with. Sometimes no pretence will be necessary!

● A good way to get your child to start using logical reasoning is to play Mastermind. You'll be surprised how absorbed they become, even when they're as young as this. If you want to make it easier for them to guess, insist on no repetitions and no blank spaces and limit yourself to just four colours. Mastermind has the added advantage of being less boring for adults to play than other games suitable for children of this age, such as Snap.

● *Minecraft* can be a good way to introduce your child to elementary programming. Ian Livingstone, one of the founders of the United Kingdom games industry, calls it 'digital Lego' and when you put it like that it doesn't sound too bad. Quite creative, even. Your child will initially spend an inordinate amount of time trying to kill Creepers in 'survival' mode, but there are plenty of more challenging things they can do, such as creating a Nether Portal – a gateway to 'The Nether' (don't ask). It's open-ended, which means players can generate their own content and, if they're really ambitious, start modifying the *Minecraft* code. Be warned, though: it's incredibly addictive and your child will happily remain in the *Minecraft* universe 24/7 if left to their own devices. Try and ration it to thirty minutes a day.

● For other apps and games designed to introduce children to programming, see Year 1 'Computing' on p. 85.

Design and Technology

In Year 2 your child will be asked to design and make more technically challenging things in DT. As in Year 1, DT is unlikely to be allocated more than one period a week, if that, and will either be combined with art or alternate with it, so your child does DT for the first half of the term, then art in the second half. Expect lots of links between DT and other parts of the curriculum, e.g. if your child is reading 'The Little Red Hen' in English, they will make a loaf of bread in DT. (For the 'Purpose of Study' and 'Aims' of the design and technology curriculum, see p. 465.)

The national curriculum divides up the content in Key Stage 1 as follows.

Pupils should be taught to:

- design useful, appealing products, communicating ideas through talking, drawing, templates, mock-ups and, where appropriate, information and communication technology

- use an assortment of tools to perform practical tasks like cutting, shaping, joining and finishing, choosing from a range of different materials

- build structures, exploring how they can be made stronger and more stable, and use mechanisms such as levers, sliders, wheels and axles

- understand where food comes from and use the basic principles of a healthy diet to prepare dishes.

There's lots of scope in DT for cross-curricular links with computing so expect your child to start designing some products on a desktop in Year 2. One of the suggested units in the old DT curriculum was 'Vehicles' and involved children being asked to design a range of different vehicles, e.g. service vehicles (fire engine, tip-up truck, milk float, ambulance), carnival floats, prams and buggies, wheelchairs, shopping trolleys, etc., and this is still being taught in a handful of schools. If your child does this, they will be encouraged to think about the number of wheels the different vehicles should have, how many moving parts and how much weight they should be able to bear. There will be some cross-curricular links here with what they're doing in maths and science, too.

To give you an example of the kinds of cross-curricular links your child will be making in DT, one of our children made an Inca mask in Year 2 because he was doing a unit called 'Machu Picchu' in Topic.

Another of the suggested units in the old DT curriculum was 'Joseph's coat' and involved the children designing and making a coat linked to the story of 'Joseph and the Coat of Many Colours'. That, too, has been carried across into the current curriculum, particularly in Church of England primaries, although textiles is more likely to be taught further up the school.

If your child has designed some vehicles with a computer program, they will also be given the opportunity to build them with construction kits. In Year 2 they may also be asked to make some hand puppets, both to illustrate a story they're reading in English such as 'Goldilocks and the Three Bears' and to use in stories they'll be asked to make up themselves.

If your child is doing 'Florence Nightingale and Mary Seacole' in Topic, they will be told something about the herbal remedies Seacole used to treat wounded soldiers in the Crimean War. In DT your child might be asked to reproduce some of these remedies, as one of ours was. In his case, it was a recipe for a drink involving ginger, sugar, water and an ice cube.

What can you do to help?

- If you have an old household appliance that you're about to throw out, like a toaster or a vacuum cleaner, why not spend an afternoon taking it apart with your

child? As you disassemble it, try to explain (guess) what
the various bits and pieces do. If the reason you're
throwing it out is because it no longer works, isolate the
part that's broken, if you can, and explain why that part
is so critical in making the appliance function properly.

● Your child probably won't realize that nearly
everything in the modern kitchen was designed or
invented by someone. Why not take them on a tour of
your kitchen while making a cup of tea, giving them a
potted history of the different items? You could start with
the tea bag (invented by an American tea merchant called
Thomas Sullivan in 1908), move on to the electric kettle
(perfected by a Birmingham engineer called Leslie Large
in 1922) and end with the fridge (refrigerators for home
use were invented by Fred W. Wolf of Fort Wayne,
Indiana, in 1913). Once you've made your cup of tea, your
child might want to dip a digestive biscuit into it.
Digestives were invented in 1892 by a Scotsman called
Alexander Grant who worked for McVitie's bakery.

● Ask your child to design their perfect bedroom. First
they can draw it (perhaps using a graphic design app
such as Home Design 3D), then they can 'model' it by
fitting out a shoebox.

Geography

As we said in Year 1 'Geography', the national curriculum in
this subject puts the emphasis firmly on teaching children
traditional geographical knowledge, such as the names of
the seven continents, the difference between latitude and
longitude, how to find places using globes, atlases and
maps, etc. So you can expect your child to, for example,

complete colouring tasks that allow them to identify the continents and oceans on a globe, and some more explicit teaching of these key facts. However, the manner in which geography is taught hasn't changed a great deal. It continues to be taught alongside history in Topic (or Humanities). That means your child will study some of the same geography units that children were taught in Year 2 under the old curriculum, e.g. 'Going to the seaside' and 'An island home' (see below). (For the 'Purpose of Study' and 'Aims' of the geography curriculum, see p. 466.)

The national curriculum divides up the content in Key Stage 1 as follows.

Pupils should be taught to:

- name and locate the world's seven continents and five oceans, as well as the four countries that make up the United Kingdom and their capital cities

- understand geographical similarities and differences through studying a small area of the United Kingdom and a small area in a contrasting non-European country

- identify seasonal and daily weather patterns in the United Kingdom and the location of hot and cold areas of the world in relation to the equator and the North and South Poles; use geographical vocabulary to refer to key physical features, including beach, cliff, coast, forest, hill, mountain, sea, ocean, river, soil, valley, vegetation, season and weather; and key human features, including city, town, village, factory, farm, house, office, port, harbour and shop

- use maps, atlases and globes to identify the United Kingdom and its countries; use simple compass directions (North, South, East and West) and locational and directional language to describe features and routes on a map; use aerial photographs to recognize landmarks and basic human and physical features; draw a simple map, including a key; and use fieldwork and observational skills to study the geography of the school and the key human and physical features of its surrounding environment.

By the end of Year 2 your child really should be able to remember the seven continents, the five oceans, etc., so keep practising this at home, making use of the mnemonics and memory aids in Year 1 'Geography' on p. 100.

Two of the geography units which children studied in Key Stage 1 under the old curriculum – 'Going to the seaside' and 'An island home' – both lend themselves to delivering the content in the second bullet point above without too much adaptation. In 'Going to the seaside', your child will be asked about bucket-and-spade holidays they've been on, how the seaside is different from their own locality (assuming you don't live by the sea), where else in the world they could have a seaside holiday, etc. In 'An island home', by contrast, your child will be introduced to a fictional Scottish island called Struay and told who lives there, what they do, the type of transport they use and so on. It will be up to the teacher to come up with contrasting beaches and islands in non-European countries.

In Year 2 your child will begin to study seasonal and daily weather patterns in the United Kingdom, particularly if the school is located in one of the areas that has experienced flooding recently. As in Year 1, your child's teacher will focus on the local area as far as possible when introducing new geographical vocabulary.

In addition to the different countries of the United Kingdom and their capitals, your child may be taught the differences between the United Kingdom (England, Wales, Scotland and Northern Ireland), Great Britain (England, Wales and Scotland), the British Islands (England, Wales, Scotland, Northern Ireland, the Isle of Man and the Channel Islands) and the British Isles (England, Wales, Scotland, Ireland and more than six thousand islands, including the Isle of Man, Shetland, Orkney and the Channel Islands).

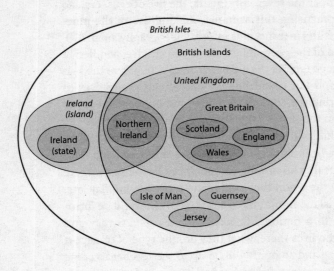

The maps your child will be asked to draw in Year 2 will become increasingly detailed and complex, and they might have an opportunity to use a simple map-making program such as *quikmaps* (quikmaps.com).

What can you do to help?

- To familiarize your child with maps and how to read them, take a map with you on a country walk and pretend to get lost on the way. Your child will enjoy the fact that you don't know where you're going and will relish the opportunity to help you get to your destination by studying the map. 'Silly Daddy . . .'

- Do a hundred-piece jigsaw puzzle of the map of the world.

- In addition to Stack the Countries (see 'What can you do to help?' in Year 1 'Geography' on p. 100), there's a more challenging geography app called Geomaster which is a good way of getting your child (and you) to learn lots of useful things, such as capital cities, the countries of Europe, the names of different mountain ranges . . . even the provinces of China. Be warned: It's *very* addictive.

- For 'Mnemonics and memory aids', see Year 1 'Geography' on p. 100.

History

In the 'Aims' section at the beginning of the history national curriculum, the first bullet point says that all children should 'know and understand the history of these islands as a coherent, chronological narrative, from the earliest times to the present day'. However, that's intended to apply to the whole of the history curriculum your child will be doing up to the age of fourteen, so don't expect them to begin with Boadicea in Key Stage 1. She probably won't make an appearance until Key

Stage 2. (For the 'Purpose of Study' and 'Aims' of the history curriculum, see p. 468.)

The national curriculum divides up the content in Key Stage 1 under the following headings.

- Changes within living memory, particularly those that reveal significant changes in our national life

- Events beyond living memory that are significant nationally or globally

- The lives of significant individuals in the past who've contributed to national and international achievements

- Significant historical events, people and places in your local area.

The units we mentioned under this heading in Year 1 'History' – 'How are our toys different from those in the past?' and 'What were homes like a long time ago?' – were commonly taught in Years 1 and 2 under the old curriculum, so don't be surprised if your child does one (or both) of these in Year 2. Other units 'within living memory' that your child's teacher may choose to do (apart from 'The Olympic Games') include 'The Diamond Jubilee', 'The 2014 Scottish Referendum' and 'Brexit'.

The authors of the current national curriculum mention the Great Fire of London under this heading and, since that's a history unit teachers were used to doing under the old curriculum, your child will study this in Year 2 in most schools. Be warned, though: your child's teacher may perform a science experiment to demonstrate just how inflammable flour is (the Fire of London started in a bakery on Pudding Lane), and that's something you don't want your child to try at home.

It's likely your child will study Florence Nightingale and Mary Seacole in Topic in Year 2, since, like the Great Fire of London, that's a unit that teachers are used to doing. The teacher will focus on Mary Seacole, the pioneering black care-giver and businesswoman who ran a 'canteen for the soldiery' in the Crimea. When the new national curriculum was being drafted there was a debate about whether Seacole should be included and, to some people's surprise, she's still there.

For the purposes of introducing your child to 'significant historical events . . . in the local area', expect your child's Year 2 teacher to organize plenty of trips to nearby museums, monuments, historical landmarks and so on.

What can you do to help?

● If your child is studying the Great Fire of London, it's worth making a trip to the Museum of London, which has plenty of artefacts devoted to the episode in its War, Plague and Fire Gallery. While you're in the area you could also visit Pudding Lane, which is a twenty-minute walk away, and Christopher Wren's Monument to the Great Fire of London, which is a stone's throw from Pudding Lane.

● The Sun produces a series of mocked-up editions called Hold Ye Front Page, imagining how the red-top would have reported famous historical events had it been around at the time. Examples include 'Ooze That in the Swamp?' (the first traces of life on Earth in 3.5 billion BC), 'Tyrannosaurus Wrecks' (the end of the dinosaurs in 66 million BC) and 'The Sea Devils' (the Viking raids on

Britain in AD 793). Available at www.thesun.co.uk/sol/homepage/hold_ye_front_page.

● There's a painting of Mary Seacole in the National Portrait Gallery and if you make the trip it's worth seeing *Florence Nightingale receiving the Wounded at Scutari* as well. There are plans to erect a statue of Seacole at St Thomas's Hospital in London, but it hasn't gone up yet. However, there is a statue of Florence Nightingale in Waterloo Place in Westminster next to the Crimean War Memorial.

MNEMONICS AND MEMORY AIDS

To help your child remember that the Great Fire of London took place in 1666, ask them to think of the three sixes as smoking chimney pots silhouetted against the London skyline.

Music

Your child should begin to get a lot more out of music in Year 2 as their fine motor skills develop. That will mean less time in class spent on singing and more time on playing musical instruments. (For the 'Purpose of Study' and 'Aims' of the music curriculum, see p. 470.)

The national curriculum divides up the content in Key Stage 1 as follows.

Pupils should be taught to:

- use their voices expressively and creatively by singing songs and speaking chants and rhymes

- play tuned and untuned instruments musically

- listen with concentration and understanding to a range of high-quality live and recorded music

- experiment with, create, select and combine sounds, using the interrelated dimensions of music.

In Year 2 singing will be the main activity that takes place in music lessons, just as it was in Year 1. Expect your child to sing the same songs and nursery rhymes you sang at this age: 'Three Blind Mice', 'The Big Ship Sails on the Ally Ally Oh', 'Once I Caught a Fish Alive', etc.

As we said in Year 1 'Music', the 'tuned instruments' your child is likely to be playing in Key Stage 1 are percussion instruments such as the xylophone, vibraphone, glockenspiel and chimes. 'Untuned instruments' means percussion instruments that don't produce a definite pitch, such as drums (snare, bass, drum set, etc.) and instruments generally used for special effects (triangle, gong, castanets, rattle, cowbell, tambourine, maracas, etc.).

In Year 2 children may be asked to interpret some well-known pieces of classical music, e.g. listen to *Peter and the Wolf* and try to match the different instruments with different characters.

Your child may go beyond playing different percussion instruments and begin to explore other uses of sound. For instance, one of our children was introduced to Morse code in Year 2, with the teacher using an electronic keyboard to produce the different sounds. Scope for some cross-curricular links with computing here.

What can you do to help?

● As we said in Year 1 'Music', you should encourage your child to learn an instrument. Apart from all the obvious benefits – a lifelong source of pleasure – they'll also learn about the link between commitment, hard work, patience and achievement.

● The piano worked well for our children as a starter instrument – and electronic keyboards can be picked up for as little as £25 on eBay – but by the time your child is in Year 2 you might want to consider the violin, or the ukulele, which has become increasingly popular. Some children don't have the physical stamina at this age to hold an instrument for very long, and others will lack the coordination. But for others this is an ideal age to start.

● There are plenty of musical instruments you can make with your child at home, using coffee cans, yoghurt pots and masking tape, e.g. a drum or a rattle. To make a drum, stretch a broken balloon over the top of a large can, then hold it in place with a rubber band. For inspiration, check out the gallery of homemade musical instruments on Pinterest (www.pinterest.com/maestroclassics/homemade-musical-instruments).

Times Tables

Learning multiplication tables is a chore, however 'fun' the approach. Nevertheless, we cannot emphasize strongly enough how important it is to master them. Your child will find many topics in maths much, much easier if they do not have to work out basic multiplication facts when trying to use a new technique for long division or for finding the lowest common multiple or a percentage.

Multiplication tables, once learnt, do not always stick. You'll find teachers revisiting them every year, or more often. Learning them second or third time round is, like most things in life, a lot easier. If you ask a teenager, who will have learnt them time and again in primary school, what 8×6 is, the chances are they will have to stop and think. Ask them again the next day and they'll instantly know the answer.

Some times tables are easier than others, so they are not taught (or learnt) in ascending order.

In Year 1 children start counting in 2s, 5s and 10s.
By the end of Year 2 they should know their 2, 5 and 10 times tables.
In Year 3 they will learn the 3, 4 and 8 times tables.

In Year 4 they will learn the 6, 7, 9, 11 and 12 times tables.

By the end of Year 4 they are expected to know all of them up to 12×12.

There are some useful tricks, most of which your child will be introduced to at school, and which we set out below. But first they need to see the patterns.

Seeing the Patterns

Use a multiplication grid or let your children create one, like this one:

	1	2	3	4	5	6	7	8	9	10	11	12
1	1	2	3	4	5	6	7	8	9	10	11	12
2	2	4	6	8	10	12	14	16	18	20	22	24
3	3	6	9	12	15	18	21	24	27	30	33	36
4	4	8	12	16	20	24	28	32	36	40	44	48
5	5	10	15	20	25	30	35	40	45	50	55	60
6	6	12	18	24	30	36	42	48	54	60	66	72
7	7	14	21	28	35	42	49	56	63	70	77	84
8	8	16	24	32	40	48	56	64	72	80	88	96
9	9	18	27	36	45	54	63	72	81	90	99	108
10	10	20	30	40	50	60	70	80	90	100	110	120
11	11	22	33	44	55	66	77	88	99	110	121	132
12	12	24	36	48	60	72	84	96	108	120	132	144

Look carefully at all of the patterns and spot the repetitions, such as 7×8 and $8 \times 7 = 56$.

Let your child practise 'fast adding', which is what multiplication is.

When they can count in 3s, 4s, 5s, 6s, etc., your child will be able to say their tables. This is not the same as knowing them, which means being able to answer correctly a times table question such as 'What is 4×7?' without hesitating, counting or working it out.

Learning Your Times Tables

The standard method for any times table is to write it out, chant it out loud a few times, see how you get on without looking, concentrate hard on the ones you hesitate over and then go on chanting it ever faster until your brain has established a memory pattern of numbers that sound, and are, right. Then comes the tricky part. Get someone to ask you the questions in a random order. After a bit, you will have established which are the 'hard' ones for this times table. Learn these by endless repetition (out loud) and have another go. Once your child has done this it's time for you to write a list of randomly ordered incomplete facts ($3 \times 7 = ?$, $7 \times 7 = ?$) for them to complete. Then get them to do it against the clock and beat their own record. Once they know a few times tables, include questions from previously learnt ones alongside questions from the new one to mix it up a bit.

Then repeat this process with the next times table.

Then repeat with all the ones they are meant to know by that stage. That's all!

(There are wall charts and card games, fact cards, etc., available to buy.)

The tricks

There aren't really any tricks for the 2, 3 and 5 times tables. Most children are so familiar with counting in steps of 2, 3 and 5, however, that learning these is not too bad.

4 TIMES TABLE

If you know how to double a number this one is easy. Just double a number then double it again.

6 TIMES TABLE

If you multiply 6 by an even number, the answer ends in the same digit you multiplied by, e.g. $6 \times 2 = 12$, $6 \times 4 = 24$, $6 \times 6 = 36$, etc.

8 TIMES TABLE

Children have been heard to chant 'I ate and ate till I was sick on the floor, eight eights are sixty-four', and they never forget it again.

9 TIMES TABLE

There are various tricks for the 9 times table, but this is most children's favourite:

Hold your hands in front of you with your fingers spread out. For 9×3, bend your third finger down. (9×4 would be the fourth finger, etc.) You have two fingers in front of the bent finger and seven after the bent finger. So the answer must be 27! This technique works for 9 times tables up to 10.

This is fine as a starter, but it is slow and requires the use of two hands. It's better just to multiply by 10 (add a

0) and then subtract the number you are multiplying, e.g. $7 \times 9 = (7 \times 10) - 7 = 70 - 7 = 63$. However, this still requires time-consuming calculation, so it's better simply to learn it by rote.

11 TIMES TABLE

For numbers between 1 and 9, the 11 times table is the easiest of all: multiply 11 by 3 to get 33, multiply 11 by 4 to get 44, etc.

For numbers between 10 and 18: write down the two digits with a space in between, then add the two digits and put that number in the middle. For instance, 11×12: Jot down 1 and 2 with a space between them. Add the 1 and the 2 and put that number in the middle. Answer: 132.

12 TIMES TABLE

In theory the only one you have to learn is $12 \times 12 = 144$ as you've already learnt all the others. Easy!

Deck 'em!

- Use a deck of playing cards for a game of Multiplication War. Initially, children may need the grid on p. 164 to become quick at the answers. Flip over the cards as though you are playing Snap. The first one to say the 'fact' based on two successive cards turned over (a four and a five = '20') takes the cards. The person with most of the cards at the end wins. Children learn their facts much more quickly when they play this game on a regular basis.

Resources

- There's a colour-by-numbers book specifically aimed at children learning their times tables called *The Multiplication Tables Colouring Book*.

- There are numerous times tables apps. One our children enjoyed is Solving Maths, which has a slot-machine format.

- There's an excellent website called Memrise (www.memrise.com), a free online learning tool that's been developed by Ed Cooke, a Grand Master of Memory, and Greg Detre, a Princeton neuroscientist. It consists of lots of courses created by its community of users designed to help people remember all sorts of stuff, using a combination of pictures and mnemonics. Go to 'Maths and Science', click on 'Times Tables with Audio' and your child will be off to the races. To give just one example, if your child wants to remember that $8 \times 8 = 64$ they can choose from a series of visual mnemonics, such as a picture of the Beatles and the song title 'When I'm 64'. After they've committed four of these facts to memory, they're then tested on them – and they can keep going for as long as they like.

Year 3

Introduction

In the three core subjects (English, maths and science), the curriculum is set out by year group – or sometimes pairs of year groups – so we have been able to give lots of detail about what your child will learn in each of these subjects in each year. However, in the foundation subjects (everything else), it isn't. It just says what children should be taught in each Key Stage, not in each year. Indeed, the law doesn't allow the national curriculum to prescribe what should be taught other than by Key Stage. Consequently, schools are under no obligation to follow even the sequence suggested in the core subjects – it's advisory, not statutory – and there's no way of knowing for certain how different schools teach the subject matter specified in the foundation subjects, short of actually visiting them. In history, for instance, the national curriculum says only that children must be taught about Ancient Greece, not which year it should be taught in. That means our descriptions of what your child will be taught in Years 3, 4, 5 and 6 in the foundation subjects have involved a certain amount of guesswork and you'll often find us saying what your child 'might' or 'should' be taught rather than what they 'will' be taught.

Having said that, it's not entirely speculative. We've spoken to lots of teachers about how the national curriculum is taught in their schools and, where it seems logical to do so, we've assumed schools will continue to do what they have done in the past. If you want to know exactly which topics in, say, history or geography will be covered in each year in your school you should look on the school website or ask the head teacher.

One significant change ushered in by the new national curriculum in 2014 is that languages are now mandatory from Year 3 onwards. Many schools have been teaching some of their children a language for years (mostly French or Spanish), but since 2014 all schools have to. Even so, don't assume your child will leave primary school with a good grasp of the basics in a particular language. Given how crowded the national curriculum is, many schools won't allot more than a period a week to languages and most won't have specialist language teachers. So if you want your child to really start learning a language in Key Stage 2 you'll need to do a lot of the after-school activities we've recommended.

And how will your children be different in Year 3? In many schools the step up to Key Stage 2 from Key Stage 1 is really noticeable. Assemblies, visiting speakers and school trips, for example, are often divided by Key Stage. For some children this rise up to the bottom of the older section from the top of the younger section is a joy. For others it's a period of anxiety and their confidence may be dented for a while. In other schools the leap from Key Stage 1 to Key Stage 2 goes entirely unnoticed. One of our nephews recalls that he was expected to remember his PE kit 'all by himself' when he entered Year 3 and the consequences for failing were draconian (sitting out the PE lesson). Another child said that Year 3 felt really different because the TAs (teaching assistants) don't help 'nearly as much'. Luckily for this child, it didn't matter because he 'never needed to ask anything'. Another said the work in Year 3 was 'way harder'. No parents we canvassed could pinpoint any behavioural changes in their child as they moved up from Year 2.

English

By the start of Year 3 your child should be a competent reader. By this we mean that they should be reading speedily and accurately enough to be focusing on the meaning of what they are reading rather than on 'decoding' individual words. The more fluent readers might even be up to tackling their first Harry Potter and every child is likely to be reading books with chapters and fewer pictures than in previous years. The emphasis on reading in English switches in Year 3 from teaching them to read to encouraging them to enjoy reading. Your child's understanding of all sorts of literature – stories, poetry, plays and non-fiction – will develop fast from this point onwards as they're exposed to a greater breadth of material. Their vocabulary will be broadened both consciously by the teacher and subliminally through reading texts with unfamiliar words.

Your child is still likely to be a better reader than writer (writing is a harder skill to master, as explained in Year 1 'English'), but by the end of Year 3 joined-up writing should be the norm. The teacher will still have to nag them about grammatical and spelling accuracy – and quite possibly letter formation, too – but the focus will now be firmly on the content of their writing. Teaching children to develop as writers involves teaching them to write more effective prose (or poetry) as well as increasing their handwriting or spelling competence.

If your child is a slow reader and still struggling compared to their peers, you should expect them to be given a lot of support with extra phonics teaching to close the gap. They'll still be taught alongside their classmates so they'll have exposure to the same books, vocabulary and grammar.

As we said at the start of Year 1 'English', there's a strong emphasis on children's spoken language in the national curriculum, not only to improve standards of verbal communication, but also because spoken language underpins the development of reading and writing. In Year 3 your child should become more confident in using language in a greater variety of situations, for a variety of audiences and purposes, including through drama, formal presentations and debate.

As in Key Stage 1, the English curriculum is divided into reading and writing. Reading is further subdivided into word reading (what we think of as reading) and comprehension (understanding what you've read). Writing is subdivided into transcription (spelling and handwriting), composition and, finally, vocabulary, grammar and punctuation.

To summarize:

- Reading = word reading; comprehension

- Writing = transcription (spelling and handwriting); composition; vocabulary, grammar and punctuation

We've tackled all of these subdivisions below, apart from the last, which is dealt with in 'Grammar and

Punctuation' on p. 375. (For the 'Purpose of Study' and 'Aims' of the English curriculum, see p. 458.)

Reading

WORD READING

In Year 3 children will apply their growing knowledge of root words, prefixes and suffixes (etymology and morphology), both to be able to read aloud and to understand the meaning of new words that crop up.

Etymology is the history or origin of words. 'Amphibian', for instance, comes from the Greek for 'both', *amphi*, plus 'life', *bios*. Morphology is the study of word structure. 'Mistrustful', for example, is made up of the prefix 'mis-', the root 'trust' and the suffix '-ful'. By Year 3 teaching comprehension should be taking precedence over the teaching of word reading so we haven't devoted as much space to the latter here as we have in Years 1 and 2. Any focus on word reading will be in order to support the development of your child's vocabulary.

When children are taught to read longer words they will be encouraged to test out different pronunciations. They will attempt to match what they 'decode' to words they have already heard but may not have seen in print, e.g. in reading 'technical', the pronunciation of 'ch' as in 'church' should sound wrong, whereas when it's pronounced properly, as the 'k' in 'king', the word should sound right. When tricky words appear (i.e. words not spelt phonetically) your child will learn to see which bit of the word is 'spelt wrong', as it were, and remember the correct way to spell it.

What can you do to help?

● Keep reading with your child. Even fluent readers will learn a lot from reading out loud to an adult. Your child will often complain, saying that it's frustrating because they can read faster to themselves by now, but if you make them read out loud to you it makes them concentrate on the meaning. We all know how easy it is to read without taking it in. This will also give you an opportunity to question them to see how much they've really understood, particularly new words they might not have seen before. And quite apart from that reading aloud is a separate skill and needs practice.

● It's in Year 3 that your child should start to use dictionaries to check the meaning of words that they have read, assuming they haven't started to do that already. When they come across a new word encourage them to look it up straightaway – on-screen if the *Oxford English Dictionary* is too off-putting – and then you can each have a go at putting the word in context in a new sentence.

COMPREHENSION

In Year 3 your child will listen to and discuss a wide range of fiction, poetry, plays, non-fiction and reference books or textbooks. The emphasis will be on developing an enjoyment of written language and of working to really understand what they read. During the year, your child will be:

• preparing poems and play scripts to read aloud and to perform, showing understanding through intonation, tone, volume and action

- discussing words and phrases that capture the reader's interest and imagination

- recognizing some different forms of poetry, e.g. free verse, narrative poetry.

In books that they read independently they will learn to check that the text makes sense to them by:

- explaining the meaning of words in context

- asking questions to improve their understanding of a text

- drawing inferences, such as inferring characters' feelings, thoughts and motives from their actions, and justifying inferences with evidence

- predicting what might happen from details stated and implied

- identifying main ideas drawn from more than one paragraph and summarizing these

- identifying how language, structure and presentation contribute to meaning.

This list doesn't change much between Year 3 and Year 6 – it's the increasing complexity of the literature studied that steps up the level of challenge.

Children will be taught to recognize themes in what they read, such as the triumph of good over evil or the use of magical devices in fairy stories and folk tales. They will also learn the conventions of different types of writing, e.g. the greeting in letters, a diary written in the first person, or the use of presentational devices such as numbering and headings in instructions.

Children will learn that the comprehension skills

needed may vary slightly when reading for different reasons – for pleasure, for instance, or to find out information or the meaning of new words.

Teachers will continue to read to the class, be it stories, poems, non-fiction or other writing. Most teachers read their way through a whole book with their class in instalments every term. In this way, your child will be introduced to books and authors they might not choose themselves. Children are encouraged to exercise discretion in selecting books to read and will be helped to do so successfully. This will entail use of the school library and probably a local library. Lots of schools encourage children to recommend books to each other, often having a session once a fortnight or so where children are asked to describe a book they've enjoyed and explain why.

In small schools there's likely to be a drama production every year in which children from Year 3 to Year 6 will have a chance to participate (in bigger primaries, it may well just be Year 6). In all schools there will be fairly frequent class assemblies led by children. The reading, rereading and rehearsing of poems and plays for presentation and performance will be part of life in Year 3. Your child may develop a lifelong love of language as a result of this, beginning with an appreciation of the resonance of the right word in the right place in a poem, or the right remark in a play. Drama and poetry give more opportunity to discuss language, including vocabulary. With any luck this will extend (or begin) your child's interest in the meaning and origin of words. Dramatic activities also provide children with an incentive to find out what kind of expression is required, and that feeds into better comprehension.

In using non-fiction as an information resource, children begin to see that it is important to know what information they want to look for before they start reading. They'll learn how to use contents pages and indexes.

What can you do to help?

● Ask your child what story their teacher is reading to the class and find out whether they like it or not. If it's one you're not familiar with, you might even read it yourself so you can talk about the good bits and the boring bits (and why the boring bits are included).

● Some parents love reading to their children (by now it will be relatively stimulating books rather than the ten-minute picture books of earlier years), but some really don't. Many parents just can't find the time. By the time your child is an independent reader it can be very tempting to leave them to it, especially if younger siblings are clamouring for story books to be read. Don't. If at all possible, keep reading to your child until he or she begs you to stop (Year 5 or Year 6, usually, and sometimes not even then). There will still be, in Year 3, shelves of books that are very good reads with lots of new vocabulary and excitement which are still too hard for your child to push on with by themselves. Most children love the time away from a screen with a parent's focused attention. Don't worry if the book seems too advanced for younger siblings to listen to as well – they will vote with their feet pretty quickly.

● Like all skills, gleaning information from non-fiction texts (whether following instructions in a recipe or searching for a new app) requires practice, so make sure you get your child to do it themselves rather than doing it for them.

● Looking words up in a dictionary is likely to be a homework task and one that's never greeted with enthusiasm. It's very tempting to do it for your child to speed them through, but that's not much help. (You can buy children's dictionaries, which are less off-putting than adult ones, but beware! All too often they don't include the word your child is looking up, and that can be very frustrating.) Try racing your child to find a word, using two dictionaries.

Writing

TRANSCRIPTION

a) Spelling

In Year 3 building on the previous year's work, your child will continue to learn how to spell many new words, both those that follow phonetic rules and those that don't. They'll learn to spell more homophones, e.g. 'ball/bawl', 'missed/mist', 'peace/piece', and near-homophones ('accept/except', 'affect/effect'). They'll learn the possessive apostrophe with plural words ('girls'', 'boys'', 'babies'') and to add more suffixes, including '-ation', '-ly', and prefixes, including 'un-', 'dis-', 'mis-'.

The national curriculum sets out lists of suffixes and prefixes that must be taught, but it is not a statutory requirement to teach the rules of spelling behind them. Some teachers may choose not to teach all the rules: they're often so cumbersome it's easier just to learn the spellings by rote. Most adults don't know the rules, but can spell the words. Whether a suffix is spelt '-sure' or '-ture', or when it's '-tion' rather than '-sion' is a good example. The rule is that when the 'root word', e.g. 'invent', ends in a 't' or '-te', the correct suffix is '-tion' (as in 'invention' or 'hesitation'). When the root word ends in a 'd' or '-se', then '-sion' is used (as in 'expansion' or 'extension'). When the root word ends in 'ss' or '-mit', then '-sion' is used (as in 'expression', 'discussion' or 'permission').

By the time they reach Year 3, your child will be used to the routines established in their school for improving their spelling. They will be used to learning spelling rules, so they'll understand that the list of new words introduced is not random. The teacher may write a list of root words, and then words with correct suffixes, and ask if the children can see a pattern. The children may then group words following one pattern, e.g. root words that take the suffix '-sion', and learn the rule. And, to finish, they'll be given a list of words and asked to add the correct suffixes by following the rules. Then they'll be set those words as the spelling homework for that week. (See the statutory word list for Years 3 and 4 in Year 4 'English' on p. 252.)

What can you do to help?

● Most schools send home weekly lists of words in your child's book bag, and they will be expected to learn how to spell them. It really helps the teacher and, more importantly, your child if you make sure they do. Children are taught a method: look, cover, write, check. It's a good technique and worth reinforcing at home.

b) Handwriting

In Year 3 your child will be taught to write with joined-up letters and will learn which letters next to each other are best left not joined up. During the year they will increase the legibility, consistency and quality of their handwriting, e.g. by ensuring that the down strokes of letters are parallel and equidistant, and that lines of writing are spaced sufficiently so that the ascenders and descenders of letters do not touch.

Handwriting will continue to be taught, with the aim of increasing speed and fluency.

Some schools teach fully cursive (joined-up) handwriting right from the start, believing that it helps children become fluent faster and that if they learn to print first and then learn to do joined-up writing it's like learning two different languages. Other schools teach children to print letters first (i.e. write them separately, without joins) and then move on to joined-up writing, thinking that teaching children to print helps them understand the concept of individual letters better. Research is inconclusive on this point. When learning joined-up writing, children are not taught letters in alphabetical order, but in groups according to their formation: for example, 'a', 'c', 'e' and 'o' are taught together because they're all based on an anticlockwise circle, i.e. you make circular movements with your pen in an anticlockwise direction when forming the letters. Joined-up writing has a number of advantages. It's not always faster than printing, but it generally has a nicer style, and does seem to help children speed up their writing, which encourages them to write more and produce better content. It also helps with spelling, as your child develops a muscle memory of the movements for each word. (For a guide to how to form letters, see the Appendix 'How to Form the Letters of the Alphabet' on p. 473.)

What can you do to help?

● Try to encourage your child to take pride in their handwriting (usually easier with girls than boys) and try not to get frustrated at the snail's pace they work at when first attempting joined-up writing. Although children usually write in pencil at school, we suggest they practise with felt-tips and gel pens, which have a nice, fluid delivery of ink. (If your child is left-handed, see Year 1 'English' on p. 65.)

● There are apps for practising handwriting. Try iTrace or abc Joined Up.

● You can buy handwriting practice books, such as *Collins Easy Learning Handwriting Practice*, or *Letterland Handwriting Practice*. Check with your school to see if they use a particular scheme. It will help your child in so much of their school life if they can write legibly and fast. Boys, particularly, often struggle. Practice really does help: the actions become better imprinted in the brain the more they are repeated. If all else fails try bribery and get your child writing at home every day.

COMPOSITION

In Year 3 children begin to plan and draft their writing more formally. Before writing something, they may first discuss a similar piece of writing to learn from its structure, vocabulary and grammar. They'll also record ideas before they start. They'll compose and rehearse sentences orally (including dialogue), building a varied and rich vocabulary and an increasing range of sentence structures. They'll start organizing paragraphs around a theme. In narratives they'll create settings, characters and plots; and in non-narrative material they'll start to use simple organizational devices such as headings and subheadings.

Self-evaluation and editing of written work begins in Year 3. Your child will assess the effectiveness of their own and others' writing and suggest improvements. They'll be encouraged to come up with changes to grammar and vocabulary to improve consistency and to proofread for spelling and punctuation errors.

Your child will read their writing aloud, either to a group or the whole class, and be encouraged to use more expression in their voice to emphasize the meaning.

Across the whole curriculum, your child will have opportunities to write for a range of purposes and audiences as part of their daily school work and will soon learn to make decisions about the form the writing should take, such as a narrative, an explanation or a description, depending on what or who the writing is for. The sequence of processes essential for writing – thinking aloud to explore ideas, drafting and rereading to check that the meaning is clear – will become familiar.

Many schools follow a writing scheme such as 'Big Writing', which encourages children's awareness of their developing skills. These are relatively new, but quite effective (or so we're told). If children know that to reach the next level they must include more sophisticated vocabulary and more complex sentence structure they will strive to do just that. This is made easier for them by lists of higher-level vocabulary – adjectives, mainly – and suggested higher-level connectives, e.g. 'meanwhile', 'besides', 'since', or more interesting 'start words', all

available on laminated sheets for them to use if they like.
It sounds prescriptive, but it generates enthusiasm.

What can you do to help?

● Give your child an appealing exercise book to use as a
journal. Diaries with locks go down well. Enforce the
writing of thank-you letters with a minimum number of
sentences and exciting vocabulary.

● Play composition games. Give your child an object, a
place and a verb and give them ten minutes to write a
(very short) story. For example, 'a vase', 'China',
'stealing'. Or 'a gardener', 'the King's bedroom',
'laughing'.

Maths

The main focus of maths teaching in lower Key Stage
2 (Years 3 and 4) is to ensure that your child becomes
increasingly fluent with number facts, e.g. 24 + 7 = 31,
the concept of place value (hundreds, tens and units) and
the four operations (addition, subtraction, multiplication and division). Having a firm base of real
understanding of these concepts is vital. This is what
ensures that children develop efficient written and mental methods so they can do calculations accurately with
progressively large numbers.

Problems with simple fractions and decimal place
value should be introduced in Year 3. Your child should
learn to draw shapes with increasing accuracy, and to
describe them confidently, using ideas such as obtuse
and acute angles and symmetry. They will try to use

measuring instruments such as rulers and scales with accuracy. And they should learn to read and spell mathematical vocabulary correctly and confidently.

The national curriculum sets out what your child should learn in Year 3 under the various headings below. (For the 'Purpose of Study' and 'Aims' of the maths curriculum, see p. 459.)

Number and place value

Your child should learn to count from 0 in multiples of 4, 8, 50 and 100 (they will already be able to count in 2s, 3s and 4s) and to find 10 or 100 more or less than a given number. They will be taught to recognize the place value of each digit in a three-digit number (hundreds, tens, units), and compare and order numbers up to 1,000. They'll read and write numbers up to 1,000 in numerals and in words.

Your child is likely to use a technique called 'partitioning' to solve increasingly complex problems, building on work from Year 2. When they partition a number, they split it into components of hundreds, tens and units that add up to make the number. Fluency in partitioning is a good indicator that a child really understands place value, e.g. 146 = 100 + 40 and 6; 146 = 130 + 16. Understanding this will help your child when they are asked to take 16 from 146, or to add 70 to 146.

Your child should continue to count in 1s, 10s and 100s, until they become fluent in the order and place value of numbers up to 1,000.

Addition and subtraction

In Year 3 your child is likely to practise solving a variety of addition and subtraction problems. They will be expected to learn how to add and subtract numbers mentally, including three-digit numbers. Then your child should learn, probably for the first time, how to add and subtract in columns. This is when problems start arising at home, as the cry goes up, 'That's not how we do it at school!' Parents will insist that their way is 'right', that the sum requires them to 'borrow' or 'carry' one. It's likely that, in addition, your child may be thinking of 'carrying', but they'll be 'carrying' ten not one. In subtraction, they are unlikely to use the term 'borrowing', but rather will be 'partitioning' a larger number into smaller parts and putting one part of a number currently in the tens column into the units column, for example, because there aren't enough tens in the tens column to subtract the required amount. Here's an example of how they'll be taught to do it:

$73 - 27$ is the same as $(70 + 3) - (20 + 7)$
Written in columns: $70 + 3$
                                   $-20 + 7$

Children start with the units, see they need to take 7 from 3, know this won't work, so they regroup, or 'partition' the numbers, so it will work:

$70 + 3$ becomes $60 + 13$
$-20 + 7$ $-20 + 7$

Now they can take 7 from 13, then 20 from 60, and get the answer: 46. And they won't have used the word 'borrow'. Some schools use the term 'exchanging' (because they are 'exchanging' one ten for ten units).

Why has the language changed? The reason is that it became clear that lots of children never understood why they were 'carrying' or 'borrowing' one and with the new system they all seem to get a better grasp of the under-lying numbers behind the method. Teachers use all sorts of tools, such as rods of different lengths to represent tens and units, to reinforce the need to 'partition' num-bers up, or 'exchange' a ten for ten units, or a hundred for ten tens, when subtracting. Here's a picture of Dienes blocks, which are very popular with teachers and children.

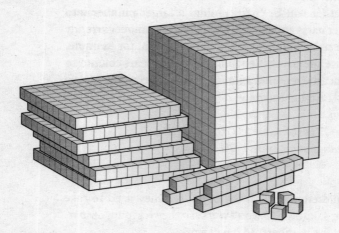

Teachers are likely to encourage your child to estimate the answer to a calculation and use inverse operations to check answers. For instance, if you think 143 − 31 = 121, then add 31 to 121 and see if you get 143. Oops, must have made a mistake.

Multiplication and division

Last year, your child should have learnt their 2, 5 and 10 times tables. These will be revised and in Year 3 it's on to the 3, 4 and 8 times tables. As we've said before (see 'Times Tables' on p. 163), there is nothing for it but to learn these by rote. Tricks abound that help in moments of uncertainty, but the facts have to be learnt. Teachers despair of those children whose parents don't help with learning tables, because although it's a chore it helps their maths enormously and needs to be practised at home – there isn't time to do them often enough in school.

Your child should learn to develop efficient mental methods. For instance, they'll use commutativity (when you can swap numbers over and still get the same answer, e.g. $4 \times 12 \times 5 = 4 \times 5 \times 12$), associativity (when it doesn't matter how the numbers are grouped, e.g. $4 \times 5 \times 12 = 20 \times 12 = 240$) and multiplication and division facts, e.g. $3 \times 2 = 6$, $6 \div 3 = 2$ and $2 = 6 \div 3$, to derive related facts, e.g. $30 \times 2 = 60$, $60 \div 3 = 20$ and $20 = 60 \div 3$. Through doubling, they will learn to connect the 2, 4 and 8 times tables.

They will probably now start to write multiplication calculations, using various formal methods, such as a multiplication grid (sometimes called the 'box' method), which will look unfamiliar to parents:

34×8

×	8
30	$30 \times 8 = 240$
4	$4 \times 8 = 32$

Answer: 240 + 32 = 272

They are likely to move on to expanded short multiplication:

34 × 8 could be written as

```
30 + 4
×    8
_____
30 × 8 = 240
 4 × 8 =  32
_____
           272
```

Eventually, but probably not until Year 4, they will start writing multiplication and division sums vertically, in the way parents are familiar with:

```
    24
×    3
_____
    72
```

Your child should also start to solve simple problems in context, deciding which of the four operations (addition, subtraction, multiplication or division) to use and why. These include measuring and scaling contexts, e.g. four times as high, eight times as long, etc., and correspondence problems, e.g. three hats and four coats make how many different outfits? Or twelve sweets shared equally between four children, or four cakes shared equally between eight children.

Fractions

In Year 3 your child should really get going with fractions. Having become familiar with halves and quarters in Year 2, they'll now learn what's meant by a tenth, connect tenths to place value, decimal measures and to division by ten. By this we mean they'll know that 'a tenth' is ten times smaller than one, in the same way that ten is ten times bigger than one (and so that the column for tenths will be to the right of the column for units).

They can then progress to other fractions, such as a $\frac{1}{6}$, or $\frac{1}{7}$, or $\frac{3}{7}$. They should learn to put these in the right place on a number line and to deduce relations between them, such as size ($\frac{1}{7}$ is bigger than $\frac{1}{10}$) and equivalence ($\frac{3}{6}$ is the same as $\frac{1}{2}$). They will see, for example, that $\frac{3}{7} + \frac{2}{7} = \frac{5}{7}$.

They'll continue to recognize fractions in the context of parts of a whole, parts of numbers, parts of measurements or parts of a shape. They'll recognize unit fractions as a division of a quantity (one sixth of a number is that number divided by six).

Your child is likely to practise adding and subtracting fractions with the same denominator (e.g. $\frac{5}{7} + \frac{1}{7} = \frac{6}{7}$) in a number of different ways to improve fluency.

Measurement

In Year 3 your child should continue to measure using the appropriate tools and units, progressing to using a wider range of measures, including comparing and using mixed units, e.g. 1kg and 200g, and simple equivalents of mixed units, e.g. 5m = 500cm.

The comparison of measures includes simple scaling up by whole numbers, e.g. a given quantity or measure is twice as long, or five times as high, and this connects to multiplication, e.g. 2kg = 10 × 200g; or 25cm × 5 = 1m 25cm.

Your child will probably continue to use money (or pictures of it) until they become fluent in recognizing the value of coins, adding and subtracting amounts (including mixed pounds and pence), and giving change using manageable amounts. They will record pounds and pence separately. (The decimal recording of money e.g. £1.23 rather than £1 and 23p is not introduced formally until Year 4.)

Children should be able to tell the time on an analogue clock, if they can't already, by the end of Year 3. Some teachers may introduce children to digital 12-hour clocks, paving the way for using digital 24-hour clocks in Year 4. Your child will, we hope, estimate and read time with increasing accuracy to the nearest minute; record and compare time in terms of seconds, minutes and hours; use vocabulary such as 'o'clock', 'a.m.', 'p.m.', 'morning', 'afternoon', 'noon' and 'midnight'. They should learn the number of seconds in a minute and the number of days in each month, year and leap year.

Geometry

Your child's knowledge of the properties of shapes should be extended in Year 3 to symmetrical and non-symmetrical polygons and polyhedra. Your child will probably draw two-dimensional shapes and make three-dimensional shapes using modelling materials. They'll learn to identify horizontal and vertical lines and pairs of perpendicular and parallel lines. They may learn to describe shapes, including the terms 'acute' and 'obtuse' for angles lesser or greater than a right angle, and to identify right angles. They'll learn that two right angles make a half-turn, three make three quarters of a turn and four a complete turn.

Statistics

In Year 3 your child should continue to learn to interpret and present data using bar charts, pictograms and tables, such as these:

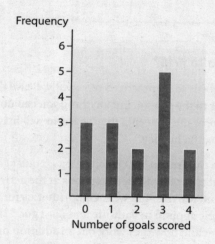

A pictogram to show the number of goals scored in fifteen football matches

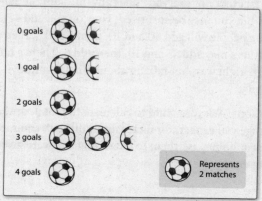

Number of goals	Tally
0				
1				
2			
3	ⅢⅠ
4			

What can you do to help?

Maths needs to be practised repeatedly. Leave the teaching to the school, but anything you can do at home to reinforce the concepts they've learnt will help your child's maths fluency.

● Some children in Year 3 will be much quicker than others at mental arithmetic, so look at the activities for Year 2 and for Year 4 as well. Opportunities for mental arithmetic abound in daily life and it's a good tactic to ask your child how they work out an addition or subtraction. They will be used to explaining, and used to the fact that not everyone does any one sum the same way, but you may be surprised. How do you add 47 + 14? Some people will add 40 and 10, then 7 and 3, then add 1. Others may add 45 and 10, then add 6. There's no single right way, but talking about it helps improve fluency.

● Shops. Ask your child to calculate the total, or the change you expect, for increasingly difficult transactions. Back at home, ask them to check that you were given the right change.

● Cards. Playing card games is great for maths. Try Blackjack, Whist, or any game where they need to score by adding numbers.

● Board games. An element of competition seems to enable quite complicated calculations. Monopoly, or the many alternatives that involve money, will improve maths skills.

● Fractions. Fruit can be a good place to start. How many segments in a satsuma? What fraction is each? Can you cut two apples into fifths? Then how much does two fifths plus four fifths make? It helps, obviously, if you have more than one child and they have to divide a piece of fruit – or a chocolate bar – between them.

● Cooking. If you have some electronic scales that can be reset to 0 every time you need to add more, that's just too easy. If you have some that can't, there are lots of additions to be worked out when adding ingredients. Ask your child to make double the quantity, or triple . . .

● Time. Help your child become good at telling the time. It doesn't take long if you keep at it. It's made easier with a 'teaching clock': a cardboard clock face with plastic hands, usually coloured differently on the 'past' and 'to' sides. Children are usually happy with 'o'clock', 'quarter past' and 'half past'. They find 'quarter to' harder. You need to make sure they understand that the minute hand always moves clockwise and that, once it's gone past the six, it's on its way back up to the top, **to** the next 'o'clock'. Once they've got that, you can go on to show that after five tiny little minutes they get to the number one. Your child will be adept at counting in fives by now, so five, ten, fifteen, twenty and twenty-five past are easy. They don't like the confusion over fifteen past always being called quarter past (can you blame them?). Only when they've become good at recognizing, say, ten past four or twenty past seven, should you move on to 'to'.

Lots of positive reinforcement ('Not bad! But not quite right . . .') is better than negative feedback ('No, you dimwit!'). Ask what time it will be in twenty minutes, or how long ago the television programme started.

And leave digital out of it until they have mastered analogue.

● Multiplication. Ask your child to show you how to multiply, say, 24×6. Pretend you've forgotten and see if they can show you how. If your child tells you they find multiplication hard ask the teacher for some guidance as to how they are being taught and for some worksheets to try at home together. (See 'Times Tables' on p. 163.)

● Bond Assessment books are very dry, but some children love solving graded puzzles with the answers in the back.

● Lots of parents swear by Kumon maths programmes. These are worksheet-based study programmes 'designed to pursue the potential of each child' (sic). Look up your local 'study centre' and if you sign up to a course (and pay!) your child will be set a series of repetitive worksheets to complete daily.

● The following apps are popular with some children: Times Table Clock, Motion Maths: Fractions, Bubble Pop Multiplication and Doodle Tables.

● A book called How to Do Maths So Your Children Can Too by Naomi Sani provides a wealth of detail if you're finding it hard to understand what your child is telling you about how they do maths now.

Science

The principal focus of science in Years 3 and 4 is on broadening your child's scientific view of the world around them. They will explore, talk about, test and develop ideas about everyday phenomena and the relationships between living things and their environments, e.g. why polar bears don't thrive in deserts. They will ask their own questions about what they observe and decide how to find answers: whether to observe changes over time, to group and classify things, or carry out simple comparative tests. In Year 3 your child will be taught how to draw simple conclusions. The national curriculum places a big emphasis on using scientific language, first to talk about and later to write about, what they've discovered. And children are expected to learn how to spell scientific words correctly.

Throughout their science work, children will begin to learn various practical scientific processes and skills, such as setting up comparative and fair tests, making systematic and careful observations, taking accurate measurements and so on. They may get to use thermometers and data-loggers during Year 3.

They are likely to spend more time than they would like recording their work – this can be off-putting, because lots of children in Year 3 will still struggle with writing stamina. 'Writing up' an investigation means explaining what you've done, *and* why, *and* recording your results (neatly) *and* writing down your conclusion. If the investigation was into 'Which paper towel is most absorbent?', this can feel like a horribly arduous task for a very straightforward test. (Teachers recognize this, but they have to be able to provide evidence that the children have these skills, so they have no choice.)

In Year 3 the national curriculum organizes the science to be covered under the headings 'Plants', 'Animals (including humans)', 'Rocks', 'Light' and 'Forces and magnets'. By this stage, most primaries will have two science lessons a week. (For the 'Purpose of Study' and 'Aims' of the science curriculum, see p. 461.)

Plants

Your child will have learnt the main plant parts in previous years. Now they will be introduced to the relationship between structure and function: the idea that every part has a job to do. They will focus on the role of the roots and stem in nutrition and support, leaves for nutrition and flowers for reproduction.

The teacher may introduce the idea that plants can make their own food, but at this stage the children do not need to understand how this happens.

The kinds of things your child is likely to do are: compare the effect of different factors on plant growth, e.g. the amount of light, the amount of fertilizer; observe the different stages of plant life cycles over a period of time to discover how seeds are formed; and look for patterns in the structure of fruits that relate to how the seeds are dispersed. They might observe how water is transported in plants (if you cut a white carnation and put the stem in coloured water you can see the water travelling up the stem to the flower).

Animals (including humans)

Your child will continue to learn about the importance of nutrition (see Year 2 'Science' on p. 139). The class might compare and contrast the diets of different animals (including their pets) and decide ways of grouping them according to what they eat. They might research different food groups and how they keep us healthy and design meals based on what they find out.

In this year your child will be introduced to the main body parts associated with the skeleton and muscles and find out how different parts of the body have special functions: skeletons for support and protection and muscles for movement, for example. They are likely to identify and group animals with and without skeletons and observe and compare their movement, and explore ideas about what would happen if humans did not have skeletons.

Rocks

This section is highly likely to be linked with work your child is doing in geography. The class will explore different kinds of rocks and soils (most schools have a good collection built up and children love adding to it with samples from their garden or the playground). They will learn how to sort different kinds of rocks into different categories – igneous, metamorphic, sedimentary – on the basis of their appearance and simple physical properties (such as what happens when rocks are rubbed together or what changes occur when they're put in water). They will think about the way soils are formed.

They will explore how and why the rocks used in buildings or gravestones might have changed over time, maybe using a hand lens or microscope to help them identify and classify rocks according to whether they have grains or crystals, and whether they have fossils in them.

Your child will learn how fossils are formed and might

research and discuss the different kinds of living things whose fossils have been found in sedimentary rock.

Light

Like most topics in science, light will crop up again and again over the years. In this first exposure (geddit?) your child will think about what light is, possibly for the first time. It's not an easy question to answer at this stage, other than to say that they need light in order to see things and that dark is the absence of light. Young children, when asked to draw how they see, will often draw light coming out of their eyes. It's interesting probing this idea with them, helping them to realize that, if light really did come out of their eyes they'd be able to see in the dark. In Year 3 your child will explore what happens when light reflects off a mirror or other reflective surfaces, including playing mirror games to help them answer questions about how light behaves. The class will look for, and measure, shadows, and find out how they are formed and what might cause the shadows to change. They will look for patterns in what happens to shadows when the light source moves or the distance between the light source and the object changes.

Forces and magnets

Your child will learn that the word 'force' in a scientific context means something that makes something else happen, e.g. a push or a pull. They will probably start this topic by comparing how things move on different surfaces and will learn that friction is a force that stops things moving so fast.

They will see that, for most forces, such as a push or a

pull (opening a door, pushing a swing), or friction, there needs to be contact between two objects. Then magnets are introduced and it will come as no surprise to your child that magnetic forces can act without direct contact. This is a very strange phenomenon, but being children they won't find it strange. They'll have fun exploring the behaviour and everyday uses of different magnets, e.g. bar, ring, button and horseshoe. The class is very likely to be asked to think up scientifically fair ways of comparing the strengths of different magnets, e.g. measure how close different magnets need to be to a paperclip to make it move; to be 'fair' it must be the same paperclip, on the same surface, from the same angle each time. They will sort materials into those that are magnetic and those that aren't. They will look for patterns in the way that magnets behave in relation to each other and what might affect this, e.g. the strength of the magnet or whether the poles are facing the wrong way or the right way, and will, no doubt, suggest creative uses for different magnets.

What can you do to help?

- By this age your child will be able to enjoy the many science kits available to buy called things such as Kitchen Science, Magnet Science, Weird Slime Laboratory, etc. They are too young for chemistry sets and won't begin to learn about electricity until Year 4.

- Fossils get some children very excited. Museum visits to see fossils are surprisingly popular. Be prepared to spend more time in the shop choosing an artificially coloured slice of crystal than you did in the museum itself.

- Let your child astound you with their powers of observation by hunting for fossils on a beach or in a stony field. The Jurassic Coast (between Exmouth in Devon and Swanage in Dorset) is the best place for this, but you may know somewhere closer to home.

- Make a museum display of local rocks at home. Your child will probably enjoy making the labels most.

- Next time you buy a chicken and roast it, cut it up with your child and talk about muscles and skeletons. You could boil the bones and try to reconstruct the bird.

- Dye some white carnations various colours by putting them in water with different-coloured food dyes.

Art and Design

In Key Stage 2 your child's teacher may introduce your child to some of the key concepts they'll need to understand and evaluate different works of art, such as 'genre', 'movement' and 'period'. Your child will also be introduced to concepts such as 'tone', 'line', 'form' and 'contrast' to help them describe their own and others' work. But don't expect any more time to be set aside for art and design than in Key Stage 1. In all likelihood, it will either be combined with DT in a single period per week, alternate with DT every half-term or be taught for just one week per term in 'Art Week'. Having said that, some schools will devote more time to the subject. For instance, at one of our children's primaries they have one period of art and design a week in addition to Art Week. During Art Week, the whole school focuses on the work of a single artist, such as Claude Monet or Pierre-Auguste

Renoir. (For the 'Purpose of Study' and 'Aims' of the art and design curriculum, see p. 462.)

The national curriculum divides up the content in Key Stage 2 as follows.

Pupils should be taught to:

- develop different artistic techniques with creativity and experimentation, showing an increasing awareness of different kinds of art, craft and design

- create sketchbooks to record observations and use them to review and revisit ideas

- improve mastery of art and design techniques, including drawing, painting and sculpture, using a range of materials

- understand the work of great artists, architects and designers in history.

The reason schools regard it as important to encourage your child to explore as many different artistic techniques as possible in Key Stage 2 – charcoal line drawing, fabric printing, beadwork, felt-making, collage – isn't just to help them understand the work of different practitioners. It's also in the hope that they'll discover the technique that works best for them. The theory is that the reason some children don't like art is because they aren't given an opportunity to discover the particular form of artistic expression they're best at.

Your child will begin Year 3 with a sketchbook – in some cases, given to him or her by the school – but it's unlikely to be a hard-backed Victorian affair with white, unlined drawing paper. Rather, your child will be encouraged to use a range of different materials to record their thoughts and ideas, including folders, artist's portfolios and spiral-bound notepads. The thinking here is that they're more likely to sustain their interest in art and design outside lesson time if they get into the habit of keeping a sketchbook, recording their observations and trying out different ideas.

Under the old curriculum some primary schools taught an art and design unit called 'Investigating pattern' in Year 3 and that has survived the transition to the current curriculum in a handful of schools. Your child will observe how patterns are made by shapes overlapping and repeating themselves, particularly in Islamic art. They may be asked to create a pattern themselves, using textiles or card based on a digital image or a photograph. There is scope for cross-curricular links with computing here.

Unless your primary is exceptional, your child won't be introduced to a large number of artists/architects/designers in Year 3. Teachers will instead choose a handful of well-known figures who are exemplars of particular movements or styles, such as Picasso (cubism) or Frida Kahlo (folk art).

What can you do to help?

● In our experience, girls are more interested in art than boys and this is borne out by the fact that girls are twice as likely to do a GCSE in the subject. One reason for this may be that girls are neater and better organized than boys at this age, with more developed fine motor skills, and enjoy showing off these attributes in drawings and pictures. Boys may be put off by their inability to master basic artistic techniques and inhibited by their all-round messiness, particularly if they have 'artistic' sisters.

Consequently, if you want your son to take as much interest in art as your daughter, you'll need to praise his efforts. Let him know that his lack of technique needn't necessarily be a barrier to self-expression. If you can bear it, encourage him to engage in more 'physical' artistic activities, such as Jackson Pollock-style 'action painting'.

● One way to develop your child's interest in art is to give them an opportunity to present their work to a larger public, not just family members and grandparents. They'll have learnt to distrust all those exclamations of 'Brilliant!' by now and crave a more reliable form of validation. Entering competitions can be a good route to this and most large public galleries organize competitions for children. For instance, there's an annual art prize for schools given by the Saatchi Gallery (www.saatchigallery.com).

● Get a pack of blank cards and create your own version of Happy Families, with every family member joining in. To make it more challenging, choose species of birds or different flowers. You could visit Kew Gardens for inspiration. One of us did this with their family as a child. Important: don't use shiny cards because the ink smudges!

● If you want to encourage your child to experiment with colour – to use those colours they want to use, not those they think they're *meant* to use – you could do worse than read him or her *The Artist Who Painted a Blue Horse* by Eric Carle. The artist in the book views the world through a child's eyes, painting a red crocodile, an orange elephant, a purple fox and a polka-dotted donkey.

● If your child is doing the 'Ancient Egypt' unit in history you could take them to see some Egyptian art.

There are permanent exhibits at the British Museum in London, the Bristol Museum and Art Gallery, the Ashmolean Museum in Oxford, the Fitzwilliam Museum in Cambridge, the World Museum in Liverpool and the Manchester Museum. We were both taken to the Treasures of Tutankhamun exhibition at the British Museum in 1972 and it made a lasting impression on us.

Computing

As in Key Stage 1, a good way of looking at the computing curriculum in Key Stage 2 is to distinguish between those components that involve teaching children computer science (the first three bullet points below) and those aimed at teaching them digital literacy (the next four). The digital literacy components are quite similar to what children used to study in ICT in the pre-2014 curriculum and some of the units schools have taught before have resurfaced. However, in most schools the focus has shifted from using word processors and towards more web-based programs, especially with the rise of Chromebooks and tablets in classrooms. (For the 'Purpose of Study' and 'Aims' of the computing curriculum, see p. 463.)

The national curriculum divides up the content in Key Stage 2 as follows.

Pupils should be taught to:

- design, write and debug programs that accomplish specific goals, including controlling or simulating physical systems; solve problems by deconstructing them into smaller parts

- use sequence, selection and repetition in programs; work with variables and various forms of input and output

- use logical reasoning to explain how simple algorithms work and to detect and correct errors in algorithms and programs

- understand computer networks, including the internet; how they can provide multiple services, such as the World Wide Web; and the opportunities they offer for communication and collaboration

- use search technologies effectively, appreciate how results are selected and ranked, and be discerning in evaluating digital content

- select, use and combine a variety of software (including internet services) on a range of digital devices to design and create a range of programs, systems and content that accomplish given goals, including collecting, analysing, evaluating and presenting data and information

- use technology safely, respectfully and responsibly; recognize acceptable/unacceptable behaviour; identify a range of ways to report concerns about content and contact.

Computer science

The way the computing curriculum is designed, your child is expected to focus on algorithms in Key Stage 1 and think about how to embed them in programs in Key Stage 2. That will involve breaking problems down into smaller parts and creating decision trees and the like which will dictate how a computer reacts to different inputs. (Think of an 'input' as being like a keyboard or a mouse and an 'output' as the computer screen.)

For instance, the teacher may ask your child to write an algorithm that describes the steps they take from waking up in the morning to arriving at school. (We're indebted to Phil Bagge, a primary school teacher, for this example.) To do that, your child will have to think about how to break down this sequence into small, discrete steps (the 'sequences', in computer science lingo) as well as producing a set of instructions to cover every eventuality (if this, then that – known as 'selection') and the need for the program to repeat certain sequences until a condition is met ('repetition'). As part of this exercise, which will take place over several weeks, your child might come up with something like the 'breakfast' pathway shown here.

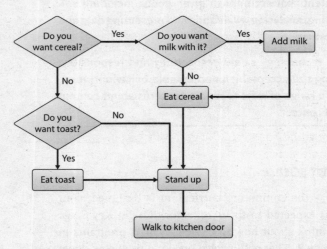

This pathway was created by Phil Bagge using Microsoft Publisher

Some seven-year-olds will find this quite challenging, but your child won't be expected to do this on their own. They'll work with others in pairs or larger groups, and their Year 3 teacher will guide them through it, step by step. There'll also be lots of opportunities for them to put their new knowledge into practice, using a simple programming language such as Scratch. You may be surprised by how quickly they pick it up.

Another computer science component in the curriculum is 'controlling or simulating physical systems' (see first bullet point on p. 204) and your child's school may choose to teach that using Lego WeDo. These are Lego construction sets that enable children to build models which they can then attach to computers and control using computer programs.

Digital literacy

This part of the computing curriculum is more like the old ICT curriculum, with the emphasis on teaching your child the skills they will need to make full use of computers and other information technology. Some of the units children used to study in Year 3 and which have survived include 'Combining text and graphics' (learning how to use software such as Microsoft Word and PowerPoint), 'Introduction to databases' (search engines, Wikipedia), 'Manipulating sound' (an opportunity to play around with some music software) and 'Email' (what it says on the tin).

One way for the teacher to bring these skills together and familiarize your child with computer networks would be to create a class blog, as they may have done in Key Stage 1 (see Year 1 'Computing' on p. 89). However, unlike before, your child may now be trusted to contribute to the blog without having to use the teacher as an intermediary. That is, they may be able to publish blog posts, upload photographs, embed video content and so on, without direct teacher supervision. How much latitude your child is granted when it comes to this sort of thing will depend on how risk averse the teacher is – or how risk averse the head is.

In addition, your child may be taught how to use the school's VLE (Virtual Learning Environment). Most secondary schools now have VLEs, and an increasing number of primaries do, too. Their main purpose is to enable children and parents to access teaching resources from home.

E-safety

The emphasis on e-safety throughout the computing curriculum may strike some parents as a bit overprotective, but the reason it's there is because your child will be actively encouraged to explore computer networks, including social networks, which is a new departure. Teachers are quite strict about children not using the school's computers to access networks such as Facebook and Twitter because of the risk of cyber-bullying or inappropriate contact, and the majority of schools will probably continue to block access to those sites. However, teachers are likely to become less paranoid about this as time goes on, given that understanding networks is a key part of the computing curriculum, so e-safety remains important. (Ofsted recommends a 'managed' rather than a 'locked down' approach.) Think of it as being like a driving licence: We'll trust you to roam around out there unsupervised, provided you take e-safety seriously.

What can you do to help?

● If your child is into Lego, why not ask them to use the instructions for building something simple, such as an action figure, as a starting point for creating a step-by-step algorithm? Tell your child to imagine the person that they're writing the instructions for is a member of an Amazonian tribe who has never seen plastic before, let alone Lego. They'll need to be told to open the plastic bags containing the pieces, empty the pieces on to a flat work surface, identify the pieces they're going to need for the first stage of construction, hold each piece the right way up, apply just enough pressure to make the pieces click together and so on. After they've written the algorithm, you can then pretend to be the Amazonian tribesman and see how far you get by meticulously following their instructions. Chances are, you'll end up with something very different to the picture on the box. That means your child will have to rewrite the program, i.e. debug it. Keep doing it until they get it right.

● Set up a family email account on gmail or hotmail. You'll have to monitor the account pretty carefully to ensure your child isn't exposed to any inappropriate junk mail, but once they've got an email address they can use they can send emails to their grandparents, as well as to aunts, uncles, cousins, etc. You can teach them how to embed photographs in emails, include links to URLs and how to copy – or blind copy – other people in.

● There are a number of apps and games designed to help children who've already mastered some basic programming skills to progress to the next level, including Sketch Nation, Move the Turtle, Hopscotch,

Cargo-Bot, Cato's Hike and Pettson's Inventions (a problem-solving app). Some of these apps are free and some are available for free in 'Lite' versions.

Design and Technology

There's a revealing sentence in the preamble to the design and technology section in the curriculum in which the authors try to justify why children should study it: 'They acquire a broad range of subject knowledge and draw on disciplines such as mathematics, science, engineering, computing and art.' Even by the standards of the national curriculum document, that's a bit over the top. Let's not forget that, until 2014, DT in Key Stage 2 didn't involve much more than getting children to make boxes. The highfalutin language is symptomatic of a subject that suffers from an inferiority complex, with its champions having constantly to justify the time it takes up in the school timetable. It's generally regarded as a 'practical' subject rather than an academic one and has suffered from the second-class status attached to vocational subjects in English schools.

The post-2014 Key Stage 2 curriculum is more technically demanding than the previous one and the descriptions of what children are expected to do makes it sound quite rigorous (see below). But it hasn't been allocated any more time in the curriculum than it was pre-2014. At one of the primaries attended by our children, for instance, it isn't allocated any dedicated time at all. That may be because the school has a laser-like focus on getting good results at the end of Key Stage 2 and, for that reason, prioritizes English and maths above everything else. But that approach is far from uncommon among primary schools, given how important Key Stage 2 results are when it comes to Ofsted and the school's standing in the school league tables. So don't expect your child's school to devote much time to DT.

Below and in the chapters that follow, we've set out how DT is likely to be studied if a school devotes a period a week to it in Key Stage 2. In reality, few schools will, and your child's exposure to the subject is likely to be more haphazard. One further thing to note is that we've described separate projects that your child might do under the general headings of 'Design', 'Make', 'Evaluate', 'Technical knowledge' and 'Cooking and nutrition' in each year to try and give you a flavour of the variety of things children are asked to do in DT. In reality, your child will only be given one project to do at a time. (For the 'Purpose of Study' and 'Aims' of the design and technology curriculum, see p. 465.)

The national curriculum divides up the content in Key Stage 2 as follows.

When designing and making, children should be taught to:

Design

- use research and develop design criteria to inform the design of innovative, functional, appealing products that are fit for purpose, aimed at particular individuals or groups

- generate, develop, model and communicate ideas through discussion, annotated sketches, cross-sectional and exploded diagrams, prototypes, pattern pieces and computer-aided design.

Make

- select from and use a wider range of tools and equipment to perform practical tasks accurately
- select from and use a wider range of materials and components, including construction materials, textiles and ingredients, according to their functional properties and aesthetic qualities.

Evaluate

- investigate and analyse a range of existing products
- evaluate their ideas and products against their own design criteria and consider the views of others to improve their work
- understand how key events and individuals in design and technology have helped shape the world.

Technical knowledge

- apply their understanding of how to strengthen, stiffen and reinforce more complex structures
- understand and use mechanical systems in their products
- understand and use electrical systems in their products
- apply their understanding of computing to program, monitor and control their products.

Cooking and nutrition

- understand and apply the principles of a healthy and varied diet

- prepare and cook a variety of predominantly savoury dishes, using a range of cooking techniques

- understand seasonality, and know where and how a variety of ingredients are grown, reared, caught and processed.

Design

Your child might start their first term in Year 3 by being given a sketchbook and asked to keep a record of everything they're learning in DT throughout Key Stage 2. Ideally, if they start sketching the products they're designing in class, the sketches won't be of the finished articles but of them at various stages in their evolution. If they're asked to design anything in Year 3 it could just as easily be for a fictional character – a wand case for Harry Potter, for instance – as for a real person.

Make

Your child will probably be given a chance to explore different materials with different characteristics – strength, flexibility, electrical conductivity – and learn that certain types of materials are more suited to some products than others. They'll also be asked to think about the characteristics that make some products attractive to look at, such as colour, pattern and texture. The teacher may ask them to bring into class a toy or product they're particularly fond of and discuss its design characteristics with them.

Evaluate

Evaluating products in Year 3 is unlikely to extend beyond asking questions about them, something the teacher will encourage your child to do. They may be presented with some iconic, ground-breaking product, such as a Sony Walkman, and be asked to think about why it had such a huge impact at the time. They might also be told about some particularly influential designers, such as Jonathan Ive, the British Chief Design Officer of Apple.

Technical knowledge

The 'complex structures' your child will learn about in Year 3 probably won't be any more complicated than cereal packets, but they'll be asked to think about some of the decisions that designers have had to make in connection with them, such as how thick and stiff the material needs to be in order to protect the cereal. There's a unit in the old curriculum called 'Packaging' they sometimes do in Year 3, in which children disassemble and evaluate a range of commercial packaging. More likely, however, your child will take on a project linked to their topic, e.g. building a Stone Age home. They might also put together a simple mechanical system, such as a moving picture with levers, linkages and pivots. Alternatively, if the school has some Lego WeDo, your child might have an opportunity to build a model with moving parts that can be attached to a computer and controlled using a simple program. There is scope for cross-curricular links with computing here.

Cooking and nutrition

When it comes to food, in Year 3 your child's teacher is likely to spend a lot of time talking about a healthy diet and encouraging them to eat lots of fruit and vegetables. They might well be introduced to the concept of the 'eatwell plate', a diagram that turns a plate into a pie chart composed of five different categories of food and indicates how much you should eat in each category every day in order to enjoy a healthy diet: fruit and vegetables; potatoes,

The eatwell plate

bread, rice, pasta and other starchy foods; milk and dairy; meat, fish, eggs and other forms of protein, such as beans and pulses; and high-fat/sugary foods. As you'd expect, the fruit and vegetables and the carbohydrates take up about a third of the plate each, with the last third being made up of the other three categories. The range of foods your child prepares or cooks in Key Stage 2 are likely to be in line with these proportions, i.e. plenty of fruit shakes and sandwiches, but not many sugary snacks.

What can you do to help?

- If you live anywhere near West London, the Design Museum on Kensington High Street is worth a visit. There are activities the whole family can do, such as Easter egg hunts, as well as courses children can do in the holidays. Check out the website (www. designmuseum.org) for more details.

- The V&A bills itself as 'the world's greatest museum of art and design' and there's plenty for young children to do. For instance, there are hundreds of 'hands-on' exhibits whereby your child can, among other things, build a replica of Crystal Palace, put their hand inside an armoured gauntlet and feel its weight, and find out how pots are made.

Geography

Under the old geography curriculum the emphasis in Key Stage 2 was on teaching higher-order thinking skills, with children expected to ask geographical questions, analyse evidence and form their own opinions. Under the current curriculum there's more focus on teaching core geographical knowledge. For instance, in the preamble to Key Stage 2 it says that children 'should extend their knowledge and understanding beyond the local area to include the United Kingdom and Europe, North and South America'. Your child will still be expected to learn some essential geographical skills, such as reading a compass and maps, but they'll also be expected to memorize a good deal of geographical knowledge. The section in the old curriculum on environmental change and sustainable development has been dropped.

As you'll see below, the content of the Key Stage 2 geography curriculum is divided up under four headings, and it's tempting to assume that schools will do 'Locational knowledge' in Year 3, 'Place knowledge' in Year 4, etc. That would certainly make the job of describing what's taught in each year a bit easier, but unfortunately it's not what most schools are doing. Rather, they teach some content under each heading in each year, gradually drilling down into the subject in more and more depth. Consequently, we've summarized what it is your child will be doing in geography each year under these headings.

Of course, your child's primary may take a completely different approach and we recommend you check the school's website if you want to know what your child will be doing in more detail. Schools are supposed to publish information about the curriculum they'll be teaching on their websites, but if it doesn't have enough information ask the head teacher. They should have a 'curriculum map' for each subject, including geography.

As in Key Stage 1, in most schools geography continues to be taught in lessons called Topic (or Humanities) and some of the units studied under the old curriculum in Key

Stage 2 are still being taught. (For the 'Purpose of Study' and 'Aims' of the geography curriculum, see p. 466.)

The national curriculum divides up the content in Key Stage 2 as follows.

Pupils should be taught to:

Locational knowledge

- locate the world's countries, using maps to focus on Europe (including Russia) and North and South America, concentrating on their environmental regions, key physical and human characteristics, countries and major cities

- name and locate counties and cities of the United Kingdom, geographical regions and their identifying human and physical characteristics, key topographical features (including hills, mountains, coasts and rivers) and land-use patterns; and understand how some of these aspects have changed over time

- identify the position and significance of latitude, longitude, the equator, northern hemisphere, southern hemisphere, the Tropics of Cancer and Capricorn, the Arctic and Antarctic Circles, the prime/Greenwich meridian and time zones (including day and night).

Place knowledge

- understand geographical similarities and differences through the study of human and physical geography of a region of the United Kingdom, a region in a European country and a region within North or South America.

Human and physical geography

- describe and understand key aspects of physical geography, including: climate zones, biomes and vegetation belts, rivers, mountains, volcanoes and earthquakes and the water cycle

- describe and understand key aspects of human geography, including: types of settlement and land use, economic activity including trade links, and the distribution of natural resources including energy, food, minerals and water.

Geographical skills and fieldwork

- use maps, atlases, globes and digital/computer mapping to locate countries and describe features studied

- use the eight points of a compass, four- and six-figure grid references, symbols and key (including the use of Ordnance Survey maps) to build knowledge of the United Kingdom and the wider world

- use fieldwork to observe, measure, record and present the human and physical features in the local area, using a range of methods, including sketch maps, plans and graphs, and digital technologies.

Locational knowledge

Your child's teacher will probably begin by revising what your child has done in Key Stage 1, making sure they can use a globe to locate and name the equator, the North and South Poles, the seven continents and the five great oceans. (See Year 1 'Geography': 'Mnemonics and memory aids' on p. 100.) The teacher may also refresh their memory about the difference between the United Kingdom, Great Britain, the British Islands and the British Isles. After that, the likelihood is they'll move on to teaching your child to locate the main countries of Europe and their capital cities, identify the highest mountains in the world, the longest rivers, the largest forests, etc., and latitude and longitude.

Place knowledge

In Year 3 the teacher may ask your child to compare a region in the United Kingdom – probably the region the school is in – with another region in Britain and not bring in Europe or North or South America at this stage. There's a unit in the old geography curriculum called 'Llandudno' which your child might be taught here, not least because it can be adapted for any region in the United Kingdom. They'll be asked to locate their school and the contrasting region on a map, noting the position of both places, how many miles apart they are, what transportation routes link them, to plan a journey between the two, etc.

Human and physical geography

It's hard to say which geographical features are likely to be picked out from the long list above in Year 3 by your child's teacher, but some of the simpler ones are: rivers, mountains, volcanoes and earthquakes (physical geography); and your child might be asked to look at the types of settlement and land-use, economic activity and trade links (human geography) in, say, Britain during the prehistoric period (Stone Age, Iron Age). There's scope here for cross-curricular links with history.

Geographical skills and fieldwork

Children will probably be asked to use maps, atlases, globes and digital mapping applications such as Google Earth to locate the countries they're studying in Year 3 under 'Locational knowledge'. In addition, they'll refresh what they've already been taught in Key Stage 1 (see Year 1 'Geography': 'Mnemonics and memory aids' on p. 100) and then learn that compasses have eight points, not four. In addition, they're likely to be taught how to find a two-figure grid reference on a map and how to interpret a rudimentary key (possibly using simplified Ordnance Survey maps). The fieldwork they do in Year 3 is likely to be limited to observing and recording some of the human and physical features in the local area, using sketch maps and a digital map-making tool such as quikmaps. They'll probably be asked to draw a map of the school, describe where the school is in relation to local landmarks and identify other features of the village, town or city where it's located. There's a unit in the old geography curriculum called 'Investigating your local area' which children are often taught in Year 3. This will likely involve a local walk, with children collecting information by filling in survey forms.

What can you do to help?

- There's a lot you can do on a daily basis to encourage your child to think geographically. Make use of maps when travelling and at home; talk to your child about where they're located, what settlements/features are around them; point out the differences between villages, towns and cities; draw attention to where amenities are located (shops, train station, ring roads) and why; and talk about the distinctive features of places you visit.

● One way to encourage your child to take an interest in geography is to get a grandparent to give them a subscription to *National Geographic Kids*, a child-friendly version of the famous magazine. Alternatively, you can explore the website (www.ngkids.co.uk) which has lots of fun stuff, including games, puzzles and quizzes.

● Play Name a Country, in which each member of your family has to take it in turns to name different countries beginning with all the different letters of the alphabet, starting with 'A' for, say, Albania. Each time it's someone's go they have to recite the entire list from the beginning before adding a new country.

● The Natural History Museum has a whole section devoted to the world of British geology called 'Earth lab' which is packed with fossils, minerals and rocks. It also contains a lab area where your child can examine the museum's specimens in more detail and has experts on hand to help them identify their finds. (Look out for the dinosaur footprint!) By looking at fossils or prehistoric tools your child might also get some insights into the Stone Age and Iron Age, which they'll be studying in history.

● There's an online children's encyclopaedia called Glossopedia (glossopedia.org) that includes lots of child-friendly information on subjects such as Antarctica, the Arctic, Central America, tropical rainforests and wetlands.

● The BBC used to have a geography section on its Schools website that included resources linked to the various units your child might have studied under the old national curriculum, such as 'Rivers and coasts' (www. bbc.co.uk/schools/websites/4_11/site/geography.shtml). It's a bit babyish – the Key Stage 2 stuff seems more suitable for children in Key Stage 1 – but might be useful for a Year 3 child. It has been archived, but you can still find it using the above URL.

● There's a better BBC resource called Bitesize, a website that contains short educational films. It has a Key Stage 2 geography section which includes areas such as 'Geography skills', 'The natural world', 'Natural processes and disasters', 'Human geography' and 'Sustainability' (www.bbc.co.uk/education/subjects/zbkw2hv).

● The Ordnance Survey website has a section called 'Fun for everyone' which includes a number of free games designed to test children's geographical knowledge, e.g. a map symbol card game (www.ordnancesurvey.co.uk/education/children/map-symbol-flashcards.html).

● For an A–Z-style map of your local area, go to streetmap.co.uk and type in your postcode (www.streetmap.co.uk).

MNEMONICS AND MEMORY AIDS

● Memrise (www.memrise.com), the online learning tool we recommended in 'Times Tables' on p. 168, has a 'History and Geography' section with subcategories such as 'Maps', 'Capitals' and 'Flags'. Click on 'Capitals' and a picture of a particular country comes up, along with the name of its capital city. Your child can then ask for a mnemonic to help them remember it. For instance, to help them remember that Minsk is the capital of Belarus it shows you a picture of a beautiful girl in a fur scarf with the phrase, 'She looks so BELA-rus with a MINsK scarf.' If they don't like that mnemonic they can choose another. There are hundreds of other courses – 'Famous Landmarks', '7 Wonders', 'Biggest Cities', etc. – and its users swear by it.

● When reading a grid reference it's important to remember that the first set of numbers refers to the lines running from left to right and the second set from bottom to top. This is true whether it's a two-grid reference, a four-grid reference or a six-grid reference. To help your child fix this in their mind, get them to memorize this saying: 'Along the corridor and up the stairs.' (Alternatively: 'Onwards and upwards.')

● To remember the difference between latitude and longitude, the phrase 'Lat is fat' is helpful. Latitude runs from east to west, like a belt – and if you visualize the line as a belt the globe it encircles looks fat.

● An acronym to help your child remember the nine longest rivers in the world in descending order of length is NAYY CLAIM. The letters stand for the Nile (4,160 miles), the Amazon (4,153 miles), the Yangtze (3,964 miles), the Yellow River (3,001 miles), the Congo (2,877 miles), the Lena (2,734 miles), the Amur (2,703 miles), the Irtysh (2,640 miles) and the Mekong (2,597 miles). If they just want to focus on the top three, they could remember the word 'NAY'.

● To remember the three longest rivers in Europe, think of the letters VDU, as in 'Visual Display Unit'. They stand for the Volga (2,292 miles), the Danube (1,771 miles) and the Ural (1,509 miles).

● To remember the world's three tallest mountains – Everest, K2 and Kangchenjunga – think of this mnemonic: 'Ever kayaked twice (2) with a kangaroo?'

● The world's largest deserts are the Sahara (8.6 million sq. km), the Arabian (2.3 million sq. km) and the Gobi (1.3 million sq. km). To remember this, think of the acronym SAG. Strictly speaking, the largest desert of all is Antarctica (14 million sq. km), but it's not typically thought of as a desert.

History

The preamble to the history curriculum in Key Stage 2 re-emphasizes the importance of studying the subject chronologically – 'Pupils should continue to develop a chronologically secure knowledge and understanding of British, local and world history, establishing clear narratives within and across the periods they study' – and in most primaries this is how British history will be taught. As you'll see from the bullet points below, there are nine units in the Key Stage 2 history curriculum overall, six British and three non-British. Of the six British units, four cover the history of these islands from the Stone Age to 1066, and two are more general, giving the teacher room to teach a topic of their choice. One obvious way to approach history in Key Stage 2, therefore, is to teach two units per year, one of the four specific British units and another, depending on what the best match is.

For instance, your child might be taught about the Stone Age and the Iron Age in Year 3, along with Ancient

Egypt; then do Ancient Greece, and the Roman conquest of Britain in Year 4; Britain's settlement by Anglo-Saxons, a local study and a non-European society – early Islamic civilization, for instance – in Year 5; and in Year 6 Vikings and another aspect of British history that extends their knowledge beyond 1066 – say, the Tudors or the Victorians.

	Year 3	Year 4	Year 5	Year 6
British	Stone Age/ Iron Age	Romans	Anglo-Saxons	Vikings
			Local Study	Victorians/ Tudors
Non-British	Ancient Egypt	Ancient Greece	Islamic Civilization	

Throughout all this, the teacher should focus on the cognitive skills mentioned in the 'Purpose of Study' section of the history curriculum: 'ask perceptive questions, think critically, weigh evidence, sift arguments and develop perspective and judgement'.

In order to summarize what will be taught in history in each year, we've assumed this is how schools will teach it – and many of them do – but your child's primary may take a completely different approach. It's worth bearing in mind that schools aren't under a statutory obligation to teach history chronologically and some will choose not to, particularly those embracing the concept of a 'creative curriculum' in which forging cross-curricular links between subjects is all-important. Your best bet is to check the school's website. If there's nothing on there – or it's not detailed enough to be of much help – ask the head.

As in Key Stage 1, in most schools history will be taught in lessons called Topic (or Humanities) and some of the units studied under the old curriculum in Key Stage 2 are still being taught. (For the 'Purpose of Study' and 'Aims' of the history curriculum, see p. 468.)

The national curriculum divides up the content in Key Stage 2 under the following headings.

- Changes in Britain from the Stone Age to the Iron Age

- The Roman Empire and its impact on Britain

- Britain's settlement by Anglo-Saxons and Scots

- The Viking and Anglo-Saxon struggle for the kingdom of England to the time of Edward the Confessor

- A local history study

- A study of an aspect or theme in British history that extends pupils' chronological knowledge beyond 1066

- The achievements of the earliest civilizations – an overview of where and when the first civilizations appear and a depth study of one of the following: Ancient Sumer; the Indus Valley; Ancient Egypt; the Shang Dynasty of Ancient China

- Ancient Greece – a study of Greek life and achievements and their influence on the Western world

- A non-European society that provides contrasts with British history – one study chosen from: early Islamic civilization, including a study of Baghdad c. AD 900; Mayan civilization c. AD 900; Benin (West Africa) c. AD 900–1300

If your child's school embraces the structure we've outlined above, they'll start with 'The Stone Age to the Iron Age' in Year 3. This is a new unit in the national curriculum so teachers won't be able to fall back on any of their pre-2014 lesson plans, worksheets, marking schemes, etc. This topic is vast, covering a 10,000-year period from the last ice age to the coming of the Romans, so there's a lot of ground to cover (though for long periods in the Stone Age and the Iron Age nothing much happened). In the first lesson, the teacher may create a living timeline across the classroom, positioning children at different points to illustrate pivotal moments: man moves from hunter-gatherer to farmer, from rural to urban, from a Hobbesian universe in which life was 'nasty, brutish and short' to the emergence of society, etc. For the remainder of the term, the teacher may divide up the material by focusing on these pivotal changes in different lessons.

The non-British unit taught in Year 3 will probably be 'Earliest civilizations', most likely 'Ancient Egypt' because that's a unit that was often taught under the old curriculum. Your child may be asked what they already know about Ancient Egypt – and they'll probably know something, if only from watching The Mummy films. The teacher can then ask them how they know it and that, in turn, will stimulate a discussion of how we come by historical knowledge – archaeological digs, ruins, ancient monuments, objects, books, eyewitness accounts, etc. Children may be taught about some of the more unusual beliefs of the Ancient Egyptians, particularly their ideas about life after death. There is plenty of scope for cross-curricular links with art and design here.

What can you do to help?

STONE AGE AND IRON AGE

- The BBC's old History site (now archived, but still accessible) has a section on 'Ancient history' that includes an essay on 'Life in an Iron Age village'. The subheadings include 'Agriculture', 'Lifestyle', 'Leisure time', 'Appearance' and 'Religion and ritual' (www.bbc.co.uk/history/ancient/british_prehistory/ironage_intro_01.shtml).

- There are plenty of Stone Age sites and ruins dotted throughout England, not just Stonehenge. (Although most of them *are* in Wiltshire.) For instance, there's the Avebury Ring, probably the largest Neolithic stone circle in the world, and Silbury Hill, the largest man-made mound in Europe (both in Wiltshire). For a fuller directory see the Historvius website (www.historvius.com/stone-age-sites/pe160).

- Butser Ancient Farm in the South Downs National Park in Hampshire is definitely worth a visit. It's both an archaeological site and a visitor attraction, a replica of an Iron Age farm with Iron Age buildings, tools, crops – even rare breeds of animals. They may not have been around in 1200 BC, but they certainly look the part. One of us has fond memories of climbing Butser and visiting the farm as a child.

- The BBC made a series called *Living in the Past* in 1978 in which a group of volunteers was filmed living on an Iron Age farm. The programme's makers went to great lengths to try to make it as authentic as possible, even insisting that the participants wore handmade clothes. It's remembered today as a forerunner of the reality shows that became popular in the nineties, a kind of *Big Brother* set in the prehistoric era. There was a documentary about the series on BBC4 in 2008 and you can see it on YouTube here: https://youtu.be/qt5ir-viCzk.

ANCIENT EGYPT

● The British Museum has a good online resource called *Ancient Egypt* that's been designed for children. They can explore a range of different areas, including 'Gods and goddesses', 'Mummification', 'Pharaohs', 'Pyramids' and 'Temples' (www.ancientegypt.co.uk/menu.html).

● There's a free app called Book of the Dead that's quite fun. It was linked to the Ancient Egyptian Book of the Dead exhibition at the British Museum, but it works as a stand-alone game. Your child will find himself alone in the Egyptian Netherworld and have to negotiate a succession of dangers in order to become immortal.

● There's a Nintendo DS game called *Jewel Master: Cradle of Egypt* in which children have to solve puzzles to unlock and build twenty different Egyptian locations, learning more about the history and geography of Ancient Egypt in the process.

● For a list of English museums with Egyptian artefacts, see 'What can you do to help?' in Year 3 'Art and Design' on p. 204.

GENERAL

● If you're looking for a good textbook to accompany the history your child will be learning in primary school, we recommend the Usborne internet-linked *Encyclopedia of World History*, with illustrations, dates and plenty of recommended websites.

● At this stage, you could start reading your child *Our Island Story*, H. E. Marshall's classic history of the British Isles – a chapter every night before bedtime. Alternatively, *Lord of the Forest* by 'BB'.

● Why not get your child to draw a history timeline on the wall of their room? It could start with the Stone Age, mark the transition from the Stone Age to the Iron Age, include the time span of Ancient Egypt, Ancient Greece, Rome, etc., leading all the way up to your child's birth. (It may need to cover more than one wall!) Once it's finished, your child can then begin to fill it in with particular historical episodes or events they've learnt about, such as the Roman invasion of Britain in AD 43. Leave room for your child to fill in more detail – facts, pictures, etc. – as they learn more about the pivotal moments in question. It is a very tangible way for your child to really understand the scales of time they are covering in history. If you're stuck for what to include, you can get some ideas from the British History Timeline (www.bbc.co.uk/history/interactive/timelines/british/index_embed.shtml), a BBC history website with a timeline stretching from before the Bronze Age to 1945 and beyond.

● If that sounds a bit too messy for your taste, or your child doesn't have their own room, you can always have them create an online timeline instead. They can do this at *Timetoast* (www.timetoast.com).

● Get your child to memorize the dates of a hundred important events in British history from 55 BC to the present day, e.g. the Magna Carta (1215), the Declaration of Rights (1689), the Battle of Waterloo (1815), etc. This is what is known as a 'schema' and when your child is then introduced to new facts and topics in history they can assimilate them into this chronological framework. According to cognitive scientists, having a schema in a particular subject will help your child to learn and retain knowledge in that subject. We suggest asking your child to memorize five dates a day over a period of twenty days, having them recite all the ones they've learnt so far each time they add another five. If you want to give them an incentive, bet them a trip to the cinema that they can't do it. As above, if you're stuck for ideas about what to include, try the British History Timeline (www.bbc.co.uk/history/interactive/timelines/british/index_embed.shtml).

● Alternatively, try Memrise (www.memrise.com), the free online learning tool we recommended in 'Times Tables' on p. 168. It has plenty of online courses (pictures and mnemonics) in its 'History' section, designed to help children commit historical facts to memory, including '43 Key Dates of Human Prehistory', '50 Key Dates of World History' and 'Ancient Egyptian Deities'. For instance, if your child clicks on 'Chronology of Ancient History', a picture of a particular period comes up, along with its dates, and they can ask for a mnemonic to help them remember it, e.g. to remember that Ancient Egypt spans the period 3100–30 BC it suggests the following: 'Look at the word "Egypt". The "E" has 3 lines jutting out horizontally, and 1 line vertically – so the period began in 3100 years BC – and 30 should be easy to remember.'

Languages

Languages have been mandatory in Key Stage 2 since 2014. Almost all primary schools will already have been teaching languages to some of their seven- to eleven-year-olds before 2014, but today all children must learn a language from the age of seven.

The national curriculum doesn't prescribe which language it should be – it can be ancient or modern, provided the teaching focuses on 'enabling pupils to make substantial progress in one language'. Most primary schools currently teach French, but Spanish is becoming increasingly popular. Some schools may teach German, while others offer more than one language, including Mandarin. Some have after-school Latin clubs. Some offer lessons in a locally relevant language, such as Somali in an area where there are many Somali speakers.

The preamble to the national curriculum document, which is intended to apply to Key Stage 3 (Years 7, 8 and 9) as well as Key Stage 2, expresses some lofty ideals. It says teachers should 'enable pupils to express their ideas and thoughts in another language' and provide opportunities for them to 'read great literature in the original language'. More realistically, the 'Aims' are that children should 'understand and respond to spoken and written language from a variety of authentic sources' and 'speak with increasing confidence, fluency and spontaneity . . . continually improving the accuracy of their pronunciation and intonation'. They are also expected to be able to write in the language 'for different purposes and audiences, using the variety of grammatical structures that they have learnt'.

This is intended to apply to your child's language

education up to the age of fourteen, so how much they will learn in primary school is an open question. According to the British Council, about a quarter of primary schools have no staff with a qualification higher than a GCSE in the language that's taught. But the national curriculum makes it clear that primary schools have got to take languages as seriously as every other area of learning – although not necessarily by teaching them in a formal way. There will need to be time and expertise dedicated to it: twenty minutes a week won't achieve the standard expected by the end of Year 6.

You will have to ask your child's school to tell you what language they'll be teaching, whether there'll be a choice and what their programme of study will be (assuming it's not on the website). The idea is to lay good foundations for further foreign language teaching at secondary school, so your primary school should teach a language that your child will be able to continue in Year 7. There will be a spoken and a written element. The focus of study will be on practical communication, so the vocabulary will be around familiar and routine matters. By the end of Year 6 your child will be expected to use some grammatical structures correctly, in speech and in writing.

Your child's school will probably follow a scheme of work available either to buy or for free that comes with lesson plans and suggested activities from Year 3 to Year 6. Your child's school may have specialist language teachers; many will not. The teachers are likely to use the chosen scheme of work differently according to teacher and school, some adhering to it rigidly, and some not.

Schemes of work we have looked at tend to follow a pattern: the work is divided into units or topics, one per half-term, so there will be six units per year for four years. Each unit is divided into six sections, so roughly one per week. (This pattern will not be the same for all schemes of work.) Some schools may spend two hours a week teaching languages but, for most it'll be one and for some just half an hour. Many schools will have a fixed slot of thirty to sixty minutes and then revisit the language taught in other lessons – if France or Spain crops up in geography, for instance. For children exposed for less than an hour a week to a new language, progress is bound to be slow. Any exposure at home will help!

Given the range of time dedicated to language teaching we expect to find across the country's schools, it's hard to say exactly what you should expect your child to learn in each year. If your child has less than an hour a week, your primary school may not be expecting to cover as much ground as we describe. (For the 'Purpose of Study' and 'Aims' of the languages curriculum, see p. 469.)

The language content of the national curriculum in Key Stage 2 can be divided up under two broad headings, spoken and written.

Spoken language

Pupils should be taught to:

- listen attentively to spoken language and show understanding by joining in and responding

- explore the patterns and sounds of language through songs and rhymes and link the spelling, sound and meaning of words

- engage in conversations; ask and answer questions; express opinions and respond to those of others; seek clarification and help

- speak in sentences, using familiar vocabulary, phrases and basic language structures

- develop accurate pronunciation and intonation so that others understand when they are reading aloud or using familiar words and phrases

- present ideas and information orally to a range of audiences

- appreciate stories, songs, poems and rhymes in the language.

The teaching in Year 3 will be an introduction to the sound of the language and your child's first attempt to master a foreign accent. The teacher will start by introducing day-to-day vocabulary and phrases, such as 'Hello', 'Goodbye', 'My name is . . .', 'I'm eight years old', 'I live in . . .', etc. The teacher will have your child copying and chanting back straight away. There will be songs and rhymes. The units in Year 3 are likely to be along the lines of: 'All about me', 'Animals', 'Friends', 'Birthdays' and 'Food'. By the end of Year 3 your child should be able to answer some basic, well-rehearsed questions in these areas, know the colours and be able to count to twenty. They may have learnt parts of the body and how to say 'I like/can/play/sing/ . . .' They will be able to ask 'How many?' and may be able to give a simple description of an animal, such as 'The cow is big' or 'That is a black dog'. They are likely to have been introduced to a map of the country, typical food and weather, the flag and so on.

To give you an idea of the kinds of activities your child may take part in, here are some examples:

- Ask and answer simple questions, using real objects, cards and games, e.g. 'How many?', 'What is this?', 'Is she called Rajida?'

- Play Bag of Tricks. Children guess what's in the bag, asking, 'Is it big/small/soft/hard/red?', 'Is it a . . . ?'

- Ask for and give objects in pairs or small groups, using appropriately polite language, e.g. adding the words 'please' and 'thank you'

- Act out simple role plays such as asking for and receiving items, introducing yourself to someone, making a telephone call, making appropriate use of terms of politeness

- Play Pass It On. Children form three lines. The child at the front starts by saying to their neighbour, 'My name is X. What's your name?' Each answers and then passes on the question down the line

- Play a circle game to practise greetings. The teacher throws a soft toy to different children and says a greeting. Children repeat it and throw the toy back to the teacher

- Act out a Mexican wave, passing single words or patterns of words around a circle

- Perform a Mexican wave in the style of an adjective, taking turns round a circle to call out 1–2–3, for example (in the language) in the manner of the adjective called out by the teacher: a new one for each child (such as happy, sad, tired, thirsty, angry, bored, frightened, shocked)

- Perform a mime to show understanding of a phrase or sentence spoken by the teacher, e.g. 'I am reading a book', 'I am skipping', 'I am jumping'

- Play Verb Bingo. The teacher calls out a variety of familiar verbs and the children match what they hear to pictures on Bingo cards, placing a counter over those they've heard

Written language

Pupils should be taught to:

- **read carefully and show understanding of words, phrases and simple writing**

- **broaden their vocabulary and develop their ability to understand new words that are introduced into familiar written material, including through using a dictionary**

- **write phrases from memory and adapt these to create new sentences, to express ideas clearly**

- **describe people, places, things and actions orally and in writing.**

As you can see, there is an emphasis in the national curriculum on being taught to write as well as speak the language so your child may be taught phonics in the new language in much the same way they are in English. However, phonetic teaching is usually confined to the pronunciation of new words as children are introduced to them, e.g. when learning the French words for different colours they might focus on the soft 'g' sound in 'rouge', 'orange', etc.

To give you an idea of the kinds of activities your child may take part in, here are some examples:

- Trace letter shapes on a partner's hand to spell well-known words

- Learn to spell key words by playing spelling games. The teacher calls out the spellings of familiar words and children identify the word

- Play Guess the Word. The teacher starts to spell a word slowly by writing it down one letter at a time. After each letter the class can have one guess at the word. All possible correct guesses score a point for the class

- Use newspapers and a computer to keep a simple class record of the weather over a short period of time in a particular place where the language that's being studied is spoken and compare it with the weather in the school's own locality

What can you do to help?

In Continental schools, where multilingual children are the norm, there is no sense of embarrassment about speaking in a foreign accent. The children who speak the most languages are considered the most cool, not 'geeks'. If only it were the same here! If your first language is one of the most widely spoken in the world, and is the language of pop music, Hollywood films and international business and finance, that puts you at a disadvantage when it comes to learning a new language – we don't have the constant exposure to other languages that others do to English. But that's no excuse for not bothering to learn. Whichever language your child is learning, if you don't speak a word of it, you won't be able to help much. Unless, of course, you take the bull by the horns and learn it, too. If you can speak it then do so to your child, even if you can only speak it a bit.

● Memrise (www.memrise.com), the free online learning tool we referred to in 'Times Tables' on p. 168, has plenty of online language courses (pictures and mnemonics) designed to help people learn a new language, including a course called 'Learn Basic French'. 'Learn French vocab, grammar, verbs and phrases,' it says. 'This course contains 300 meticulously selected French words and phrases, broken up into lessons by subject, to help you begin learning how to speak French.'

● Talk about the country where the language is spoken: make it seem real. Find a funny YouTube clip of children in that country doing something normal and silly to help your child understand that it's just like home, that children just like them actually speak this language. Show them where the country is on a globe, try some typical food, etc.

● Bingo. Make a couple of bingo boards, divided into sections with the words for different colours or numbers or days of the week in the foreign language. Take it in turns with your child to pull out cards marked the same way and race to be the first to fill your board. If you want to make it more difficult, have the English words for the colours, numbers and/or days of the week on the cards you're pulling out so you and your child have to match them with the French words on the boards.

- Snap. Make or buy cards with colours or numbers on one set, and the words for those colours or numbers on another. Shuffle and play Snap, matching the right colour or number to the written word.

- Count steps in the foreign language whenever you and your child walk upstairs or down.

- Count everything that can be counted in the foreign language instead of in English.

- Play Shops with your child in the language.

- Join an after-school language club. There will be a more relaxed atmosphere, possibly some food from the country, and usually some physical games.

- Listening to CDs or MP3 downloads in the car, or watching children's DVDs in the foreign language, helps enormously. Getting used to the sound of the language and hearing the intonation will attune your child's brain to it. After that, they'll be more likely to be able to 'hear' different words in a sentence. Some examples you could try are:

Little Pim – French Bop is a French audio CD with a selection of new and classic French songs for children

Let's Sing and Dance in French! is ecstatically reviewed by parents and teachers

Music Lingua is a music-based French, Spanish or German programme for children up to the age of eight

Escucha, Escucha (Kids Learn Spanish) has songs in Spanish

Canciones en Español by Music with Sara has short, easy-to-remember songs sung by children

Some DVDs we like:

First Fun with Spanish is a beginner's guide to Spanish for young children, based on the best-selling book First Hundred Words in Spanish published by Usborne. Each scene in the DVD corresponds to a double-page spread in the book

With Allons vite à Bethléem, your child can learn eight traditional and original French carols while watching the Christmas nativity story unfold

As you'd expect, there are many apps and books to help in every language. Some apps you could try are:

French: LinguPinguin, Frenchie Teachie or French Start

German: Learn German by MindSnacks

Spanish: Fun Spanish, Rosita y Conchita in 3D, Spanish Kids – Speak and Learn Pro

Music

Primary schools will differ widely in how they teach music in Key Stage 2. Some schools may be large enough to employ a specialist music teacher, in which case there's likely to be a well-worked-out scheme of work progressing from Year 3 to 6. Others may employ a peripatetic teacher – sometimes known as a 'peri' – who comes in on one day a week and teaches an instrument such as the recorder to each class, while some may offer subsidized lessons in various instruments, with the ukulele, guitar, piano and flute being the most common. If your child's school doesn't set aside any dedicated time for music lessons in Key Stage 2, don't worry. Their teacher will probably let your child leave classes during the school day if they have private instrumental lessons and there are many opportunities for learning about music across the primary curriculum.

The national curriculum suggests that learning about music should happen mostly through practical experience. 'Creativity' is of central importance and the many interrelated processes, such as performing, composing, improvising, singing, manipulating, combining, listening and appraising, underpin the essentially practical nature of the subject. 'Interrelated' means that these activities are usually bundled up together.

The phrase 'musical canon' in music's 'Purpose of Study' may cause mild panic, as if children are going to be taught only about the great classical composers. Don't worry – your child will be taught about a wide range of historical periods, genres, traditions, composers and musicians. (If anything, your child's teacher will err in the opposite direction and focus on pop music.) Children are also expected to 'develop an understanding of the history of music'. (For the 'Purpose of Study' and 'Aims' of the music curriculum, see p. 470.)

The national curriculum divides up the content in Key Stage 2 as follows.

Pupils should be taught to:

- play and perform in solo and ensemble contexts, using voice and playing musical instruments with increasing accuracy, fluency, control and expression

- improvise and compose music for a range of purposes, using the interrelated dimensions of music

- listen with attention to detail and recall sounds with increasing aural memory

- use and understand staff and other musical notations

- appreciate and understand a wide range of high-quality live and recorded music drawn from different traditions and from great composers and musicians

- develop an understanding of the history of music.

One of the 'Aims' of the music curriculum is that children should learn to sing and use their voices so expect your child to do a lot of singing in Key Stage 2, just as they did in Key Stage 1. Most schools have at least one piano and a member of staff who can play it. Some schools spend a fair amount of time on hymn practice, particularly Church of England schools, and most will put on a Christmas carol concert. Some will prefer a multi-faith concert of some kind, but nearly all will have children singing in assemblies throughout the year.

In Key Stage 1 your child will have made a lot of noise using a variety of percussion instruments, with little or no instruction about how to use them. As they progress through Key Stage 2, that's likely to change and in Year 3 they may have class recorder lessons. Individual pupils will already be able to play some instruments a bit, so when the teacher wants music to be made there should be enough talent and equipment in the classroom to make that possible.

In Year 3 your child might listen to music that's associated with particular animals, e.g. 'Colonel Hathi's March' and 'Trust in Me' from The Jungle Book, or The

Carnival of the Animals by Camille Saint-Saëns. They may be asked to compare the animal described with the sounds used and think about how the music helps us imagine its size, how it moves, what it looks like and how it behaves. After commenting on the more obvious musical features (louder, quieter, higher, lower, faster, slower), they might be asked to concentrate on the use of rhythm and melody: is the rhythm jumpy, creeping, regular, hopping or gliding? They may then work in pairs to create sounds and movements to describe an animal, first selecting an appropriate untuned instrument, then working out a sequence of sounds and movements – one child plays and the other moves. They'll then perform their animal compositions to other members of the class.

What can you do to help?

- Sing songs with your child. Not just 'Ten Green Bottles' or 'Hot Cross Buns', but the songs that you listen to. Almost everyone likes singing, however bad they are at it, so encourage your child by singing in the car, in the shower, in the kitchen, or to ads on TV. Try being each other's backing group. It's great fun when they join in, and you should enjoy it while you can. By the time they're nine or ten they'll beg you to stop.

- Try doing some karaoke after supper on a Saturday night. If you don't have a karaoke machine there are plenty of online karaoke sites, such as the Karaoke Channel (www.thekaraokechannel.com), with lots of free songs. Be warned, though: your child may become a passionate karaoke enthusiast and a little can go a long way.

- Expand the repertoire of music your child listens to. Listen to Radio 3 or Classic FM in the car. Try to identify the instruments. If they groan when you ask them to listen to something classical, cheer them up by getting them to say which is the most painful instrument they can hear.

● Take your child to hear live music. The London Symphony Orchestra has special concerts and events for families that are listed on its website: www.lso.co.uk/ lso-discovery/discovery-families.html

● Toc and Roll is an app designed to help children start composing songs. They can mix different instruments on a virtual multi-track, add sound effects, record their voices and then share the results with the world.

● My Rockin Fairy is an app (currently available from US iTunes only) designed to help young girls gain confidence in music. It includes instruments that your child can play alone or with friends, with background rhythms that work in any combination.

How to Survive Class Assemblies, Parents' Evenings and Sports Days

Class assemblies

This title, suggested by one of us to the other, speaks volumes. Some of us find an involuntary grin fixed across our faces at the sight of our little darling (or anyone else's offspring) speaking, singing, dancing or acting in public. But some of us can't help but think that, as an adult, there are more enriching ways of spending an hour than listening to the fifth consecutive rendition of 'Twinkle, Twinkle, Little Star' on an out-of-tune piano played by *someone else's* child. (What was that school thinking? To have *no* selection process . . . to allow anyone who wanted to perform, when they all wanted to, and they had all learnt the same piece . . .)

Schools put a huge amount of effort into dramatic or musical productions – even into the regular class assemblies. Your child will go through the same heady mixture of exciting castings, boring rehearsal and terrifying public performance as you probably did at school. Your duty is to attend, and to express delight. It's not that hard!

Parents' evenings

There are likely to be two parents' evenings a year. You will be given an appointment time and you will inevitably have to wait around while the parents before you take much longer talking about their child than is reasonable or polite. During this waiting you will probably have the opportunity to look through your child's exercise books and to admire the work on display. This is well worth doing. You will (we hope) be amazed at how much your child writes/draws/makes/etc. at school that you were completely unaware of. If your child is not with you, mentally note down a few pieces of work you can compliment them on when you get back home.

The wall displays are an interesting window into the range of attainment in the class and will give you a much better fix on how your child is getting on than any level or assessment system the school report contains.

To get the most from the one-to-one moment with the teacher, prepare some questions in advance. Remember that the teacher may well have spoken to twenty other parents already that evening so allow them time to think about your child before they start talking and listen carefully to what they have to say. They spend hours more in your child's company than you do during weekdays and your child may well be a different person at school than they are at home.

If you have questions or worries between parents' evenings, good schools welcome parents contacting them. Teachers generally prefer you to address concerns as and when they arise so don't wait for the next fixed date. You may have to be patient, however. Not all teachers are good at replying to emails promptly.

Sports days

At every sports day we've been to there are two or three parents who make themselves very visible by their extreme enthusiasm. This takes the form of loud verbal support, or inappropriate flouting of the where-to-stand guidelines in order to capture the best video footage. For your child's sake, try not to be one of those parents. One of us recalls practising the egg-and-spoon race with his daughter for weeks beforehand and then, on race day, becoming more and more agitated when her classmates dropped their eggs and carried on running regardless. He ended up remonstrating with the PE teacher, trying to get all the competitors disqualified apart from his daughter – who finished last, but with her egg still resting firmly in its spoon. In future years, he learnt to channel all this competitive energy into the dads' race and not burden his daughter with it.

The difficult thing to get right as a parent is the management of your child's expectations. If they are competitive or quite sporty they may find it hard to cope with the disappointment of not winning. If they are hopeless at sport they may dread taking part. The PE teacher (who may well be their class teacher as well) will have discussed this with them and done their best to allay fears and generate excitement and enthusiasm. Your job is to tread the fine line between minding too much or not enough, to praise achievement and shrug off failure. But, then again, not to shrug it off too much, either. After all, part of the point of competitive sport is to teach your child how to cope with failure.

Year 4

Introduction

A lot of academic progress will be expected of your child in Year 4. They should be fluent readers by now and adept at basic mathematical manipulations. This year they'll be chanting times tables to you and producing extended pieces of writing. Their increasing articulacy may mean they talk more about the things they're doing at school (but don't hold your breath). In Year 4 boys tend to play with boys and girls with girls. That split usually happens in about Year 2 and from that point onwards even the oldest, 'bestest' childhood friends probably won't associate with each other in the playground if they're not the same sex.

Traditional stereotypes will be visible in the playground: boys' play will be centred around ball games and girls' around chat-related activities, such as role play (or gossip!). This is a grotesque generalization, of course, and a good game of British Bulldog or Tag will get them all swooping around together.

Parents we've spoken to bear out our own experience: the Year 4 child tends to have grown in confidence and be noticeably (if only slightly) more mature than they were in Year 3. A boy in Year 4 said the girls became 'weirder', playing games like 'Horses' and doing lots of skipping. He, of course, played football. In his class, they would still all play It together. Mention of British Bulldog was met with a frown: 'Not allowed: health and safety.' A Year 4 girl thought the boys were a bit rough and babyish. (It was ever thus.)

English

The national curriculum doesn't distinguish between Years 3 and 4 in English. This is not because nothing new happens in Year 4, but because the type of learning that takes place in Year 3, as described in our previous chapter, remains the same in Year 4. The difference is one of degree rather than kind. Children will read and study more complex literature in Year 4 than in Year 3 and they will make further progress in their spelling, composition, comprehension and their ability to discuss texts.

We suggest that, if your child is in Year 4, you read Year 3 'English' on p. 171. We will add a little here under the same headings as before.

- Reading = word reading; comprehension

- Writing = transcription (spelling and handwriting); composition; vocabulary, grammar and punctuation

We've tackled all of these subdivisions below, apart from the last, which is dealt with in 'Grammar and Punctuation' on p. 375. (For the 'Purpose of Study' and 'Aims' of the English curriculum, see p. 458.)

Reading

WORD READING

In Year 4 your child should be reading fluently, encountering difficulties only with words that are entirely new to them and not spelt phonetically, or with unclear emphasis, e.g. 'eyrie' and 'eerie'. They'll probably still need to pause while they work out the meaning of what they're reading if the text is difficult or unfamiliar.

COMPREHENSION

Your child will continue to develop their understanding of how language, structure and presentation contribute to meaning.

Writing

TRANSCRIPTION

a) Spelling

Words such as 'business', 'particular', 'potatoes', 'weight', 'imagine' and 'separate' will be learnt. There is a statutory word list for Years 3 and 4, which we reproduce here.

WORD LIST: YEARS 3 AND 4

accident(ally)	believe	caught
actual(ly)	bicycle	centre
address	breath	century
although	breathe	certain
answer	build	circle
appear	business/busy	complete
arrive	calendar	consider

continue
decide
describe
different
difficult
disappear
early
earth
eight/eighth
enough
exercise
experience
experiment
extreme
famous
favourite
February
forward(s)
fruit
grammar
group
guard
guide
heard
heart
height
history

imagine
important
increase
interest
island
knowledge
learn
length
library
material
medicine
mention
minute
natural
naughty
notice
occasion(ally)
often
opposite
ordinary
particular
peculiar
perhaps
popular
position
possess(ion)
possible

potatoes
pressure
probably
promise
purpose
quarter
question
recent
regular
reign
remember
sentence
separate
special
straight
strange
strength
suppose
surprise
therefore
though/
thought
through
various
weight
woman/
women

b) Handwriting

Your child should increase the legibility, consistency and quality of their joined-up writing. (See Year 3 'English' on p. 179 for more detail on handwriting.)

COMPOSITION

Your child will produce pieces of creative writing, be it prose or poetry, of increasing sophistication and length. Their stamina for writing should increase over Year 4 so that producing a side of writing in an A4 exercise book is no longer a Herculean task, but a matter of routine. Children will be encouraged to use ever more varied vocabulary and to alter the style of their writing to match different needs (descriptive prose, a formal letter, an account of an event written once for a friend to read, and then again for a head teacher).

They will continue to learn to edit and evaluate their own work.

What can you do to help?

In this section we've put all these suggestions together instead of putting them under each subsection as in previous sections, because the majority apply to all areas of English.

● Everything we said in Year 3 'English' still applies. Listen to your child reading aloud and read challenging texts to them. Draw their attention to nuances in meaning between similar words. Look words up together to show that even you can't always put into words these nuances without some help. Try and encourage them to take pride in having an unusually large vocabulary.

● Spelling. By now, if the look-cover-write-check process doesn't do it for your child it's time to come up with some imaginative extras. Try getting your child to write their spelling words on fluorescent Post-its and sticking them in amusing places around the house (on the fridge door handle, on the TV remote, by the loo) where they will see them often. Try asking them to spell a word at every red light when in the car, or only let them take another handful of crisps after getting another one right. Whatever it takes!

- Take your child to the theatre. Most big towns have a theatre that caters for children and the events are usually imaginative and thought-provoking, and children remember shows they've seen for years. Most theatres offer reduced prices at certain times for children.

- Play Charades, either acting out just one word, for example, 'caterpillar' (which splits nicely into actable syllables), or a favourite film or book title.

- Play Articulate. There's a junior version, but why not just use the adult one and allow your child double time, or the freedom to reject cards with words they don't know?

- Play Boggle.

- Use an app to practise joined-up writing. We recommend abc Joined Up.

- Subscribe to a newspaper for children. We like First News, which comes out once a week and gets children used to the idea of an actual newspaper. Our children love receiving post that's addressed to them personally – an increasingly rare event. If your child prefers the glamour of the iPad you can become a digital subscriber to First News. Or even a broadsheet newspaper if you think having it on your iPad will make your child more likely to read it.

- If your child doesn't much like reading, try comic books. Our children loved The Adventures of Tintin by

Hergé and the Asterix books by Goscinny and Uderzo. Posy Simmonds has written some lovely books for children, such as *Fred*, and she's illustrated Hilaire Belloc's 'Matilda, Who Told Such Dreadful Lies, and was Burned to Death'. Comics of the type we used to buy with pocket money at the newsagent's are often very expensive, yearned for mostly for the useless toy attached to the cover, and rarely read. Avoid if possible.

● Subscribe to *The Week Junior*, which aims to explain news and events in ways children can understand without patronizing them.

● Subscribe to *Scoop*, a 'kaleidoscope of creative genius for kids', which has short stories, book reviews and more, and is a joy to look at and hold.

● We've found that some children love reading poetry. There are countless anthologies of poems for children. We like *The Spot on My Bum* by Gez Walsh and Carol Ann Duffy's children's anthology. Hilaire Belloc, mentioned above, has an irresistible collection of *Cautionary Verses*, although some children may find them disturbing.

● Some children who find handwriting a real struggle may benefit from learning to touch type. Not only is this a useful skill, but it will free them up to compose stories, poetry, etc., without being held back by their difficulties with putting pen to paper. You should talk to your child's teacher before you start and find out what the rules are about typing in school. The school SENCO (Special Educational Needs Coordinator) may have some advice, particularly if you or they think your child may have dysgraphia (a learning difficulty that affects writing). (For more details on this learning difficulty, see 'Special Educational Needs' on p. 113.)

- You may find a local small touch-typing business, but a full-blown course can be expensive. If the cost is too much, try a touch-typing app, such as Mavis Beacon Teaches Typing or Dance Mat Typing. The first of these isn't cheap, but the second, a BBC site, is free (www.bbc.co.uk/schools/typing). Another free site is www.typingclub.com.

Maths

The introductory paragraph in Year 3 'Maths' on p. 183 applies here, too. The national curriculum sets out what your child should learn in Year 4 under the various headings below. (For the 'Purpose of Study' and 'Aims' of the maths curriculum, see p. 459.)

Number and place value

By now, your child should be very familiar with units, tens and hundreds. In Year 4 they'll expand this to thousands, if they haven't already. They'll become competent at ordering and comparing numbers beyond a thousand and finding a thousand more or less than a given number, e.g. $3764 + 1000 = 4764$; $3764 - 1000 = 2764$. They'll learn to count in multiples of 6, 7, 9 (in preparation for their remaining times tables), and 25 and 1,000.

The national curriculum says that in Year 4 your child should be taught to read Roman numerals to 100 (I to C), and so understand that concepts we take for granted, such as 0 and place value, are relatively new. (They'll probably do this during a history lesson rather than maths, as they're likely to be studying the Romans in Year 4 anyway.)

Negative numbers are likely to be introduced for the first time, so your child will learn to count backwards through 0 (5, 4, 3, 2, 1, 0, –1, –2, etc.). Some teachers use the term 'negative' instead of 'minus' (as in 'negative 1, negative 2', etc.) because they'll have already taught the class that 'minus' means 'subtract' and they won't want to confuse children by introducing another meaning of the word.

Your child will practise rounding numbers up or down to the nearest 10, 100 or 1,000. They'll use this technique while estimating, probably starting with measuring lengths or capacities (the volume of water in this jug is about 270ml).

Also in Year 4 your child will begin to see where the decimals and fractions they have already come across fit in the number system, e.g. 33¼ comes a quarter of the way between 33 and 34. It may seem blindingly obvious to you, but . . .

Addition and subtraction

Your child should continue to practise both mental arithmetic and columnar addition and subtraction with increasingly large numbers (with up to four digits) to aid fluency. They will probably be expected to estimate answers before working them out, and to use inverse operations to check their answers, e.g. if they calculate that 357 – 212 = 145, they check by adding 212 + 145 = 357.

Multiplication and division

This year's times tables are the 6s, 7s, 9s and 12s. By the end of Year 4 your child should know all their times tables up to 12 × 12.

In Year 4 children will continue practising mental methods of multiplying and dividing to derive 'facts', e.g. $600 \div 3 = 200$ can be derived from $2 \times 3 = 6$. They'll learn that multiplying or dividing by one doesn't change a number, and that multiplying by 0 results in 0.

They will also repeatedly practise the formal written method (columnar) of short multiplication and short division ('short' here means multiplying or dividing a multi-digit number by just a single-digit number). At this stage, the division calculations will have exact answers (no 'remainders'). (Examples of short and long multiplication and division are given in the Appendix 'Addition, Subtraction, Multiplication and Division' on p. 474.)

Your child will learn to write statements about the equality of expressions, e.g. use of the distributive law: $39 \times 7 = (30 \times 7) + (9 \times 7)$; and associative law: $(2 \times 3) \times 4 = 2 \times (3 \times 4)$, and do problems using these, such as: $2 \times 6 \times 5 = 10 \times 6 = 60$.

They will learn to solve two-step problems in contexts such as the number of choices on a menu, or three cakes shared equally between ten children.

Fractions (including decimals)

Because your child is already familiar with fractions, it's likely that teaching the next bits about fractions will happen before decimals are introduced. (This won't necessarily be the case: some teachers will teach decimals along with place value at the start of the year.) Children will learn to show families of common equivalent fractions, e.g. $\frac{1}{2} = \frac{4}{8}$ or $\frac{8}{16}$; $\frac{2}{3} = \frac{6}{9}$, etc., by shading pie charts or sections of rectangles.

They already know about tenths; now they'll also count up and down in hundredths. They'll recognize that hundredths arise when dividing an object by one hundred and when dividing tenths by ten.

Your child will start to solve problems involving adding increasingly complex fractions and using fractions to divide quantities (but only where the answer is a whole number). (For example, ⅛ of 24 is ²⁴⁄₈ = 3.) They'll use factors and multiples to recognize equivalent fractions and simplify where appropriate, e.g. = ⅔ or ¼ = . They'll add and subtract fractions with the same denominator (number on the bottom). This is straightforward, e.g. ⁶⁄₉ + ²⁄₉ = ⁸⁄₉).

And then they'll move on to decimals. They will be taught throughout that decimals and fractions are different ways of expressing numbers and proportions.

First, they'll learn to write decimal equivalents of any number of tenths or hundredths, then decimal equivalents to ¼, ½ and ¾. They'll compare numbers such as 0.87 and 0.89. They'll round up decimals with one decimal place to the nearest whole number.

They will practise counting, using simple fractions and decimals, both forwards and backwards.

Through all this work your child will learn decimal notation and the language associated with it, including in the context of measurements, e.g. 10cm = 0.1m, 1 cm = 0.01m, etc. They will be taught to represent decimal numbers in several ways, such as on number lines. (See Year 3 'Maths' on p. 189.) By this time they'll be ready to tackle simple measurement and money problems involving fractions and decimals to two decimal places.

Measurement

Now that your child has been introduced to decimals to two decimal places they will begin to use the decimal point for money (£3.63 rather than £3 and 63p) and to record metric measures (1.23m rather than 1m and 23cm). They'll probably learn to convert between different units of measurement, e.g. kilometre to metre; hour to minute.

After learning to measure and calculate the perimeter of a rectilinear figure (including squares) in centimetres and metres, they will learn that the perimeter of a rectangle is 2 × (length + breadth). They should be shown that this can be expressed algebraically as $2(a + b)$ where a and b are the dimensions in the same unit. Note that this is the very first use of the term 'algebra' in the maths curriculum, even if it's not used to your child, and note also that your child is unlikely to find it daunting. It's worth bearing in mind that this is all algebra is – using letters to represent numbers.

The concept of 'area' is introduced and children will find the area of rectilinear shapes ('rectilinear' includes shapes made up of rectangles, such as L-shapes) by counting squares:

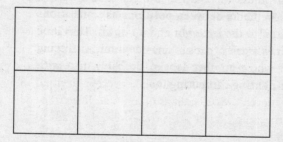

The area of this 4cm by 2cm shape is 8cm². It has 8 separate 1cm² squares (not to scale).

Your child can probably already tell the time. In Year 4 children learn to read, write and convert time between analogue and digital 12- and 24-hour clocks, and to solve problems involving converting from hours to minutes, minutes to seconds, years to months and weeks to days.

Geometry

Some new shapes should be introduced in Year 4: different triangles, e.g. isosceles, equilateral, scalene, and quadrilaterals, e.g. parallelogram, rhombus, trapezium.

Your child will learn to compare and order angles (in preparation for using a protractor next year) and compare lengths and angles to decide if a polygon is regular or irregular.

Children will learn about lines of symmetry, draw symmetrical patterns and recognize line symmetry in a variety of diagrams, including where the line of symmetry does not dissect the original shape.

Your child should be taught how to plot pairs of coordinates, e.g. 2, 5, on a two-dimensional grid. They'll probably be given a set of coordinates and asked to join the plotted points to reveal a mystery shape. They'll describe movements between positions as translations of a given unit to the left/right and up/down. They'll be taught to draw a pair of axes in one quadrant, with equal scales and whole-number labels (probably also with coordinate-plotting computing tools).

Statistics

In Year 4 your child should be shown how to draw graphs with time along the bottom (x) axis for the first time so they will be able to plot continuous data (such as the temperature of a cup of tea as it cools down), as well as bar graphs of discrete data (eye colour in the class).

Children will become more skilled at using information presented in bar charts, pictograms, tables and other graphs to solve problems.

What can you do to help?

- Fractions are probably the thing that will cause your child the most anxiety this year. It's really worth doing what you can to help your child get a good grounding in these before they move on in Year 5. Some children find this work comes very easily, but many who seem to understand at the time can turn out to have some misconceptions, or just not to have seen a particular pattern.

To see if your child has understood, ask them which is bigger, $\frac{1}{3}$ or $\frac{1}{8}$? If they think it's $\frac{1}{8}$, because eight is a bigger number than three, they haven't understood that an eighth is just one of eight pieces when something is divided into eight. Get some pieces of toast and show them. Then go on to explain what is meant by $\frac{2}{8}$. They may 'see' it as two bits of toast shared between eight, or as two portions from one piece of toast divided into eight. You can easily show them that these are both right: the answer is the same amount of toast. Keep going with the toast to see what happens if you have $\frac{3}{8}$ and someone gives you another $\frac{7}{8}$, although you'll need two pieces of toast for this. Can they see that 1 and $\frac{2}{8}$ is the same thing as 1 and $\frac{1}{4}$?

Working tricky calculations into everyday speech is not easy, but simple questions like 'Can you pour one fifth of this apple juice into each cup?' equates a fraction with the kind of sharing your child will be used to if they have siblings.

● Decimals crop up mostly in relation to money. You might try reinforcing what your child is learning at school by practising the facts that 0.25 is the very same thing as ¼, 0.5 is the same as ½ and 0.75 is the same as ¾.

● Play Battleships to get good at coordinates.

● Keep on with times tables (see 'Times Tables' on p. 163).

● Ask your child to explain what a parallelogram, a rhombus and a trapezium are. Then try to spot examples together around the house or from your car window.

● Dig out the NHS red record book you will have assiduously filled in during the first few months of your child's life, which will have line graphs showing weight and height growth. Get your child to draw up a blank version to start filling in every month to show their changing height from now on. You could have your child measure everyone in the family and plot their growth in different colours. It makes a change from recording heights against a door jamb (although that's always fun, too).

● Subscribe to Mathletics (www.mathletics.co.uk), an 'inspiring and engaging' online platform for improving and reinforcing maths skills. You can try for free with a ten-day 'guest pass'. Or it may be that your school already has a school-wide subscription, so it won't cost you anything. It's worth checking.

● A similar online maths resource – but with better graphics – is Manga High (www.mangahigh.com).

● Use Bond Assessment papers in maths and non-verbal reasoning. The thrill wears off pretty quickly, but lots of children quite like the fact that there are timed papers with answers in the back so they can compete against themselves.

● Fraction Action Snap. This is the standard card game, except you match fractions with percentages – ½ and 50 per cent, ¼ and 25 per cent, etc. Available to buy for £2.99.

● Have a look at Thinking Blocks, an app for modelling maths problems, especially good for fractions. Go to www.thinkingblocks.com for the website that explains the app.

Science

The current national curriculum introduces some topics in Year 4 (such as electricity) that used to be taught in science at an earlier age. By this stage, it's hoped that children will learn some important basics without forming some of the misconceptions that often arise (and stick) when they are taught to younger children.

The Year 4 science curriculum is divided into five sections: 'Living things and their habitats', 'Animals (including humans)', 'States of matter', 'Sound' and 'Electricity'. In your child's primary school, the science topics may be given different names and not all the activities will be as we predict or suggest. But the scientific knowledge set out below and in Year 3 'Science' should have been covered by the end of Year 4. (For the 'Purpose of Study' and 'Aims' of the science curriculum, see p. 461.)

Living things and their habitats

Your child will have looked at plants in their habitats in Years 1 and 2, had a rest from the topic in Year 3, and will take it up again this year. This time they should study how the habitat in the local environment changes throughout the year and be taught ways to identify and study the plants and animals in it (easier for rural schools). Children will see that there are many possible ways of grouping a wide selection of living things. They may begin to put vertebrate animals into groups such as fish, amphibians, reptiles, birds and mammals; and invertebrates into snails and slugs, worms, spiders and insects. Plants can be grouped into categories such as flowering plants (including grasses) and non-flowering plants, such as ferns and mosses. Your child is likely to use or design classification keys, or make a guide to local living things.

Your child will explore examples of human impact on environments, such as the positive effects of nature reserves, ecologically planned parks and garden ponds, and the negative effects of population increase and development, such as litter and deforestation.

Animals (including humans)

Your child should learn the main body parts associated with the digestive system (mouth, tongue, teeth, oesophagus, stomach and small and large intestine) and be taught their particular functions. They might draw and discuss their ideas about the digestive system and compare them with models or images.

Your child is likely to compare the teeth of carnivores and herbivores and suggest reasons for the differences between them. They'll find out what damages teeth and how to look after them (prepare for plaque-revealing blue pills).

States of matter

Your child will observe a range of everyday materials and develop simple descriptions of the states of matter (solids hold their shape; liquids form a pool, not a pile; gases escape from an unsealed container). They're bound to look at ice, water and steam and describe how water changes when it's heated or cooled. Scope for cross-curricular links with geography here.

There's the opportunity for some fun while exploring the effect of temperature on substances such as chocolate, butter and cream (to make food such as chocolate crispy cakes and ice-cream for a party, for instance). Your child could research the temperature at which materials other than water change state, e.g. when iron melts or when oxygen condenses into a liquid (not all schools will manage this). They might observe and record evaporation over a period of time (a puddle in the playground or washing on a line) and investigate the effect of temperature on laundry drying or snowmen melting.

Sound

Your child will learn by exploring the way sound is made by a range of different musical instruments from around the world that there is always vibration involved (including their own voice if they put a finger on their voice box); and find out how the pitch and volume of sounds can be changed in a variety of ways (altering the length, thickness or tension of a guitar string, or the length of the column of air in a flute to change pitch; making a 'bigger' vibration to increase volume). They'll be taught that sound is not only caused by vibrations, but that it's because the vibrations travel through air, water or liquid to their ears that they can hear it. They'll have to take this on trust, unless the school has a glass bell jar with an electric bell in it which the air can be removed from (using a vacuum cleaner in reverse) so the bell can no longer be heard ringing . . .

They are likely to experiment with readily available sound-makers like saucepan lids of different sizes or elastic bands of various thicknesses. They might make earmuffs from a variety of different materials to investigate which provides the best insulation against sound. They may well make and play their own instruments by using what they have found out about pitch and volume. (You have been warned.) There's lots of scope for cross-curricular links with music here.

Electricity

Your child will construct simple-series circuits (everything in a row, joined at each end to one of the two terminals of a battery), trying a range of different components (bulbs, buzzers, motors and switches), and use their circuits to create simple devices, e.g. a circuit where the buzzer sounds when the switch is pressed, or the buzzer sounds and a light comes on. They'll put non-conductors (such as their pencils or a plastic spoon) into their circuits and so learn the difference between an insulator and a conductor. They'll predict whether the lamp will light in a simple series circuit, based on whether or not it's part of a complete loop with a battery. They'll draw the circuit as a pictorial representation, not necessarily using conventional circuit symbols at this stage (wait until Year 6).

The terms 'current' and 'voltage' might crop up, but these should not be introduced or defined formally at this point. Pupils should be taught about precautions for working safely with electricity.

They'll test their predictions about what happens to a bulb's brightness if more cells (a battery is made up of a number of cells, if we're being pedantic) are added.

What can you do to help?

● Electrify your daughter's doll's house (or a house she's made out of a shoe box for her Sylvanians). Don't follow the online tutorials, which make it as complicated as possible and would be no good for a child, but ask your school if you could buy a couple of lamps (bulbs) and a switch from them and make it up as you go along with some copper wire and a 2.5V battery. Keep it simple, with one or two lights, and your child should be able to 'advise' you how to get it right.

● If they haven't already done so at school, help your child make an instrument. Talk about ways to make the vibrations bigger so it increases the volume. This could be a guitar (shoe boxes are so versatile) or pan pipes made from narrow-topped bottles filled to different depths. There are many ideas online. Look at www.kinderart.com and type 'musical instrument' in the search bar, or homemade musical instruments on Pinterest (www.pinterest.com/maestroclassics/homemade-musical-instruments). One of our favourites (because it's easily done and fun to use) is to make a didgeridoo (a long wooden trumpet-like instrument used by the Aboriginal peoples of Australia). A real didgeridoo is made from a hollow wooden branch and has a beeswax mouthpiece. Get a length of PVC pipe (like plumbers use), or just two cardboard wrapping-paper tubes taped together. The length should be manageable: say, a metre or so. Decorate using bright, exciting paints or markers. Glue buttons, glitter, stickers, etc. on it at will. You can create a mouthpiece by rolling a piece of paper into a cone and glueing it to the end of your pipe or tube. To play it, stand or sit with the instrument straight out in front of you with one end resting on the ground. Place your mouth inside the tube (or on the beeswax mouthpiece) and make a loose motorboat sound with your lips.

● This is the age of the tooth fairy, but she can have a night off. Keep a tooth back to see if Coca-Cola really does have a damaging effect (it doesn't, at least not overnight, but it's fun discovering that). You could then try extending the experiment to a fortnight or so, taking the tooth out and brushing it and photographing it every day for a fortnight. It will look horrid after this amount of time, very stained and showing signs of decomposition. It'll offer plenty of opportunity for discussion: in real life, the Coca-Cola's only in contact with your teeth for a short period, so do you need to worry if it only begins to look bad after a fortnight of constant contact?

● Try an experiment to see if adding salt changes the temperature at which water boils. Or, if you don't have the right kind of thermometer, see if it takes longer or is quicker to come to the boil. This gives lots of opportunity for 'fair test' discussions (same pan, same heat supply, same temperature of pan to begin with, same amount of water, same starting temperature of water, same amount of stirring . . .)

● Ask your child why astronauts on space walks need radios to talk to each other. Sound needs a 'medium' to travel through, like air, water or even a solid. Sound cannot travel through a vacuum, and space is a vacuum. Ask what they should do if they drop their radios (answer: touch helmets while speaking). You may need to gloss over how sound travels via the radio as this would require a GCSE-level understanding of what an electromagnetic wave is.

● Kindle any interest in science by conducting some experiments at home, even if unrelated to this year's school curriculum:

Magic coloured milk. If you add food colouring to milk, not much happens, but it takes only one simple ingredient to turn the milk into a swirling colour wheel. Pour enough milk on to a plate to cover the bottom. Drop food colouring on to the milk. Dip a cotton bud in Fairy Liquid, then touch it to the milk in the centre of the plate. Watch the colours swirl on their own as soon as the detergent contacts the milk. (Why? Milk consists of a lot of different types of molecules, including fat, protein, sugars, vitamins and minerals. When you introduce detergent to the milk, the detergent lowers the surface tension of the liquid and the food colouring is free to flow throughout. The detergent reacts with the protein in the milk, altering the shape of those molecules and setting them in motion. The reaction between the detergent and the fat causes molecules to be formed that help to lift grease off dirty plates. As the molecules form, the pigments in the food colouring are pushed around. The swirling of the colours continues for quite a while before stopping.)

Colour density column. Coloured sugar solutions made at different concentrations will form layers, from least dense on top to most dense (concentrated) at the bottom of the glass. Line up five glasses. Add one tablespoon of sugar to the first glass, two tablespoons to the second, three to the third, and four to the fourth. The fifth glass remains empty. Add three tablespoons of water to each of the first four glasses. Stir each solution. If the sugar does not dissolve in any of the four glasses, then add one more tablespoon of water to each. Add two to three drops of red food colouring to the first glass, yellow to the second glass, green to the third and blue to the fourth. Stir each solution. Fill the last glass about a quarter full with the blue sugar solution. Carefully layer some green sugar solution above the blue. (Do this by putting a spoon in the glass just above the blue layer and pouring the green solution slowly over the back of the spoon. If you do this right, you won't disturb the blue solution much at all.) Add the green solution until the glass is about half full. Now layer the yellow solution above the green liquid, using the back of the spoon. Fill the glass to three quarters full. Finally, layer the red solution above the yellow liquid. You should have a glass with four separate rings of colour.

Buy a science kit such as Kidz Labs Kitchen Science from Great Gizmos, or suggest it as a birthday or Christmas present. It'll show you how to launch a rocket fuelled by baking soda and vinegar, how to build a table-top volcano and how to light a bulb using electricity generated by a lemon and a fork.

There are apps that measure the volume of sounds. These may not seem highly educational, but an appreciation of a decibel gets your child thinking about measurement and how to make sounds louder or quieter. Try Decibel Meter Pro, or Sound Meter.

Art and Design

In Year 4 your child will be asked to immerse themselves more fully in the range of artistic activities available at the school. So expect them to use digital cameras or tablets to record visual data, create printing blocks, try their hand at dyeing, weaving and stitching, and experiment with a range of collage techniques, such as tearing, overlapping and layering. (For the 'Purpose of Study' and 'Aims' of the art and design curriculum, see p. 462.)

The national curriculum divides up the content in Key Stage 2 as follows.

Pupils should be taught to:

- develop different artistic techniques with creativity and experimentation, showing an increasing awareness of different kinds of art, craft and design

- create sketchbooks to record observations and use them to review and revisit ideas

- improve mastery of art and design techniques, including drawing, painting and sculpture, using a range of materials

- understand the work of great artists, architects and designers in history.

One of the ways in which your child will be encouraged to stretch their artistic muscles in Year 4 will be to make some quite complex 3D shapes with cross-curricular links to the work they're doing in other subjects. For instance, if they're doing 'Ancient Egypt' in history, it's a racing certainty that they'll be asked to make pyramids in art and design.

To encourage your child to make use of their sketchbook, they may be asked to keep a 'visual diary' of a particular experience, such as a seaside holiday or an overseas school trip. For inspiration, they might be shown examples of the diaries and sketchbooks of local artists, designers, architects or filmmakers. (For more on sketchbooks, see Year 3 'Art and Design' on p. 201.)

There is a unit which some schools taught in Year 4 in art and design under the old curriculum called 'Can we change places?' that might be pressed into service here. The teacher will ask your child to study sculpture in public buildings, squares and parks in the local area with a view to making a model of a sculpture for a site in the school or somewhere nearby. This is likely to appeal to boys in particular, as it will involve using clay, Plasticine, salt dough or papier mâché.

If your child is doing the sculpture unit, expect him or her to be introduced to the work of Henry Moore or Georges Braque. (For some reason, twentieth-century artists are preferred by most primary school teachers.)

What can you do to help?

- Throughout England there are lots of opportunities to see public sculpture and statuary, from the Henry Moores in Dartington Hall Gardens in South Devon to Antony Gormley's *Angel of the North*. We particularly recommend a visit to the Yorkshire Sculpture Park in Wakefield (www.ysp.co.uk), where families can wander the estate's 500-acre grounds looking at sixty different pieces. Your child can touch the sculptures, which makes it a different experience to a typical gallery or museum visit. There's a Young Explorers' Trail children can do that will lead them round the grounds and tell the history of the estate. Take welly boots because it can be very muddy!

● Introduce your child to the work of Thomas Heatherwick, the celebrated British designer of the Olympic Cauldron, and take them for a bus ride on the new Routemaster, which Heatherwick was responsible for. The Routemaster was the first new double-decker London bus design for fifty years and presented a number of design challenges. Draw attention to all the details of the bus's overall design, from the fabric on the seats to the buttons on the driver's uniform, and try to get your child to imagine the choices that Heatherwick made and think about why he made them.

● Children love making costumes, even if their contribution is largely supervisory, and there'll be plenty of occasions in the school calendar for them to produce costumes, such as World Book Day. However, they needn't confine their costume-making to school activities. Get them to design a Halloween outfit that isn't a witch, a vampire or a skeleton. Here's an example one of us spotted last Halloween – a *Minecraft* Creeper:

Computing

Your child is more likely to work with programmable toys such as Bee-Bots, Roamers and Pro-Bots in Key Stage 1 and with screen-based programming tools such as Scratch in Key Stage 2. By Year 4 they should be familiar with the school's preferred programming language and able to write some simple programs, such as games and quizzes. (For the 'Purpose of Study' and 'Aims' of the computing curriculum, see p. 463.)

The national curriculum divides up the content in Key Stage 2 as follows.

Pupils should be taught to:

- design, write and debug programs that accomplish specific goals, including controlling or simulating physical systems; solve problems by deconstructing them into smaller parts

- use sequence, selection and repetition in programs; work with variables and various forms of input and output

- use logical reasoning to explain how simple algorithms work and to detect and correct errors in algorithms and programs

- understand computer networks, including the internet; how they can provide multiple services, such as the World Wide Web; and the opportunities they offer for communication and collaboration

- use search technologies effectively, appreciate how results are selected and ranked, and be discerning in evaluating digital content

- select, use and combine a variety of software (including internet services) on a range of digital devices to design and create a range of programs, systems and content that accomplish given goals, including collecting, analysing, evaluating and presenting data and information

- use technology safely, respectfully and responsibly; recognize acceptable/unacceptable behaviour; identify a range of ways to report concerns about content and contact.

Computer science

In Year 4 the teacher might ask the class to write a simple program in Scratch for a game that tests a player's ability to add fractions to tie in with the work they're doing in maths. To do that, the pupils will need to develop an algorithm for fractions, as well as make use of the concepts they were introduced to in Year 3 – sequencing, selection and repetition, among others. Alternatively, they might be asked to create a game to help younger pupils practise the maths they're doing in Year 1 or Year 2.

Digital literacy

The teacher may help your child use search engines to solve problems they are encountering in programming by typing in an error message or a pithy summary of the problem.

Your child is likely to be taught some more advanced word-processing skills in Year 4, such as how to copy and paste, how to undo and redo, how to save documents and make copies, how to italicize, embolden or under-line a piece of text, how to change the font or the font size, how to highlight a piece of text in colour, how to create a bullet-pointed list, how to use spellcheck, how to insert a picture into the text, how to save a copy of a document as a pdf file, etc.

There's a unit in the old ICT curriculum called 'Collecting and presenting information: questionnaires and pie charts' which your child might be taught in Year 4, although this is becoming increasingly rare. They'll be asked to use a simple software package to create bar charts, pie charts and line graphs and learn how to present this information in the context of a report or argument. There's scope for cross-curricular links here with geography, maths and science.

What can you do to help?

- There's a network of after-school coding clubs called Code Club which your child can participate in from the age of nine. For more details, see www.codeclub.org.uk.

- If your child has a particular interest – in Lego, say, or the Nickelodeon series *House of Anubis* – you could encourage them to look it up on Wikipedia and see if the entry is both accurate and complete. If it isn't, you could help them set up their own Wikipedia account so they can correct it or add to it. Alternatively, they might be interested in a subject that doesn't have a Wikipedia page or, if it does, just a stub. (There is no entry for Lego WeDo, for instance.) If so, they could become the first person to write a proper article about it on the site. Wikipedia bills itself as 'the encyclopedia that anyone can edit' and there are no age restrictions on who can edit it or write new articles. However, there are some fairly strict guidelines and before embarking on this project you and your child should familiarize yourselves with them by visiting the 'Guidance for younger editors' page (http://en.wikipedia.org/wiki/Wikipedia:Guidance_for_younger_editors).

- You could think about creating your own blog at home with your child, focused on a specific area such as 'Cooking for children' or 'Arts and crafts'. In developing this, your child could use the digital literacy skills they've been learning at school, such as word processing, using digital cameras and sound recorders and how to upload digital content. For inspiration, you could show them NeverSeconds (www.neverseconds.blogspot.co.uk), the famous school-dinners blog created by Martha Payne, a primary school pupil in Scotland, which has recorded over 10 million hits (although it hasn't been updated since 2014). Children should be able to use Blogger and WordPress (with a bit of help), but if you want to retain control over the blog, there's a blogging site that enables you to do that called Kidblog (www.kidblog.org).

● For apps and games designed to help children develop their programming skills, see Year 3 'Computing' on p. 209.

Design and Technology

By the age of eight or nine, some children will have developed a passionate interest in making things and may be beginning to feel a bit socially isolated by virtue of their all-consuming hobby. If your child suffers from this, the best antidote is to introduce them to the community of 'mini-makers', a burgeoning international subculture of children with a similarly obsessive interest in DT. They tend to gather at mini-maker faires (always spelt like that for some reason), where they can go and see lots of weird and wonderful things and show off their own inventions in Show and Tell-style competitions. There's a big annual faire in Edinburgh that's part of the Edinburgh International Science Festival, but there are also lots of other ones all over the UK, including Brighton Mini-Maker Faire, Bristol Mini-Maker Faire, Derby Mini-Maker Faire, Dundee Mini-Maker Faire, Elephant & Castle Mini-Maker Faire, Machynlleth Mini-Maker Faire and Manchester Mini-Maker Faire. (For the 'Purpose of Study' and 'Aims' of the design and technology curriculum, see p. 465.)

The national curriculum divides up the content in Key Stage 2 as follows.

When designing and making, children should be taught to:

Design

- use research and develop design criteria to inform the design of innovative, functional, appealing products that are fit for purpose, aimed at particular individuals or groups

- generate, develop, model and communicate ideas through discussion, annotated sketches, cross-sectional and exploded diagrams, prototypes, pattern pieces and computer-aided design.

Make

- select from and use a wider range of tools and equipment to perform practical tasks accurately

- select from and use a wider range of materials and components, including construction materials, textiles and ingredients, according to their functional properties and aesthetic qualities.

Evaluate

- investigate and analyse a range of existing products

- evaluate their ideas and products against their own

design criteria and consider the views of others to improve their work

- understand how key events and individuals in design and technology have helped shape the world.

Technical knowledge

- apply their understanding of how to strengthen, stiffen and reinforce more complex structures
- understand and use mechanical systems in their products
- understand and use electrical systems in their products
- apply their understanding of computing to program, monitor and control their products.

Cooking and nutrition

- understand and apply the principles of a healthy and varied diet
- prepare and cook a variety of predominantly savoury dishes, using a range of cooking techniques
- understand seasonality, and know where and how a variety of ingredients are grown, reared, caught and processed.

Design

In Year 4 your child may be asked to produce a simple cross-sectional or exploded diagram of a familiar object, such as a torch, although these are likely to be nothing more sophisticated than annotated sketches. They might conceivably be introduced to a computer program that helps them create diagrams for designers, such as SketchUp, although that's more likely to happen in Year 5.

Make

There was a unit in the old DT curriculum called 'Musical instruments' in which children learnt how a range of instruments are made that has been known to resurface here, not least because of its cross-curricular links with the work children will be doing on 'Sound' in science. The aim of the unit is for your child to produce a musical instrument by the end of term and, if the teacher's really ambitious, to collaborate with their classmates on composing and performing a piece of music.

Evaluate

There's a unit in the old DT curriculum called 'Storybooks' which used to be taught in Year 4 that has been recycled in some schools. It involves assessing different pop-up books with a view to making one. Your child will be asked to bring in an old pop-up book from home, disassemble it and try to discover how the internal mechanisms work. They'll then be asked to put it back together – or, if they're feeling confident, produce a pop-up book of their own from scratch. (In general, making books is more likely to be taught in computing using a digital book-making app like Book Creator.)

Technical knowledge

One of the things your child is supposed to be learning about in DT is electrical systems and in Year 4 they may be asked to design a simple electrical product for a specific consumer, such as a battery-powered night light for children who want to read under the covers in bed. They'll be asked to think about what sort of switch to use, how the beam of light will be directed towards the reading matter and how the bulb is going to be protected. Finally, they may be invited to explore what materials will dim the brightness of the bulb, creating an ambient effect and making it less likely that they'll be caught by their parents.

Cooking and nutrition

Your child will be introduced to some rudimentary cooking skills in lower Key Stage 2, such as grating, mixing, spreading, kneading and baking, and you may be surprised by how enthusiastically they embrace these skills, particularly if you also sit down as a family to watch the *Great British Bake-off*.

What can you do to help?

- Check out Greek Pot Painter (www.show.me.uk/interactive_game/949-greek-pot-painter), a website where your child can try their hand at painting a Greek pot. Less messy than trying it in real life.

- You can make a large Roman mosaic at this website: http://gwydir.demon.co.uk/jo/mosaic/mkmosaic.htm. In addition to teaching you about mosaics, it might throw some light on what your child is doing in Year 4 history.

● If you're a camping family, why not get your child to design and make a toilet-roll holder out of a coffee can or large baked-bean tin. All they need to do is cut a slit that's the width of the can, insert the loo roll, thread the paper through the slit. For convenience, they can add a string handle so it can be hung from a nearby tree. You can find more than forty ideas for 'camping hacks that are borderline genius' on BuzzFeed (www.buzzfeed.com/peggy/camping-hacks-that-are-borderline-genius).

Geography

As we said in Year 3 'Geography', one of the key differences between the old and the new geography curriculum is that there's less emphasis on teaching children skills, including higher-order thinking skills, and more emphasis on geographical knowledge. However, many teachers have been reluctant to abandon the old approach and continue to encourage children to ask geographical questions, analyse evidence and draw their own conclusions about a range of issues. If there's been any change in the way teachers approach the subject, it's about *when* they focus on these skills, not *if*. Year 4 is when they'll start introducing your child to issues such as anthropogenic global warming, deforestation, fair trade, intensive farming and renewable versus non-renewable energy. One consequence of this is that your child may start policing the contents of your shopping basket, admonishing you for not being more eco-friendly.

The national curriculum divides up the content in Key Stage 2 as follows.

Pupils should be taught to:

Locational knowledge

- locate the world's countries, using maps to focus on Europe (including Russia) and North and South America, concentrating on their environmental regions, key physical and human characteristics, countries and major cities

- name and locate counties and cities of the United Kingdom, geographical regions and their identifying human and physical characteristics, key topographical features (including hills, mountains, coasts and rivers) and land-use patterns; and understand how some of these aspects have changed over time

- identify the position and significance of latitude, longitude, the equator, northern hemisphere, southern hemisphere, the tropics of Cancer and Capricorn, the Arctic and Antarctic Circles, the prime/Greenwich meridian and time zones (including day and night).

Place knowledge

- understand geographical similarities and differences through the study of human and physical geography of a region of the United Kingdom, a region in a European country and a region within North or South America.

Human and physical geography

- describe and understand key aspects of physical geography, including: climate zones, biomes and vegetation belts, rivers, mountains, volcanoes and earthquakes and the water cycle

- describe and understand key aspects of human geography, including: types of settlement and land-use, economic activity including trade links, and the distribution of natural resources including energy, food, minerals and water.

Geographical skills and fieldwork

- use maps, atlases, globes and digital/computer mapping to locate countries and describe features studied

- use the eight points of a compass, four- and six-figure grid references, symbols and key (including the use of Ordnance Survey maps) to build knowledge of the United Kingdom and the wider world

- use fieldwork to observe, measure, record and present the human and physical features in the local area, using a range of methods, including sketch maps, plans and graphs, and digital technologies.

Locational knowledge

Your child may be asked to study a map of the world and locate areas with similar environmental features, e.g. the Arctic and Antarctica (although they're not that similar!). They may learn about the main regions of the United Kingdom – East, East Midlands, London, North-east,

North-west, Northern Ireland, Scotland, South-east, South-west, Wales, West Midlands, Yorkshire and the Humber – and the largest cities in each region. They may also learn about the Greenwich meridian and how it relates to different time zones around the world.

Place knowledge

In Year 4 the teacher will probably ask your child to compare a region in the United Kingdom – almost certainly the region their school is in – with another region in Europe and not bring in North or South America at this point. For instance, if the school is close to Wales, the comparison might be between two mountainous areas, e.g. the Snowdonia National Park and the Swiss Alps, paying attention to things such as density of population, climate, vegetation, etc. There's a unit in the old geography curriculum called 'The mountain environment', which your child might study in this context. If your child is studying French in languages and the school has established a link with a partner school in France, the teacher may well choose to study the region that school is in.

Human and physical geography

In Year 4 your child is likely to study earthquakes, volcanoes and the water cycle (physical geography); and types of settlement, land-use, trade links, etc. in Roman Britain (human geography). There is scope here for cross-curricular links with science in physical geography, because children will be learning about ice, water and steam in Year 4, and examining what happens when water is heated and cooled; and for cross-curricular links with history in human geography because children are likely to be studying the Roman occupation of Britain.

Geographical skills and fieldwork

As in Year 3, your child will probably use maps, atlases, globes and digital mapping applications to locate the countries they're studying in Year 4 under 'Locational knowledge'. Your child will continue to do exercises involving the eight points of a compass and may progress from two-figure grid references to four-figure ones. The fieldwork they do may involve a school trip to a national park or nature reserve, where they'll continue to develop their map-making skills and observe, measure and document the area's distinctive geographical characteristics. There's a unit in the old geography curriculum called 'How and why do we spend our time?' which your child might be taught in Year 4. It focuses on how to design and carry out a local survey and how to collate, interpret and present the findings.

What can you do to help?

- If you're taking your child to a museum or a visitor attraction, find it beforehand with your child on Google Maps and print out the directions. Then, on the way, give the directions to your child and have them direct you. If you have a motorway atlas in your car, get them to follow the route you're taking on a map.

- Why not ask your child to make a 3D map? Go around your local area with a map and ask your child to make half a dozen small sketches of various landmarks and points of interest on the map itself. When you're back at home, place the map on a wooden board and cut around the sketches, leaving the base of each image uncut. Then fold each image so it's standing upright, creating a pop-up effect. (This will only work if the map is on thick paper to begin with.) You and your child can watch a short video that explains how to do this in more detail on the BBC's Bitesize website (www.bbc.co.uk/education/clips/zwfcd2p).

● One way for your child to find out more about a different part of the world is for them to find a pen-pal. Most schools are twinned with other schools and some will match up your child with a pen-pal as a matter of course. If not – or if you'd like your child to have another pen-pal – you can sponsor a child via Plan UK (www.plan-uk.org), a charity that helps children in the world's poorest countries. You can sponsor a child for less than 50 pence a day and your child can then enter into a correspondence with them.

MNEMONICS AND MEMORY AIDS

To remember that the Arctic is at the North Pole and Antarctica at the South Pole, think of the first syllable of each word. The 'Arc' of Arctic makes you think of an arc shape, i.e. a shape that resembles the top half of the Earth, and the Arctic is at the very top. The 'Ant' of Antarctica, by contrast, makes you think of a tiny, six-legged creature that lives on the ground, i.e. on the bottom, and Antarctica is at the bottom of the Earth.

History

As we said in Year 3 'History', the four specific British units are likely to be taught chronologically, though probably not all nine units, taken as a whole. In Year 4 your child may study the Roman conquest of Britain and then another non-British unit, possibly Ancient Greece. Apologies for the vagueness here, but we've seen a lot of variation in when the different units are taught. (For the 'Purpose of Study' and 'Aims' of the history curriculum, see p. 468.)

The national curriculum divides up the content in Key Stage 2 under the following headings.

- Changes in Britain from the Stone Age to the Iron Age

- The Roman Empire and its impact on Britain

- Britain's settlement by Anglo-Saxons and Scots

- The Viking and Anglo-Saxon struggle for the kingdom of England to the time of Edward the Confessor

- A local history study

- A study of an aspect or theme in British history that extends pupils' chronological knowledge beyond 1066

- The achievements of the earliest civilizations – an overview of where and when the first civilizations appear and a depth study of one of the following: Ancient Sumer; the Indus Valley; Ancient Egypt; the Shang Dynasty of Ancient China

- Ancient Greece – a study of Greek life and achievements and their influence on the Western world

- A non-European society that provides contrasts with British history – one study chosen from: early Islamic civilization, including a study of Baghdad c. AD 900; Mayan civilization c. AD 900; Benin (West Africa) c. AD 900–1300

Under the old curriculum, the Romans, Anglo-Saxons and Vikings were all lumped together in a single unit, with schools having to choose which of the three to cover, whereas in the current curriculum they've been separated into different units, allowing for each to be studied in turn. Assuming your child has done Britain's prehistory in Year 3 – 'Changes in Britain from the Stone Age to the Iron Age' – we think they're likely to do 'The Roman Empire and its impact on Britain' in Year 4. There's some overlap here with a popular unit in the old history curriculum – 'Why have people invaded and settled in Britain in the past? A Roman case study', usually known to children as 'Invaders!' – and most teachers have understandably adapted it for the purposes of teaching the new unit. Material they're likely to cover includes: Julius Caesar's attempted invasions in 55–54 BC, the rise of the Roman Empire, the successful invasion by Claudius, the resistance led by Boadicea (we told you she'd crop up in Key Stage 2!) and the erection of Hadrian's Wall. The teacher will probably arrange a visit to a Roman site (the Roman baths in Harrogate, say) and point out that the Romans were responsible for importing many of the things we now take for granted: towns, baths, plumbing, new forms of religion and farming methods, etc. If there are some Roman remains close to the school, the teacher may ask the whole class to do a local study. Conceivably, your child's teacher may even get permission from the head to build a Roman road in the school's grounds, giving your child an opportunity to develop their historical research skills.

The other unit we think your child will do in Year 4 is 'Ancient Greece', a natural companion to the Roman unit and – you never know – they may even teach them in the correct order. There are two units in the old curriculum that teachers can reuse here – 'Who were the Ancient Greeks?' and 'How do we use Ancient Greek ideas today?' – and they should have plenty of material to hand. They might begin by asking what words in common usage today have Greek origins, including the word 'history', and segue from that into a discussion of what institutions and cultural practices which originated in Ancient Greece are now dominant features of contemporary life, particularly in politics, education and sport. Your child may also be taught something about Greek mythology, the differences between Athens and Sparta, Greek seamanship and warfare, the Persian Wars, Xerxes, King Leonidas and the legend of the three hundred Spartans.

What can you do to help?

ROME

● The BBC's Bitesize site has a section on 'Romans' that includes areas called 'The Roman army', 'Roads and places', 'Families and children', 'Roman remains' and 'Roman defence of Britain' (www.bbc.co.uk/education/topics/zwmpfg8).

● There are a number of video games for PCs set in Ancient Rome. One of the most educational (and none of them are that educational) is *CivCity Rome*, in which the player has to create the city of Rome from scratch, building homes, growing and harvesting crops, raising tax revenues, developing civic amenities and keeping the populace happy with bread and circuses. You can find it on Steam here: http://store.steampowered.com/app/3980/.

● There's an online game called *Battlefield Academy* (www.bbc.co.uk/history/british/launch_gms_bfacademy.shtml) in which your child will fight as a British soldier in four historical battles, one of which is set in Britain during the Roman invasion. It's been designed in consultation with the Royal Military Academy, Sandhurst.

● Google Earth has an 'Ancient Rome layer'. Under 'Gallery' tick the 'Ancient Rome layer' box and it then appears in your 'Places' list. You can zoom in on buildings, temples, amphitheatres, etc., either seeing them from above or from inside in 3D.

● The Museum of London has combined forces with the History Channel to create a free app called Streetmuseum: Londinium that directs users to various landmarks of Roman London, such as the amphitheatre and the Temple of Mithras. Your child can even 'excavate' archaeological finds by using their fingers to dig, revealing ancient artefacts. The app includes a map of Roman London created by Museum of London Archaeology which the user can superimpose on a modern map of London, revealing how much the city has changed in the last two thousand years.

● We've included a list of historical novels written for children in 'What can you do to help?' in Year 6 'History', including Rosemary Sutcliff's *Eagle of the Ninth*, which is set in Roman Britain. If your child is an avid reader, you could try that out on them now. Also worth a try are Rick

Riordan's Percy Jackson novels, a great way to introduce children to Greek mythology.

GREECE

● The BBC Bitesize site has a section called 'Ancient Greeks' that includes areas such as 'Growing up in Greece', 'The Olympic Games', 'Greeks at war', 'Sea and ships' and 'Gods and heroes' (www.bbc.co.uk/education/topics/z87tn39).

● The British Museum has a good online resource called *Ancient Greece* that's been designed for children. They can explore a range of different areas, including 'The Acropolis', 'Athens', 'Sparta', 'Festivals and games' and 'Gods and goddesses' (www.ancientgreece.co.uk/menu.html).

● Odyssey Online (www.carlos.emory.edu/ODYSSEY/GREECE/home.html) is an excellent website where your child can explore different aspects of Greek culture – 'Death and burial', 'Victory and conquest', 'Gods, goddesses and heroes', etc. – and click on different historical artefacts to learn about life in Ancient Greece. (Includes extensive quotes from *The Iliad*.)

● Roger Lancelyn Green's versions of the Greek myths – *Tales of the Greek Heroes* and *The Tale of Troy* – are still the best way to introduce your child to these stories in our view but if you fancy something a bit less old-fashioned, you could try the *D'Aulaires' Book of Greek Myths* by Ingri and Edgar d'Aulaire, which is beautifully illustrated.

● There's a PC video game called *Zeus: Master of Olympus* that's worth taking a look at if your child is a gamer. The player has to build and develop a city in Ancient Greece. It's historically accurate up to a point, with a wealth of detailed information about the kinds of crops that were grown at the time and the sort of homes people lived in, but there's also a fantasy element. For instance, the city you've built is vulnerable to attack by gods and monsters and you must summon heroes to protect the citizenry. However, you shouldn't let the blurring of the line between fantasy and reality put you off. As most historians of the period will tell you, it's almost impossible to completely separate facts from myths when it comes to Ancient Greece.

MNEMONICS AND MEMORY AIDS

Most people can remember Julius Caesar, but there were five more emperors after him:

Augustus (31 BC–AD 14)
Tiberius (14–37)
Caligula (37–41)
Claudius (41–54)
Nero (54–68)

You can remember them by committing this sentence to memory: **A**nother **T**om **C**at **C**aught **N**apping.

Languages

Rather than repeat ourselves, we recommend you read the introduction to Year 3 'Languages' on p. 233. In case you don't, it's important to repeat one paragraph here:

Given the range of time dedicated to language teaching that we expect to find across the country's schools, it's hard to say exactly what you should expect your child to learn in each year. If your child has less than an hour a week, your primary school may not be expecting to cover as much ground as we describe.

Year 4 will be your child's second year of language lessons. He or she should start the year already familiar with the sound of the language, some songs and rhymes in the language, able to count to twenty, say the colours, maybe know the days of the week, and be able to ask and answer questions such as 'What is your name?' and 'Where do you live?' Perhaps they will be able to say what they like or don't like about various animals and foods. (For the 'Purpose of Study' and 'Aims' of the languages curriculum, see p. 469.)

The language content of the national curriculum in Key Stage 2 can be divided up under two broad headings, spoken and written.

Spoken language

Pupils should be taught to:

- listen attentively to spoken language and show understanding by joining in and responding

- explore the patterns and sounds of language through songs and rhymes and link the spelling, sound and meaning of words

- engage in conversations; ask and answer questions; express opinions and respond to those of others; seek clarification and help

- speak in sentences, using familiar vocabulary, phrases and basic language structures

- develop accurate pronunciation and intonation so that others understand when they are reading aloud or using familiar words and phrases

- present ideas and information orally to a range of audiences

- appreciate stories, songs, poems and rhymes in the language.

In Year 3 after starting with an introductory topic on themselves, your child will have focused on topics such as 'Animals', 'Friends', 'Birthdays' and 'Food'. In Year 4 some possible topics (remember, each topic lasts about half a term, or six weeks) might be 'Travel', 'Weather', 'Pocket money', 'Sport' and 'Telling the time'. The weekly lesson will probably follow a pattern. After a warm-up game revising the previous week's progress, your child will be introduced to new content. What follows will probably be different games, the format of which your child will become familiar with – singing, asking and answering questions, drawing and labelling pictures.

By the end of Year 4 your child will probably have been taught how to ask and answer questions such as 'What is your favourite sport?', 'What do you do on Mondays?', 'Do you like chicken?' and 'How do you get to school?' They should be able to count to forty (or even to one hundred in multiples of ten), say 'I have . . .' and 'I haven't . . .', use adjectives such as 'fast' and 'slow', and maybe say the date.

To give you an idea of the kinds of activities your child may take part in, here are some examples:

- The Fruit Salad Game. Children are each given a word denoting a fruit to remember in the language. When the teacher calls out a word, every child with that word must change places. When the teacher calls out 'Fruit salad' all children must change places

- Sort words into categories by criteria such as how many syllables they have. So, for example, your child will be asked to place a mixture of cuddly toys (for which they have learnt the word denoting the particular animal) in different circles according to whether they have one syllable, two or three

- Sort objects into categories by the sound of the first or last letter

- Play the Singular and Plural Game. Listen to spoken language and identify ideas which are singular or plural, e.g. choose whether to stand on the singular mat or the plural mat when you hear 'Five elephants are dancing' or 'One elephant is sleeping' in the language being learnt

- Answer aloud a question which the teacher mouths silently

- Ask how to say something in the language and then practise, using pictures and props

- Turn statements into questions, paying close attention to intonation

- Play Chinese Whispers

Written language

Pupils should be taught to:

- **read carefully and show understanding of words, phrases and simple writing**

- broaden their vocabulary and develop their ability to understand new words that are introduced into familiar written material, including through using a dictionary

- write phrases from memory and adapt these to create new sentences, to express ideas clearly

- describe people, places, things and actions orally and in writing.

In each of the topics they're doing in Year 4 – 'Travel', 'Weather', 'Pocket money', 'Sport', etc. – your child is likely to focus on a new phoneme or two, and to learn to read and write words that use that phoneme, and learn some other vocabulary, too. By the end of the year they should be writing short sentences using grammar they're familiar with.

To give you an idea of the kinds of activities your child may take part in, here are some examples:

- Play Anagram Jigsaws. Familiar words are cut up into individual letter cards and, in small groups, children work together to rebuild the words

- Play Pass the Anagram Parcel. Listening to music or songs, the children pass around the circle a bag containing letter cards which, when they're all out of the bag, can be used to spell a familiar word. Each time the music stops, the child holding the bag takes out one letter card, identifies it by its name and places it in the middle of the circle. The music restarts and the game continues until all the letters are in the middle of the circle. All the children try to guess which word can be spelt with the letters

- Complete a reading jigsaw by putting text cards in the correct order, reading some of the words aloud

- Play Find the Missing Words. Looking at a familiar written poem with all the rhyming words removed and written on word cards, children rebuild the poem correctly, then read it aloud. They then jumble up the rhyming words and reread the nonsense poem aloud

- Write labels for work on wall displays and books

- Fill in lists of likes and dislikes

- Complete a dream shopping list for a party or a picnic

- Make a personal language dictionary or word bank

What can you do to help?

All of the suggestions in Year 3 'Languages' also apply to Year 4.

● Try BBC Languages (www.bbc.co.uk/languages), which covers French, German, Spanish, Italian, Chinese . . . and many more. Click on, for example, 'School French' then 'Primary French' then 'Videos' and you will see video clips of children talking about themselves in their own language, using very simple vocabulary.

● Practise the phrases your child has been learning at school. If they can't remember what they are, have a look at their exercise book or ask the teacher.

● Play Bilingual Zingo (available in French and Spanish). This is straightforward Bingo, but in two languages. See how the game works at www.youtube.com/watch?v=TVdyGTZMQBs.

● Keep an Usborne book of *My First 1,000 Words in* . . . in the car. As long as you keep nothing else in the car (except maybe CDs in the new language), your child may have a look.

● Find local activities your child can do in the language.

● Only allow your child to play FIFA football games on a tablet, phone or hand-held device when switched to the foreign language.

● Below is a list of things you can do to help if your child is learning French or Spanish, which are the most common languages taught in primary schools.

Try www.french-games.net/

Watch *Heidi and Tonton* videos on YouTube

The Putumayo *French Playground* is a popular CD

Try www.queondaspanish.com

Some apps you could try are:

Rosetta Stone Kids Lingo Letter Sounds. You repeat a word in, say, Spanish and if the speech recognition bot thinks the pronunciation is correct the GoGo Lingo characters carry out your request

Learn French by eFlashApps. This is a flashcard game where you have to match the words to the correct images. (Search 'French Flash Cards' on iTunes)

Ana Lomba's French for Kids

Le Grand Imagier de petit ours brun. This app requires you to find objects in particular settings – family, outings, at home – and match them with pictures. If you get them right, you hear how to say the object in French. (Genuine French accent!). Available on French iTunes.

Spanish kids – Speak and Learn Pro

Little Pim Spanish

InstaSpanish Kids Lessons (Android apps on Google)

Music

In Year 4 children are likely to be asked to pay particular attention to the expressive use of pitch and rhythm in different pieces of music, e.g. 'Samuel Goldenberg and Schmüyle', the sixth movement from *Pictures at an Exhibition*, Mussorgsky's suite in ten movements. The teacher may clap out rhythms which the class then has to copy and they may introduce the class to the concept of an 'ostinato', which involves clapping the same rhythm over and over again. Alternatively, the teacher may play the class a piece of music that has a clear, repeated rhythmic pattern, such as the accompaniment to the tune in Mike Oldfield's *Tubular Bells*, and ask them to clap along with the repeated pattern. Some other examples might be 'Unsquare Dance' by the Dave Brubeck Quartet, or the second movement of Beethoven's *Seventh Symphony*. (For the 'Purpose of Study' and 'Aims' of the music curriculum, see p. 470.)

The national curriculum divides up the content in Key Stage 2 as follows.

Pupils should be taught to:

- play and perform in solo and ensemble contexts, using voice and playing musical instruments with increasing accuracy, fluency, control and expression

- improvise and compose music for a range of purposes, using the interrelated dimensions of music

- listen with attention to detail and recall sounds with increasing aural memory

- use and understand staff and other musical notations

- appreciate and understand a wide range of high-quality live and recorded music drawn from different traditions and from great composers and musicians

- develop an understanding of the history of music.

As in earlier years, a lot of time will be spent on singing in Year 4 and your child may be played examples of music in which a song is accompanied in different ways, e.g. by voices, large orchestras, small groups or electronic instruments. They'll probably then learn to sing one of these songs, paying attention to how different versions of it can be arranged, e.g. taking a given melody and finding ways to make it more interesting by layering in different sounds.

In Year 4 your child may be introduced to the concept of 'time signature' (the numbers at the beginning of a piece of written music). At this stage, they're likely to refer only to the top number, which generally gives the metre, e.g. a 3:4 beat pattern. The stave may be described as a 'ladder', with notes placed higher or lower to match higher or lower sounds, and your child will be shown how you can follow a song or piece of music by moving along the line from left to right, just like in reading. They may be shown the different shapes of the notes and the way they denote how long or short the note should be, e.g. ♩ ♩ ♫. The teacher will probably discuss the meaning of musical phrases such as 'duration', 'tempo' and 'pitch' and encourage your child to think about them when devising their own compositions. Of course, if your child has been learning a musical instrument for some time all this is likely to be familiar.

One of the bullet points above says that children should be able to 'use and understand staff and other musical notations' by the end of Key Stage 2 and your child will probably be introduced to staff notation in Year 4 (in some cases earlier). Some teachers won't introduce this subject in its totality all in one go but will break it down into units. That might mean starting with the rhythmic symbols in Year 4 (see A in the diagram below) and then exploring melodic lines and the ways pitch is shown in Year 5 (see B below). Only when both aspects are secure – when children can 'read' them confidently – should they be brought together in the established form of Western staff notation.

Something else your child might do in Year 4 is to match music to paintings. For instance, the teacher could choose a painting that clearly conjures up a particular feeling – *The Fighting Temeraire* by Turner, or something by Jackson Pollock – then ask them to come up with descriptive words and phrases that apply to the picture and think about what sounds those words and phrases conjure up. The teacher might then ask them to choose some instruments to match the mood and subject of the picture and compose a piece of music.

What can you do to help?

● Encourage your child to pay attention to the detail in a piece of music they're listening to or a song they happen to enjoy. When listening to a CD in the car, try to identify the different instruments. If it's pop music, ask if they can hear the bass or drum their hands on their legs in rhythm with the drums. You might even introduce them to the concept of 'air drumming'. For inspiration, check out Thai sensation Weerachat Premananda on YouTube: www.youtube.com/watch?v=0OJ24YAKuGo, or search 'Rez Power – Israel and New Breed (drum wall)'.

● Memrise (www.memrise.com), the free online learning tool we recommended in 'Times Tables' on p. 168, has a 'Music' section. Most of the music courses (made up of pictures and mnemonics) are aimed at GCSE and A-level students, but there's a course on 'Grade 1 Theory Words' that could be useful if your child is learning about musical phrases such as 'duration', 'tempo' and 'pitch'. Click on the word 'accelerando' and the definition 'Gradually getting faster' comes up. Your child can then choose a mnemonic to help them remember it, such as a picture of a jaguar running at full speed.

● A great way to interest your child in music is to go to a music festival in the summer, though these can be expensive. All are child friendly to a greater or lesser extent (okay, maybe not Glastonbury), but the particularly child-friendly ones are Camp Bestival (Dorset), Larmer Tree (Wiltshire), Standon Calling (Hertfordshire) and Sunrise Celebration (Monmouthshire).

● There's an app called My Note Games that 'listens' to you playing your instrument – it tells you to play a particular note and you then have to play it. It's a good way to remember musical notation and phrases. It won an innovations award in 2012.

● An app called Jellybean Tunes is an introduction to reading and composing music for children.

School Dinners

Since September 2014 all primary schools offer a free school meal to every child in Reception, Year 1 and Year 2. There are exacting guidelines governing the nutritional content of average weekly consumption: maximum number of grams of salt, minimum number of grams of zinc, etc. It's up to the school governors to ensure that your chef/catering company is following the guidelines, and Ofsted may ask them (the governors) to show that they do. So, in theory, you can rest assured that the nutritional content is healthy. However, children are picky eaters and some parents will prefer to provide a packed lunch (if it's allowed) because they know their child will eat it. The cost of a school dinner varies from county to county and even from school to school. Currently, it's between £2 and £3.

Lunchtime can be fraught with difficulty (who to sit next to, whether 'packed-lunch children' are separated from school-dinner eaters, how to hide the broccoli) and in the early years lunch is often the only bit of the school day your child insists on telling you about. We've known children terrified of the dinner ladies (now called 'mid-day supervisory assistants' or 'MDSAs'), or too nervous to ask for a drink. It's worth making an effort to check that your child isn't enduring an unnecessary trial.

Schools operate in many different ways at lunchtime. In some, the staff will eat with the children. In others, the older children police the younger ones. Some schools have a finish-your-plate policy; most don't.

You won't know whether your child eats much of what they are given without finding the right person to ask, which can be tricky, and this can be another reason that some parents prefer to provide a packed lunch. But, beware, children are good at emptying their lunchbox into the bin, or giving the bits they don't want (carrot sticks, anything green, the apple) to a hungrier friend. And they are good at telling you that they are the only child in the whole school not to have whatever that month's expensive and non-nutritious craze is. Some children find it very hard to eat as quickly as their friends – one of our children asked for less and less in their packed lunch every week and finally admitted that they just wanted to get the eating done fast enough to be let out to play with their speedy-munching friends.

There's lots of guidance on the perfect packed lunch. Try the Children's Food Trust at www.childrensfood-trust.org.uk/parents/schoolfood/packedlunches, or the BBC's good food section at www.bbcgoodfood.com/howto/guide/school-packed-lunch-inspiration, or the NHS's 'Live Well' section at www.nhs.uk/Livewell/childhealth6-15/Pages/Lighterlunchboxes.aspx (Google 'NHS healthier lunchboxes').

Year 5

Introduction

The pace of progress will pick up in Year 5. Now that a degree of reading, writing and maths fluency is taken as given, your child will be expected to apply their mind to harder concepts across the board. There's not much difference in behavioural terms between a Year 4 and a Year 5 child: girls play with girls on the whole, and boys with boys. Some boys become noticeably bigger and stronger (with associated surges in testosterone and temper tantrums) and this is the year when some girls shoot upwards so they start towering over the boys. (This doesn't usually right itself until about Year 9, by which time both sexes are fed up with both girls and boys looking silly next to what might then be their boyfriends and girlfriends.)

The Year 5 teachers brace themselves for not-very-nice behaviour among some girls. The girls often seem to need to have ownership of their particular best friends and that can result in crude power plays that cause more hurt than they intend. One of us remembers their Year 5 daughter forever going on about who got to sit next to whom on the coach on a school trip, or at lunch, and, usually, how unfair it was. Then there was the awkward year when a few Year 4 children were taught with the year above to help balance class sizes in a very small school. The children they joined were really friendly until it came to which area of the playground the newcomers were allowed to be in at break. Not the Year 5s' area, that was for sure.

Year 5 (if not before) is when most schools send children to change in segregated changing rooms, rather than all together in the classroom. This is sensible: by Year 5, the chances are that one or two girls may have hit early puberty. Parents report that some girls become more aware of their appearance round about this time and a certain amount of 'liking' certain boys might be discussed. This is absolutely not across the board. With any luck, you still have a few years before girls express a special interest in boys, and vice versa.

Team sports become ever more important for those who enjoy sport (and are good at it) and most primary schools participate in competitive events against other schools. If your child is on the school council their increasing maturity becomes evident and a source of pleasure and pride to them.

Nits and head lice

Since you were a child the head louse population of our fair island has exploded. It is no longer shameful for you or your child to find that they are hosting a hamlet or a village of head lice with a healthy maternity ward of nits. It is simply an inevitable part of primary school life (and secondary school life as well). It is, however, shameful and selfish if you allow the village to become a city or a small nation state. When head lice start dropping on to the page of your child's reading book (yes, it does happen), or the eggs are visible at a casual glance, or your child is scratching their head non-stop, things have gone too far.

You need to check for nits every week. There's lots of advice on how, both online and in doctors' surgeries. Your school will remind you to check when an infestation becomes particularly bad. We are not going to recommend products, because in our experience they often don't work and new ones seem to appear on the shelves regularly. Ask your pharmacist. If, like us, the expense wears you down, just keep industrial quantities of conditioner in the house and a good nit comb (Nitty Gritty is the best) and comb repeatedly through wet, conditioned hair. If you have a daughter with long, tangly hair . . . bad luck.

English

By the start of Year 5, says the national curriculum, your child should be able to read most words 'effortlessly' and to work out how to pronounce unfamiliar written words with 'increasing automaticity' (great word!). The hope is that by now your child reads widely and frequently, both for information and for pleasure. They should be able to write down their own ideas quickly, with (broadly) accurate grammar and punctuation, and even spelling.

So what will happen in Years 5 and 6? Helping your child increase their fluency as a reader and facility as a writer is the general idea, alongside improved comprehension. The national curriculum stresses 'enjoyment' – teachers are supposed to 'emphasize the enjoyment and understanding of language, especially vocabulary' and 'enhance the effectiveness' of your child's writing, as well as their competence.

As before, if your child is less fluent at reading and writing than the rest of the class they should be getting lots of extra phonics help so they can catch up. Otherwise, they should be exposed to the same teaching as the others, listening to and discussing the same material, with their grammar and vocabulary keeping pace.

In Years 5 and 6, your child's confidence, enjoyment and mastery of language should be extended through public speaking, performance and debate.

The English curriculum at this stage, as before, is divided into reading and writing. Reading is further subdivided into word reading and comprehension. Writing is subdivided into transcription (spelling and handwriting), composition and, finally, vocabulary, grammar and punctuation.

To summarize:

• Reading = word reading; comprehension

• Writing = transcription (spelling and handwriting); composition; vocabulary, grammar and punctuation

We've tackled all of these subdivisions below, apart from the last, which is dealt with in 'Grammar and Punctuation' on p. 375. (For the 'Purpose of Study' and 'Aims' of the English curriculum, see p. 458.)

Reading

COMPREHENSION

As in Year 4, your child will continue to apply their growing knowledge of root words, prefixes and suffixes (etymology and morphology), both to be able to read aloud and to understand the meaning of new words that they're introduced to.

Your child will be encouraged to work out any unfamiliar words. They will be taught that the accurate reading of individual words, which might be key to the meaning of a sentence or paragraph, improves comprehension. They'll be told to focus on all the letters in a word so that they do not misread words, e.g. 'invitation' for 'imitation', because they're more familiar with the first word.

Reading Age

Some schools measure children's reading skills with a reading test and may assign a 'reading age' to your child. These tests vary enormously, from reading words in a list out of context to more complicated combinations of reading and comprehension. Good readers often end up with reading ages far beyond their years. If the test is a rigorous one that includes comprehension, there's usually a high correlation between how much the child reads for pleasure out of school and how high their reading age is. But without knowing anything about the specific test used you won't know what your child's 'reading age' means, so take it with a pinch of salt.

What can you do to help?

- Your child's reading will only improve if they do a lot of it, so make sure they always have a book on the go. Be aware of their nightly reading habits: if your child is not allowed a CD player or an electronic gaming machine in their bedroom at night they are much more likely to read a book. Keep abreast of what they are currently reading and ask in the morning what happened in the book the night before. No one in the real world will manage to do this every day, but asking even occasionally sends the message that you expect them to be reading. Some of our children have been reading fiendishly from about Year 2 onwards and the younger ones need to have their lights firmly switched off after half an hour or so. Often, they'll use torches, or just turn the light back on once we've gone downstairs and continue reading until their eyes close. Others, by contrast, can barely read a page before succumbing to sleep. It's the routine expectation that reading is what you do before you sleep, rather than listening to music or playing games on screens, that is important.

- Help your child choose the next book whenever they finish one. We've known weeks to go by when a child doesn't read because they haven't been able to decide what to read. If you are stumped for ideas, use the book lists at the back of this book, ask the class teacher or tell your child to ask their friends for recommendations. And there's no harm in rereading a much-loved favourite.

- Read the book your child has just finished, or the next in the series (if there is one). Lots of new children's literature is very good and it's a great pleasure (for you and your child) to talk about a book you've both enjoyed reading for the first time. Try *Mortal Engines* by Philip Reeve or *The Wind Singer* by William Nicholson.

COMPREHENSION

In Year 5 your child will continue to read and discuss an increasingly wide range of fiction, poetry, plays, non-fiction and reference books or textbooks. The emphasis, as in Years 3 and 4, will be on enjoying what they read.

During the year your child will be:

- reading books that are structured in different ways and reading for a range of purposes

- increasing their familiarity with a wide range of books, including myths, legends and traditional stories, modern fiction, fiction from our literary heritage, and books from other cultures and traditions

- recommending books that they have read to their peers, giving reasons for their choices

- identifying and discussing themes and conventions in and across a wide range of writing

- making comparisons within and across books

- learning a wider range of poetry by heart

- preparing poems and plays to read aloud and to perform, showing understanding through intonation, tone and volume so that the meaning is clear to an audience.

In books your child reads independently, they will learn to check that the text makes sense to them by:

- asking questions to improve their understanding

- inferring characters' feelings, thoughts and motives

from their actions, and justifying those inferences with evidence

- predicting what might happen from details stated and implied

- summarizing the main ideas drawn from more than one paragraph

- identifying how language, structure and presentation contribute to meaning.

They will also learn to:

- discuss and evaluate how authors use language

- distinguish between statements of fact and opinion

- retrieve, record and present information from non-fiction

- participate in discussions about books that are read to them and those they can read for themselves, building on their own and others' ideas, and challenging views courteously

- explain and discuss their understanding of what they have read, including through formal presentations and debates, maintaining a focus on the topic and using notes where necessary

- provide reasoned justifications for their views.

The list above is very similar to that for Years 3 and 4. The expectation is that the texts studied will be more challenging and your child will become more adept at demonstrating their appreciation and understanding. Themes such as loss or heroism will feature. Children will compare characters, consider different accounts of the same event and discuss viewpoints (both of authors and of fictional characters) within a text and across more than one text.

Your child will continue to learn the conventions of different types of writing, such as the use of the first person in diaries and autobiographies. They will be taught technical terms such as 'metaphor', 'simile', 'analogy', 'imagery', 'style' and 'effect', and how to compare characters, settings, themes and other aspects of what they've read. By now the focus will have moved on to discussing the craft of different authors, e.g. discussing why authors have chosen particular words or sentence structures, and what impact that has on the reader.

In using reference books, children will be taught to focus on what information they need to look for before they begin, a skill that requires them to understand the task they've been set. They should be shown how to use contents pages and indexes to locate information.

Your child's skills of information retrieval will, of course, also be applied in reading history, geography and science textbooks, and in any context where they are genuinely motivated to find out information, e.g. reading information leaflets before a gallery or museum visit, or reading a theatre programme or review. Teachers will probably make good use of any library services and local expertise provided by museums and the like.

Teachers will give feedback to children on the quality of their explanations and contributions to discussions, and guidance for improvement.

What can you do to help?

- Keep stretching your child's comprehension by reading challenging texts to them – or with them.

● Quote from newspaper articles that might interest them and ask what they think about what's being discussed. Sporty children's literacy can be brought on in leaps and bounds by drawing their attention to an 'interesting' piece about the football or rugby team they support – we've seen very young children poring over the football results even in dense, tiny print.

● Ask them to read the next bit of a recipe and tell you what you need to do (i.e. precis the information) while you're cooking.

● When a question is raised, maybe to do with something in the news they've heard or seen on TV, encourage them to find the answer on Wikipedia and tell you. Or do it with them. It won't do children any harm to discover that you're not omnipotent and there are many things you are not afraid to admit ignorance of. Learning to glean the level of information they want from a dense Wikipedia page is a very useful skill, so show them how to do it.

● Subscribe to *The Week Junior*, which aims to explain news and events in ways children can understand without patronizing them.

● Subscribe to monthly children's magazine *Scoop*, a 'kaleidoscope of creative genius for kids', which has short stories, book reviews and more, and is a joy to look at and hold.

● If you or your child needs medicine, ask them to read the dosage and possible side effects to you. Get your child to read in new contexts wherever possible and check they've understood the meaning.

Writing

TRANSCRIPTION

a) Spelling

Your child will learn further spelling rules and guidance, including suffixes such as '-cious', '-tious', '-ence', '-ance' and '-ible' and '-able'. They'll learn words with silent letters such as 'doubt', 'island' and 'thistle'. They'll learn to spell more homophones such as 'morning/mourning' and easily confused pairs such as 'advice/advise' and 'prophecy/prophesy'.

In Year 5 your child will continue to become more adept at using a dictionary and will start using a thesaurus (if they don't already).

(See the statutory word list for Years 5 and 6 in Year 6 'English' on p. 392.)

What can you do to help?

- Keep going with their spelling homework. Lots of schools will ask children to write a sentence with the word they have to spell in it to demonstrate an understanding of the word's meaning as well as how to spell it. Encourage them to write imaginative sentences.

b) Handwriting

In Year 5 your child will be taught to write legibly, fluently and with increasing speed. They will choose which pen or pencil is best for which task.

In Year 5 your child may still have handwriting lessons to increase their speed. They should be clear by now that unjoined-up writing is more appropriate in some contexts, e.g. algebra, email addresses. They'll know that different standards are appropriate for different tasks – not to get bogged down by the desire for perfection when jotting down notes. It's always been the case that girls tend to be much more obsessed with neatness than boys (who err in the opposite direction). Teachers at this stage often struggle to stop girls wasting too much time producing an immaculate page at the expense of content.

What can you do to help?

- Not much. Make sure your child has a good pen or pencil and discourage the (girly) habit of love hearts instead of dots above 'i', the backward sloping 'd' or an 'e' that looks like a Greek epsilon. Like most bad habits, they're easily acquired and then hard to drop.

COMPOSITION

In Year 5 your child will develop further the skills and processes essential for writing, such as thinking aloud to generate ideas, and drafting and rereading to check that the meaning is clear. They may first discuss a piece of writing that's similar to the one they're planning, hoping to learn from its structure, vocabulary and grammar. They'll be encouraged to then note and develop their initial ideas, drawing on research where necessary. They may compose and rehearse sentences orally (including dialogue). In writing narratives, they'll be asked to consider how authors have developed characters and settings in texts they have read, listened to or seen performed.

They'll use grammar and vocabulary to achieve a particular effect and integrate dialogue to convey character and advance the action.

They'll be taught to precis and use headings, bullet points and underlining to guide the reader.

Evaluating and editing their work continues. Your child will assess the effectiveness of their own and others' writing and propose changes either to clarify meaning or enhance an effect. They'll be taught to proofread for consistent use of tense throughout a piece of writing, and for spelling and punctuation errors.

Your child will perform his or her own compositions, using intonation, volume and movement to clarify the meaning.

The routines around composition will be well established by Year 5. Your child should be very used to planning, noting, writing, proofreading and editing. Planning is never popular: children, like adults, would much prefer just to get going. A plan, so you know, is usually allowed 'in rough', i.e. no brownie points for neatness, and is meant to show more than just a rough plot outline. It should include a list of vocabulary and phrases your child might use, and possibly a (brief) character outline, or at least a list of the cast. If they haven't been asked to produce a plan as part of their homework, they'll (rightly!) be irritated if you insist that they do. They shouldn't be offended by suggestions made by their peers to improve their work, or feel shy about providing the same service to others (which doesn't mean they'll act on them or expect others to). It is well worth it, when you have the chance, to go into school and read your child's compositions and those of some of their friends if they'll let you. It can be a revelation: more imaginative and sophisticated than you would have thought.

What can you do to help?

● Show an interest. If they have composition homework make some vocabulary suggestions, or try to guess what happens next. This can be sticky territory as great offence is often taken, in our experience, at the most casual, unintended slight, e.g. 'Is that supposed to be a full stop or a comma?' 'Mum, you're so horrible.'

● It's a long shot, but why not see if you can get your child and a couple of friends to write a play. They'll prefer to use iMovie to make a film, and you'll probably prefer watching it, too, but at least try to encourage them to script it rather than ad-lib.

● Play First Line with the whole family. Pick a book (aimed at your child's age group) and all write down what you think the first line might be. One person writes down the real first line, collects in all the suggestions and reads them out in a random order. Everyone votes for which they think is the right one, and you win a point if yours is chosen. If you stick to their kinds of book, you might find that your Year 5 child will beat you at this.

Maths

In the last two years of primary school your child should learn to solve a wider range of problems using increasingly complex properties of numbers and arithmetic. There'll be ever-bigger numbers, more fractions and decimals, long division and long multiplication. They'll learn about percentages and ratios and even start using algebra. In the current national curriculum the use of calculators has almost been dropped altogether. They might be used in Year 5 and Year 6 for more complex problems once children have become fluent at solving them, but will not be allowed in the tests at the end of Year 6 from 2016 onwards.

The national curriculum sets out what your child should learn in Year 5 under the various headings below. (For the 'Purpose of Study' and 'Aims' of the maths curriculum, see p. 459.)

Number and place value

In Year 5 your child should be taught to write, order and compare numbers to at least a million and determine the value of each digit, e.g. know that the fourth digit in 364,872 represents 800. They'll learn to count forwards or backwards in steps of powers of ten (hundreds, thousands, ten thousands, etc.) for any given number up to a million, and to round any number up to a million to the nearest ten, hundred, thousand, ten thousand and hundred thousand.

They'll read Roman numerals up to a thousand (M) and recognize years written in Roman numerals (test them!). To remind you how to do this, we've included a chart at the end of this section, but we've gone up to a million.

Your child should start to recognize and describe linear number sequences, including those involving fractions and decimals. This means that, for a sequence such as 2, 4, 6 . . . , they'll be able to say what the term-to-term rule is, by which we mean what you have to do to one number in the sequence to arrive at the next. Answer:

add 2, or '+2'. What is the nth term? Answer: $2 \times n$, or $2n$ (same thing). What is the tenth term of the sequence? Answer: $2 \times 10 = 20$.

Addition and subtraction

Your child will probably continue to practise both mental methods and columnar addition and subtraction with increasingly large numbers (more than four digits) to aid fluency. (See Year 4 'Maths' on p. 257.) They will be expected to estimate answers before working them out, using rounding-up or rounding-down techniques.

Multiplication and division

Your child is bound to carry on with short multiplication and short division (see the relevant sections in the Appendix 'Addition, Subtraction, Multiplication and Division' on p. 474). As they will know all their times tables by now (oh yes), this will become speedy. They'll learn what's meant by the terms 'factor', 'multiple' and 'prime', by 'square' and 'cube' numbers and might use them to construct equivalence statements, e.g. $4 \times 35 = 2 \times 2 \times 35$; $3 \times 270 = 3 \times 3 \times 9 \times 10 = 9^2 \times 10$, although, if not, this does crop up again in Year 8 at secondary school. They'll learn to find all factor pairs of a number (the factor pairs of 24 are 2 and 12; 6 and 4; 8 and 3) and common factors of two numbers (3 is a common factor of 9 and 21), and to recall prime numbers up to 19.

In case you've forgotten, a prime number is one that is divisible only by itself and by 1. The prime numbers up to 19 are 2, 3, 5, 7, 11, 13, 17 and 19. (20 is not a prime number because it can be divided by 5, and by 4, and by 2 and by 10.)

This year, some divisions will have 'remainders' and your child will learn to write results in different ways, e.g. $98 \div 4 = {}^{98}\!/_4 = 24 \text{ r } 2 = 24\frac{1}{2} = 24.5 \approx 25$.

Long multiplication should be introduced (multiplying numbers of two or more digits together). Your child is likely to start with the grid method and move on to the formal columnar method. (See the relevant sections in 'Addition, Subtraction, Multiplication and Division' on p. 474 for examples.)

Here's an example of using the grid method to work out 32×26:

$\times$	30	2
20	$20 \times 30 = 600$	$20 \times 2 = 40$
6	$6 \times 30 = 180$	$6 \times 2 = 12$

(We've included the intermediate calculations for clarity: your child should, by now, be confident enough to put the right number in each box.) Answer: $600 + 180 + 40 + 12 = 832$.

Your child probably already understands the rule of distributivity (that 3×7 is the same as $3 \times 5 + 3 \times 2$). This year, they may learn to express this as $a(b + c) = ab + ac$ if their teacher thinks this is a good time to introduce some algebra. (Probably not.)

Your child will do missing-number problems, e.g. $13 + 24 = 12 + \square$; $35 = 5 \times \square$, which bring home the meaning of the equals sign.

Fractions (including decimals and percentages)

Your child should learn throughout Year 5 that percent-ages, decimals and fractions are different ways of expressing proportions.

They are likely to do a lot of work on fractions, first with the same denominator (bottom number), then with different denominators. They'll learn how to deal with top-heavy fractions, how to add, subtract and multiply them. They'll probably start with a number line (that old favourite) to help them visualize what they are doing.

Traditionally, children find decimals easier and once they've grasped that a decimal is a fraction ($0.71 = ^{71}/_{100}$), that can help them deal with fractions, too. Your child will practise adding and subtracting decimals, including a mix of whole numbers and decimals, decimals with different numbers of decimal places and complements of 1, e.g. $0.83 + 0.17 = 1$.

Percentages should be introduced in a way that allows your child to understand the close connections between percentages, fractions and decimals, e.g. 100 per cent represents a whole quantity; 1 per cent is $^{1}/_{100}$; 50 per cent is $^{50}/_{100}$; 25 per cent is $^{25}/_{100}$, and relate this to finding 'frac-tions of'.

Measurement

Your child should learn to convert between standard units, e.g. kilometre and metre; centimetre and metre; gram and kilogram; litre and millilitre. They should also understand roughly how these relate to imperial meas-urements such as inches, pounds and pints. They will be taught how to calculate the perimeter of rectangles (add all the lengths going round the edge, so it's

$2 \times$ length $+ 2 \times$ width) and of more complicated straight-sided shapes. 'Missing measures' questions can be expressed algebraically, e.g. $4 + 2b = 20$ for a rectangle of sides 2cm and $b$cm and perimeter of 20cm.

They will probably calculate the area of, say, a room (given measurements), and for the first time will be introduced to volume measured in cm^3 (rather than capacity, which is all they've had to think about so far). Area is length $\times$ width, in case you've forgotten.

Children will solve problems involving time and money, including conversions, e.g. days to weeks, expressing the answer as weeks and days.

Geometry

Your child should become adept at drawing lines with a ruler to the nearest millimetre and (rather harder) measuring with a protractor. They'll learn that there are 360° in a circle and 180° on a straight line and half a turn. They'll estimate acute, obtuse and reflex angles, and learn how to find the angles formed between the sides, and between diagonals and parallel sides of quadrilaterals, possibly using dynamic geometry computing tools. Your child will be taught to work out missing angles.

Reflection and translation of shapes will be taught, so your child will recognize and use reflection and translation in a variety of diagrams (they'll continue using a grid and coordinates). Reflection should be in lines that are parallel to the axes.

The triangles below have been reflected in the × axis:

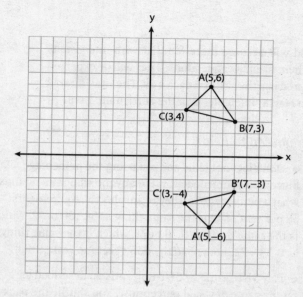

The triangle below has been translated by (3,4) (i.e. each point on the triangle has moved along 3 and up 4)

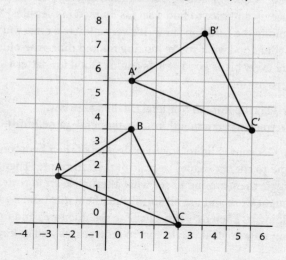

Statistics

Your child will become more familiar with line graphs and use them to answer questions. They will be expected to notice and use the scale on each axis. The vital life skill 'ability to read a timetable' is in the curriculum here.

What can you do to help?

- Don't let your child see you using the percentage button on your calculator. For anyone who understands what a percentage is, they're surplus to requirements. 58 per cent of 72 is the same thing as 58/100 of 72, which is the same thing as 0.58 of 72, which is the same thing as 0.58×72. Lots of adults don't seem to realize that.

- Play SET Game by SET Enterprises, described as 'a family game of visual perception'. You shuffle the pack of special cards (each card has between one and three shapes, shaded and coloured variously), lay twelve out face up and race to find a set (as defined in the rules) among the cards on show. It's very addictive once you've understood what you're looking for and nine-year-olds are every bit as good at it as adults. Good for pattern recognition.

- Play the Roman Numeral Challenge (www. factmonster.com/math/roman-numeral-game.html).

- Get your child to draw a scale plan of their bedroom and to cut out shapes to scale of their furniture. They can jiggle them around to see what alternative arrangement might work and use all sorts of mathematical skills while doing it. Then they can calculate the floor area and find out how much it would cost to recarpet, as well as how many litres of paint to redecorate, work out the total cost, etc. At which point the game is over, obviously. You're not made of money!

● Tell your child they can spend, say, 25 per cent of their pocket money on sweets, but only if they can tell you how much that is. Get them to work out what percentage of their waking hours they spent on screens on a particular day, and how much less time it would be if they dropped it by 10 per cent.

ROMAN NUMERALS/LETTER	VALUE
I	1
II	2
III	3
IV	4
V	5
VI	6
VII	7
VIII	8
IX	9
X	10
XX	20
XXX	30
XL	40
L	50

LX	60
LXX	70
LXXX	80
XC	90
C	100
D	500
M	1,000
$\overline{V}$	5,000
$\overline{X}$	10,000
$\overline{L}$	50,000
$\overline{C}$	100,000
$\overline{D}$	500,000
$\overline{M}$	1,000,000

Science

In the last two years of primary school some new science topics are introduced and some from previous years will be revisited in more depth. Much of science teaching is cyclical – children build on previous understanding to move on to more abstract or mathematical ideas in areas they've already touched on (sometimes this continues all the way up to the sixth form).

Alongside the acquisition of scientific knowledge, and not spelt out as such (so the children may be unaware of it), they'll be learning how to 'work and think scientifically', i.e. to analyse functions, relationships and interactions more systematically, to form ideas and design and carry out fair tests, draw conclusions and justify their ideas with evidence. They'll begin to see that abstract ideas help them to understand and predict how the world operates. (For the 'Purpose of Study' and 'Aims' of the science curriculum, see p. 461.)

Living things and their habitats

By Year 5 your child will have done a fair bit of looking at their local environment with their science hats on – they'll have studied the local habitats and micro-habitats of various animals and collected leaves and woodlice. This year's focus will be on life cycles, so they may well be closely observing local flora and fauna again. They will study and compare the life cycles of various animal groups – a mammal, an amphibian, etc. – and may be asked to produce some potted biographies of naturalists and animal behaviourists, e.g. David Attenborough, Jane Goodall.

Your child will learn about different types of reproduction, including sexual and asexual reproduction in plants, and sexual reproduction in animals. However, this will be very much focused on rabbits rather than humans. It's not the same as Sex and Relationship Education (SRE), which is statutory only in secondary schools (though may well be taught in your primary). SRE is part of the PSHE (personal, social and health education) programme and as PSHE is not part of the primary national curriculum we haven't addressed it in this book.

They might try to grow new plants from different parts of the parent plant, e.g. seeds, stem and root cuttings, tubers or bulbs. They might observe changes in an animal over a period of time, e.g. by hatching and rearing chicks, and compare how different animals reproduce and grow.

Animals (including humans)

Puberty is tackled in Year 5. Most children (secretly or otherwise) are fascinated. Stereotypically, the boys snigger and the girls take it all very seriously because they enjoy being too grown-up to laugh. Or they all giggle helplessly. Boys and girls are usually separated to provide an environment where they feel more comfortable to ask what might be awkward questions. Your child might draw a timeline to indicate stages in the growth and development of humans.

They may research the gestation periods of other animals and compare them with humans' or find out and record the length and mass of a baby as it grows.

Properties and changes of materials

There is likely to be more comparing and grouping of materials on the basis of their properties (hardness, solubility, conductivity, etc.). A host of new vocabulary will be introduced when children start talking about reversible changes: 'evaporating', 'filtering', 'sieving', 'melting' and 'dissolving'. The notion that 'melting' and 'dissolving' are different processes may be a new one. Your child will see that some processes are difficult (or impossible) to reverse, such as burning, rusting or adding vinegar to bicarbonate of soda (a great way to model a volcano). They may find out how chemists create new materials, e.g. Spencer Silver, who invented the glue for Post-it notes, or Ruth Benerito, who invented wrinkle-free cotton, or Margaret Thatcher, who some say helped to invent Mr Whippy ice-cream.

Your child is likely to carry out tests to answer questions such as which materials would be the most effective for making a warm jacket, for wrapping ice-cream to stop it melting, or for making blackout curtains. They might compare the electrical conductivity of different materials in order to make a switch in a circuit. They might research and discuss how chemical changes have an impact on our lives (as in cooking), and discuss the creative use of new materials such as polymers, super-sticky and super-thin materials. Scope for cross-curricular links with DT here.

Earth and space

Using models of the sun and Earth, and no doubt torches (and YouTube clips), your child will learn how to explain day and night. They should learn that the sun is a star at the centre of our solar system and that it has eight planets: Mercury, Venus, Earth, Mars, Jupiter, Saturn, Uranus and Neptune (Pluto was reclassified as a 'dwarf planet' in 2006 and your child will love telling you this), and that a moon is a celestial body that orbits a planet (Earth has one moon; Jupiter has four large moons and numerous smaller ones). Their class will probably make models of the planets to scale and create simple models of the solar system. Some schools construct simple shadow clocks and sundials, calibrated to show midday and the start and end of the school day.

Your child may research the way that ideas about the solar system have developed, understanding how the geocentric model of the solar system gave way to the heliocentric model. Ptolemy, Alhazen and Copernicus will probably get a mention. The teacher will probably link this with the work they're doing on seasons and the movement of the Earth around the sun in Year 5 geography.

Forces

Friction and gravity are the forces looked at in Year 5. Your child will learn that it is the force of gravity between Earth and an unsupported object that makes things fall. They will have a lot of fun 'exploring' falling objects and thinking about the effects of air resistance. They'll think about how different objects such as parachutes and syca-more seeds fall. They'll test their ideas with falling paper cones or cupcake cases and design and make a variety of parachutes and carry out fair tests to see which designs are the most effective. They might find out how scientists such as Galileo Galilei and Isaac Newton helped to develop the theory of gravitation (apples and leaning towers will come into it).

Your child should explore the effects of friction on movement and find out how it slows or stops moving objects, by watching the effects of a brake on a bicycle wheel, or how a piece of carpet slows down a toy car. They will probably look at the effects of levers and pulleys on movement and might even design and make things that use levers, pulleys, gears or springs. Scope for cross-curricular links with DT here.

What can you do to help?

- Take out a subscription for your child to *Aquila* (a magazine written for this age group) or ask your library if it will stock it. Alternatively, ask a grandparent or aunt or uncle to give it to them as a present.

• Take your child to the Science Museum in London as often as you can bear to. For children in Year 5 there are brilliantly designed hands-on exhibits in the gallery called Launchpad. It's tempting to treat the whole thing as a playground and leave your child to race around pressing buttons and pulling levers, but if you take the trouble to read the instructions at each exhibit, there is a lot more fun to be had. It's a good idea to get some notion of particular galleries or objects you want to see before you arrive (the Science Museum is huge), so look at the website first (www.sciencemuseum. org.uk).

• If you don't live in or near London, there are lots of alternatives. Find your nearest Science and Discovery Centre by searching at sciencecentres.org.uk/centres/. Some excellent examples are the Magna Science Adventure Centre in Sheffield; At-Bristol; and the Winchester Science Centre and Planetarium.

• Watch *The Blue Planet* and other David Attenborough documentaries together.

• Encourage your child to watch science programmes aimed at children. The BBC's *Springwatch* and *Autumnwatch* are good examples. Our children also like *Nina and the Neurons*.

• Allow your cat to have kittens, your dog to have puppies (or your guppy to have little guppies).

• Make a sundial (look it up on WikiHow), or follow this link for a really straightforward pdf you can print off and construct with very little effort: www. skyandtelescope.com/astronomy-resources/ how_to_make_a_sundial/

● Use pulleys and rope (if you get the chance) to raise toys to a high platform, e.g. a treehouse, or do it on a smaller scale using a Playmobil crane.

● The University of Manchester's website has a great children's section. Look at the section on 'The Earth and Beyond' (www.childrensuniversity.manchester.ac.uk/interactives/science/earthandbeyond). There are some interactive activities and your child may be tempted into looking at the other science areas, too.

● Take your child out in the dark. Look up. Talk about what you see! Even if you live in a bright city you'll see some stars on a clear night. Take a city child to the depths of the country on a clear night and they will be staggered at the number of stars and how bright they are. A simple pair of binoculars could lead to a lifetime of wonder and curiosity. It doesn't matter if you don't know much about what you are seeing: you may be inspired to get a star chart and start trying to identify constellations. Try the Constellation Secret Explore the Night Sky app.

● Toys R Us sells a Planetarium Projector by EDU Science. It's not cheap, but may kindle a lifelong interest in space.

● Visit NASA's children's website (www.nasa.gov/audience/forkids/kidsclub/flash/index.html#), or that of the European Space Agency (www.esa.int/esaKIDSen).

Art and Design

In Year 5 your child will begin to explore some of the more cerebral aspects of the subject, such as the roles and purposes of different artists, craftspeople and designers in other periods and cultures. (For the 'Purpose of Study' and 'Aims' of the art and design curriculum, see p. 462.)

The national curriculum divides up the content in Key Stage 2 as follows.

Pupils should be taught to:

- develop different artistic techniques with creativity and experimentation, showing an increasing awareness of different kinds of art, craft and design

- create sketchbooks to record observations and use them to review and revisit ideas

- improve mastery of art and design techniques, including drawing, painting and sculpture, using a range of materials

- understand the work of great artists, architects and designers in history.

Your child's school should continue to introduce them to new artistic techniques in Year 5. When one of our children was in Year 5, his teacher showed the class how to create designs on tiles which were then used to make prints. The idea was to produce dramatic, black-and-white images to illustrate the story of 'Hansel and Gretel', which they were reading in English lessons.

At this stage, by which time your child will be nine or ten, they may be asked to use perspective in their work, learning how to draw with reference to a single focal point and a horizon. They can use their sketchbooks to practise this, drawing furniture, houses, landscapes and so on. (Expect to see lots of cubes and three-dimensional letters.)

A unit in the old national curriculum called 'Objects and meanings' would complement the introduction of perspective. It involves asking your child to select and arrange objects in a still-life painting, such as old iron-ware, objects from the coast or sea, crockery, fabric remnants and bottles. They'll probably be asked to work with other children in groups, first arranging a tableau and then seating themselves in a semicircle to paint it. Afterwards, they may be asked to evaluate each other's work.

If your child is doing the 'Objects and meanings' unit, expect them to study some of the great still-life painters, such as Jan Brueghel, Rembrandt and Vincent van Gogh.

What can you do to help?

- Take your child to see some great still-life paintings if you can. There are Bruegels at the National Gallery, the Royal Collection, the Courtauld Institute and the British Museum, all in London; Rembrandts at the National Gallery in London, the Walker Art Gallery in Liverpool and the Hunterian Museum and Art Gallery in Glasgow; and you can see van Gogh's *Sunflowers* at the National Gallery in London.

- The Pitt Rivers Museum in Oxford organizes some family-friendly activities. For instance, there are 'family trails' in which you and your child can go round the museum together, hunting for particular artefacts, such as shields, masks or magical charms. The museum provides maps and activity sheets.

- By the time your children are in Year 5 they'll probably be ready to try some origami. We recommend a beginner's guide called *Origami Kit for Dummies* by Nick

Robinson (comes with twenty-five sheets of origami paper).

● At Christmastime, you could try making your own Christmas decorations. You can find an easy-to-follow twelve-step guide to making 3D paper snowflakes at www.instructables.com/id/3d-PAPER-SNOWFLAKE/.

● There'll be plenty of costume-making opportunities in the school calendar, such as World Book Day, on which children may be asked to come into school as their favourite literary character. Below is a picture of one of the authors' children on World Book Day 2014. They are, from left to right, Mr Bump, The Mad Hatter, Captain Hook and Gangsta Granny.

Computing

By the time they reach Year 5 it's possible that your child will be fluent enough in visual programming languages such as Scratch, Snap! and Kodu to be introduced to a text-based programming language, such as Logo, TouchDevelop or Python (named after Monty Python). Among the many bloggers and experts who've weighed in on how to teach the new computing curriculum, the consensus is that 'upper Key Stage 2' (Years 5 and 6) is the time when children will be introduced to a text-based programming language (though many schools will lack teachers with the training and experience to do this). Instead of dragging programming blocks to create algorithms and programs, as children do with Scratch, they'll write lines of code. Children often get frustrated when first trying to program using text, because it's easy to introduce bugs by making syntax errors. However, with patience and attention to detail, such problems are soon eliminated. (For the 'Purpose of Study' and 'Aims' of the computing curriculum, see p. 463.)

The national curriculum divides up the content in Key Stage 2 as follows.

Pupils should be taught to:

- design, write and debug programs that accomplish specific goals, including controlling or simulating physical systems; solve problems by deconstructing them into smaller parts

- use sequence, selection and repetition in programs; work with variables and various forms of input and output

- use logical reasoning to explain how simple algorithms work and to detect and correct errors in algorithms and programs

- understand computer networks, including the internet; how they can provide multiple services, such as the World Wide Web; and the opportunities they offer for communication and collaboration

- use search technologies effectively, appreciate how results are selected and ranked, and be discerning in evaluating digital content

- select, use and combine a variety of software (including internet services) on a range of digital devices to design and create a range of programs, systems and content that accomplish given goals, including collecting, analysing, evaluating and presenting data and information

- use technology safely, respectfully and responsibly; recognize acceptable/unacceptable behaviour; identify a range of ways to report concerns about content and contact.

Computer science

By now your child should be able to create some quite sophisticated programs using a visual programming language like Scratch, such as a program to calculate the perimeter of regular shapes, an advent calendar with boxes programmed to open one day at a time in the month of December and a music machine that plays different notes when different buttons are clicked with a mouse. There is scope for cross-curricular links with music here.

If your child is introduced to Python they may find it quite challenging to begin with, particularly if their keyboard skills are poor. Making an elementary mistake, such as inserting an unnecessary space or using single inverted commas instead of double, will mean the program won't work.

Here's an example of a Python program:

```
print ("Hello, world.")
print ("\n")
print ("I am learning Python.")
```

The sort of programs your child might be asked to create in Python in Year 5 are a simple version of a Snakes and Ladders game, a fortune-telling program (in which a child enters their name and then is told whether they'll be rich, famous, married, etc.) and a basic adventure game.

To help your child understand the new programming language, their teacher may deliberately insert syntax errors into a line of code or leave out a crucial instruction and then ask the class to 'debug' the program. (Alternatively, your child might insert plenty of mistakes all by themselves!) Children might be asked to work in pairs, 'debugging' each other's programs. Don't expect the teachers to help them solve these problems. Part of learning how to code involves working out how to fix problems yourself as they arise.

Digital literacy

In Year 5 your child may be taught to treat the results thrown up by search engines with a degree of scepticism. Just because a page is given a high ranking by Google doesn't mean the information it contains is true or relevant. Your child will need to develop strategies for assessing how reliable the information is, such as asking themselves whether a person, company or organization might have a vested interest in publishing something misleading or by comparing it with another source. (If the page in question is 'sponsored', i.e. if it's a thinly disguised advertisement, that's a good reason to treat it as unreliable.)

Don't be too concerned that your child may come across age-inappropriate content while searching the Web at school. Teachers are likely to use child-friendly search engines, such as Safe Search Kids, Yahoo for Kids, Kids Click and Ask Kids. In addition, your children will be taught that including the word 'kids' in a search will return more child-friendly results.

It might well be that your child's teacher explains some of the more technical aspects of how search engines – and the internet – work in Year 5. Don't be surprised if your child comes home and asks if you knew that the Web was invented by an Englishman.

There are some other units from the old ICT curriculum that are taught in Year 5, such as 'Introduction to spreadsheets' (basic Excel), 'Graphical modelling' (learning to use an object-based graphics package) and 'Controlling devices' (learning how to control buzzers, small motors and lights with control boxes). But don't expect your children to become whizzes at creating Excel spreadsheets.

What can you do to help?

- There are a number of beginner's guides to Python that you might want to read yourself – or read with your child – if they are introduced to Python in Year 5. You can find a selection of books on the website https://wiki.python.org/moin/IntroductoryBooks. Most of the books on that page are available for sale, but there are some free beginner's guides available, such as *Invent with Python*. (https://inventwithpython.com).

- Now might be a good time for your child to join Codecademy (www.codecademy.com), a website that offers free tutorials in six different programming languages, including Python. It's not specifically designed for children, but a child of nine or ten should be able to cope with it well enough. It includes forums where people stumped by a particular problem can ask more experienced coders for help.

- If you have a daughter, her interest in computing might be hampered by gender stereotypes – she may have got the impression (wrongly) that it's a male-only field. To counter this, you could introduce her to some of the pioneering women in computer science, such as Ada Lovelace, Grace Hopper and Dame Wendy Hall. You can read about Ada Lovelace (1815–52), generally considered the world's first computer programmer, on Wikipedia (https://en.wikipedia.org/wiki/Ada_Lovelace).

- At Christmastime, or on their birthday, you might think about buying your child an e-book reader, such as a Kindle. Some of these, such as the Kindle Fire, double up as tablets, so if you want to control the amount of time your child spends playing video games you should probably limit yourself to the most basic, entry-level device. Some parents dislike the idea of their children spending even more time staring at a screen and, in any case, have a sentimental attachment to paper. But if our experience is anything to go by, some reluctant readers are more likely to read books if they're onscreen, particularly boys.

● If your child is a fan of *Wallace and Gromit* you could encourage them to create some stop-motion films of their own, using one of the many stop-motion video apps, e.g. Smoovie, StopMotion Studio or Animation Creator. If they are a fan of Lego, they could try making a Lego stop-motion film. For inspiration, check out *Lego Shark Attack!*: www.youtube.com/watch?v=AaaitgKbr8k. Or rent *The Lego Movie*, now regarded as a modern children's classic.

● There are a number of quite sophisticated apps and games designed to help children whose programming skills have already reached an intermediate level, including Machinarium, The Tiny Bang Story, Creatorverse, Monster Physics and Hakitzu.

Design and Technology

By Year 5, if not before, your child is likely to be introduced to computer-aided design – or CAD, as it's known. CAD involves using computer systems to come up with design blueprints and is used in a range of industries, including the automotive, shipbuilding and aerospace industries. Some CAD software is extremely complicated to use and requires lots of training, but there are also some web-based packages that are suitable for children, such as Tinkercad (www.tinkercad.com) and 3DTin (www.3dtin.com). (For the 'Purpose of Study' and 'Aims' of the design and technology curriculum, see p. 465.)

The national curriculum divides up the content in Key Stage 2 as follows.

When designing and making, children should be taught to:

Design

- use research and develop design criteria to inform the design of innovative, functional, appealing products that are fit for purpose, aimed at particular individuals or groups

- generate, develop, model and communicate ideas through discussion, annotated sketches, cross-sectional and exploded diagrams, prototypes, pattern pieces and computer-aided design.

Make

- select from and use a wider range of tools and equipment to perform practical tasks accurately

- select from and use a wider range of materials and components, including construction materials, textiles and ingredients, according to their functional properties and aesthetic qualities.

Evaluate

- investigate and analyse a range of existing products

- evaluate their ideas and products against their own design criteria and consider the views of others to improve their work

- understand how key events and individuals in design and technology have helped shape the world.

Technical knowledge

- apply their understanding of how to strengthen, stiffen and reinforce more complex structures

- understand and use mechanical systems in their products

- understand and use electrical systems in their products

- apply their understanding of computing to program, monitor and control their products.

Cooking and nutrition

- understand and apply the principles of a healthy and varied diet

- prepare and cook a variety of predominantly savoury dishes, using a range of cooking techniques

- understand seasonality, and know where and how a variety of ingredients are grown, reared, caught and processed.

Design

In Year 5 your child's teacher may ask the whole class to try their hand at designing a fashionable consumer product, such as a handbag. They'll be asked to think about who they're designing the bag for and what their needs, wants and values are. How is the bag meant to be carried, and what compartments should it have? What are the sorts of things consumers take into account when choosing what bag to buy? Is how it looks more important than how practical it is? How much priority should be given to its durability?

Make

Your child might be asked to make something using recycled textiles, such as a bedspread or pillowcase out of old clothes. They'll be encouraged to take creative risks with their ideas, think about the problems thrown up by the particular product they're making and avoid hackneyed solutions. The aim will be to come up with a final product that is original, functional and appealing.

Evaluate

By now, your child should be quite practised at evaluating other people's work and, more importantly, having their own work evaluated. Learning how to take criticism is an important life skill that most adults would benefit from (including us!). To tie in with the work they're doing on Earth and space in science (and on the seasons in geography), your child might learn something about the inventor of the telescope. It's a popular misconception that telescopes were invented by Galileo. He was the first person to use a telescope for stargazing purposes, but it was actually invented by Hans Lippershey, a sixteenth-century German spectacle maker.

Technical knowledge

Your child might be presented with a particular technical challenge, such as being asked to come up with some packaging to protect a fragile product that will be on sale in supermarkets. They'll have to consider the practical and aesthetic aspect of the packaging. They'll be invited to explore how much protection is provided by different 3D shapes – are rectangular boxes better than square boxes? – and road-test different techniques for reinforcing the protective shell, such as stiffening the card they're using through laminating, ribbing or corrugating. Finally, they might be asked to think about the different fonts to use on the packaging and where to include a window so consumers can see the product.

Cooking and nutrition

In Year 5 your child may be introduced to some more intermediate cooking skills, such as peeling, chopping and slicing. Your child might also be introduced to the idea of using seasonal ingredients, e.g. peppers, tomatoes and runner beans in summer and root vegetables in the winter. There's scope here for cross-curricular links with the work they're doing on seasons in geography and science.

What can you do to help?

- There's quite a cool website aimed at children called How Stuff Works (www.howstuffworks.com) that unlocks the secrets of various hi-tech gizmos, from Google Glasses to the Oculus Rift (3D gaming headset). If your child wants to know how to land a spacecraft on a comet travelling at 83,885mph, this is the site for them.

- If your child is interested in Lego, there's a design website called LDraw (www.ldraw.org) where they can use CAD software to create virtual Lego models. Not only that, but they can design sets of instructions, create 3D photorealistic images of their models and include them in animations.

- If your child is introduced to CAD in Year 5, there's plenty of CAD-for-kids software they can download for free, such as CB Model Pro (https://cb-model-pro.en.softonic.com), which they can use to create 3D action figures.

- There's a selection of short films on 'Textiles' in the DT section of the BBC's Bitesize site (www.bbc.co.uk/education/topics/zkjwxnb). Try the three-minute film on designing and making your own cushion covers (www.bbc.co.uk/education/clips/zb6w2hv).

Geography

By the time your child is in Year 5 they should have developed a basic 'schemata' in geography which they can start building on (see p. xxv in 'Introduction' for an explanation of what a 'schemata' is). Their teacher will have introduced them to some of the basics, such as the

North and South Poles, the equator and the seven continents, and will now begin to explain why different parts
of the world have different seasons at different times of
year, why it's hotter on either side of the equator than it
is on the equator and why it's so bitterly cold in the Arctic
and Antarctica. Once your child has grasped that the
Earth's axis is tilted at 23.4 degrees, that it rotates once
on its own axis every 24 hours and orbits the sun once
every 365 days – and when they've understood why so
many of the differences between the various parts of
the world are explained by this – they'll have a framework
in place which they can continue adding to for the
remainder of their education. There is scope here for
cross-curricular links with the work they're doing on
Earth and space in science.

The national curriculum divides up the content in Key
Stage 2 as follows.

Pupils should be taught to:

Locational knowledge

- locate the world's countries, using maps to focus on
  Europe (including Russia) and North and South
  America, concentrating on their environmental regions,
  key physical and human characteristics, countries and
  major cities

- name and locate counties and cities of the United
  Kingdom, geographical regions and their identifying
  human and physical characteristics, key topographical features (including hills, mountains, coasts and
  rivers) and land-use patterns; and understand how
  some of these aspects have changed over time

- identify the position and significance of latitude, longitude, the equator, northern hemisphere, southern hemisphere, the tropics of Cancer and Capricorn, the Arctic and Antarctic Circles, the prime/Greenwich meridian and time zones (including day and night).

Place knowledge

- understand geographical similarities and differences through the study of human and physical geography of a region of the United Kingdom, a region in a European country and a region within North or South America.

Human and physical geography

- describe and understand key aspects of physical geography, including: climate zones, biomes and vegetation belts, rivers, mountains, volcanoes and earthquakes and the water cycle

- describe and understand key aspects of human geography, including: types of settlement and land use, economic activity including trade links, and the distribution of natural resources including energy, food, minerals and water.

Geographical skills and fieldwork

- use maps, atlases, globes and digital/computer mapping to locate countries and describe features studied

- use the eight points of a compass, four- and six-figure grid references, symbols and key (including the use of

Ordnance Survey maps) to build knowledge of the United Kingdom and the wider world

- use fieldwork to observe, measure, record and present the human and physical features in the local area, using a range of methods, including sketch maps, plans and graphs, and digital technologies.

Locational knowledge

Your child will probably be asked to locate and name the counties of the United Kingdom and the main countries in North and South America, including their capital cities. In addition, they may be asked to compare and contrast a region in the United Kingdom with the same region in the past, e.g. Hampshire as it is today with Hampshire in the Anglo-Saxon era, linking up with what your child may be doing in history in Year 5. The teacher might ask them to imagine that they're the son or daughter of an Anglo-Saxon farmer and write a letter about their daily life to a child in the present. Your child will probably also learn about the tropics of Cancer and Capricorn, the northern and southern hemispheres and why the Earth is hotter towards the middle than it is at either end.

Place knowledge

The teacher might ask your child to choose a region of the United Kingdom and compare it to a region in South America, contrasting a developed area with a developing one, e.g. Herefordshire in the West Midlands with the Pampas in Argentina, Uruguay and Brazil. How different would a beef farm in Herefordshire be from a cattle ranch in the Pampas? Alternatively, your child might be asked to compare two regions that share the same latitude, say, the north-east coast of the United States with Western Europe.

Human and physical geography

Your child might return to volcanoes and earthquakes (physical geography), but learn about them in greater depth, e.g. begin to study tectonic plates and the ring of fire. They might also look at trade between the United Kingdom, Europe and the rest of the world, with the teacher introducing them to the concept of 'fair trade' (human geography).

Geographical skills and fieldwork

The teacher will probably have your child using maps, atlases, globes and digital mapping applications to locate the countries they're studying in Year 5. In all likelihood, your child will be asked to use the eight points of a compass and four-figure grid references to find different places in the United Kingdom. In fieldwork, your child will continue to observe, measure and record the physical and human features in the local area, using a range of different methods.

What can you do to help?

● There are numerous websites that will help you explain how the Earth's tilt creates the seasons. As a starting point, try this seven-minute film on the BBC's Bitesize site: www.bbc.co.uk/education/clips/zj8pyrd. The graphics from the five-minute point onwards are particularly good.

● There's more in the same vein on the Bitesize site (www.bbc.co.uk/education). Try this seven-minute film with the irresistible title 'How planet Earth was hit by meteorites, causing Earth's tilt and its seasons' (www.bbc.co.uk/education/clips/z67rkqt). Good special effects!

● If your child wants to test their knowledge of England's counties, there's a website where they can play a game in which they have to identify various counties on a map of England (www.geography-map-games.com/geography-games-Geography-Counties-of-England-_pageid161.html).

● Play the geographical version of *Just a Minute*. One person starts and they have to try to name as many countries or capital cities as they can in the space of a minute. If they pause to think, or repeat themselves, another player can shout 'Hesitation' or 'Repetition' and, if they're right, it's their turn to fill what remains of the minute without pausing or repeating themselves (though they are allowed to repeat countries or capital cities named by the other players). This game only works if an adult is acting as timekeeper and referee. You don't need to buy a stopwatch – you've almost certainly got one on your mobile phone.

● Create a weather station in your garden – or, if you don't have a garden, in a window box. Use a cut-open plastic bottle as a rain gauge, with centimetres marked up the side, a thermometer to measure the temperature, and cut the toe off an old sock to create a windsock. Have your child make a chart, recording the average weekly rainfall and temperature over the course of three months.

● The geography section of a BBC website called GCSE Bitesize includes a short film on the banana industry in Ecuador with specific reference to fair trade (www.bbc. co.uk/learningzone/clips/the-wealth-of-the-banana-trade/501.html). The website is aimed at GCSE students, but it's still useful.

MNEMONICS AND MEMORY AIDS

● To remember the names of the seven Central American countries – Guatemala, Belize, Honduras, El Salvador, Nicaragua, Costa Rica and Panama – think of the following mnemonic phrase: '**G**reat **B**ig **H**ungry **E**lephants **N**early **C**onsumed **P**anama.'

● The Tropic of Cancer is roughly 23.5 degrees north of the equator and the Tropic of Capricorn is roughly 23.5 degrees south of the equator. To remember which is north and which is south, focus on the fact that 'Cancer' has an 'n' in it for 'north' and Capricorn an 'o' for 'other side':

Cancer is north of the equator –
Capricorn is on the other side.

History

If schools are following our curriculum map in history (and not all of them will, obviously), your child will cover Anglo-Saxons in Year 5, beginning with the migration in the fifth and sixth centuries, as well as one of the non-British units, possibly early Islamic civilization. (For the 'Purpose of Study' and 'Aims' of the history curriculum, see p. 468.)

The national curriculum divides up the content in Key Stage 2 under the following headings.

- Changes in Britain from the Stone Age to the Iron Age

- The Roman Empire and its impact on Britain

- Britain's settlement by Anglo-Saxons and Scots

- The Viking and Anglo-Saxon struggle for the kingdom of England to the time of Edward the Confessor

- A local history study

- A study of an aspect or theme in British history that extends pupils' chronological knowledge beyond 1066

- The achievements of the earliest civilizations – an overview of where and when the first civilizations appear and a depth study of one of the following: Ancient Sumer; the Indus Valley; Ancient Egypt; the Shang Dynasty of Ancient China

- Ancient Greece – a study of Greek life and achievements and their influence on the Western world

- A non-European society that provides contrasts with British history – one study chosen from: early Islamic civilization, including a study of Baghdad c. AD 900; Mayan civilization c. AD 900; Benin (West Africa) c. AD 900–1300

Assuming your child is studying 'Britain's settlement by Anglo-Saxons and Scots' in Year 5, the subject matter they're likely to cover will probably include: the Roman withdrawal from Britain; the fall of the Roman Empire; the invasion of Scotland; and the migration of Germanic tribes to England from the western coasts of Europe.

They might also cover the revival of Christianity, Lindisfarne Priory, the oldest example of English historical writing (an anonymous biography of St Cuthbert), Old English, the introduction of regional government and the establishment of the English nation. Expect the teacher to draw parallels with contemporary Britain, inviting your child to compare immigration in the fifth and sixth centuries and the social tensions it gave rise to with immigration today.

The authors of the national curriculum have made it clear that 'local history' could include a 'depth study' linked to a unit children have already done, and we think it's more likely this will happen in Year 5 than Year 6 because there'll be less time to spend on the foundation subjects at the end of Key Stage 2. (Exactly what a 'depth study' is hasn't been made clear in the curriculum, but we think it means studying something for a whole term rather than just a few lessons.) So it's likely to be a study of something local connected with the Stone Age, the Iron Age, the Romans or Anglo-Saxons. Whether your child's school does this – and which of the above units is revisited – will depend on what there is of interest near the school, if anything. For instance, if your child's school is in North Cornwall they might well study the legend of King Arthur for a term, visiting Tintagel Castle, which bills itself as his birthplace.

If your child studies a 'non-European society' in Year 5 it's hard to predict which of the suggestions the teacher will take up. Some schools might opt for the Maya and combine it with doing South and Central America in geography. However, we think the rise of Islamic civilization will be a popular choice, particularly in areas with high Muslim populations. Teachers are likely to cover the emergence of Muhammad, the Koran, the different factors that led to the rapid growth of Islam, the death of the prophet and the impact of Islam on neighbouring states.

What can you do to help?

ANGLO-SAXONS

● The BBC Bitesize site has a section on Anglo-Saxons that includes areas called 'Invasion and settlement', 'Anglo-Saxon life', 'Alfred the Great', 'Anglo-Saxons at war' and 'What happened to them?' (www.bbc.co.uk/education/topics/zxsbcdm).

● If you live near the north-east coast of England you could take your child to see the ruins of Lindisfarne Priory on Holy Island. It can be reached via a causeway at low tide and is an English Heritage site. There are lots of activities for all the family. You can pray at St Cuthbert's graveside (supposed to bring you luck), see the Lindisfarne Stone (which commemorates the monks killed in the Viking raid) and take in the spectacular coastal views.

● Visit the permanent Anglo-Saxon exhibition at the British Museum. Before you go it's worth downloading a pdf from the museum's website, which is intended as a resource for Key Stage 2 teachers to help them prepare their classes beforehand (www.britishmuseum.org/PDF/Visit_Anglo_Saxons_KS2.pdf). Among other things, it contains this excellent Anglo-Saxon timeline:

5th century AD	407–11	Roman Emperor Constantine III takes the field army of Britain to the Continent to fight continental peoples and to support his claim on the Empire. This leaves Britain with fewer troops, mostly garrisoned on the frontiers
6th century AD	597	St Augustine converts King Ethelbert of Kent to Christianity
7th century AD	600	The Anglo-Saxons control most of central and western England
	635	Aidan founds the monastery on Lindisfarne Island
	c. 595–640	Ship burial at Sutton Hoo, probably a burial for a member of local nobility
8th century AD	760	Offa organizes the building of a dyke between England and Wales
	793	Vikings raid the monastery on Lindisfarne, beginning of a period of raids on the British Isles
9th century AD	850	Vikings make permanent settlements in Britain
	867	Vikings establish the kingdom of York
	878	The Danes agree to leave Wessex after Alfred defeats them at the Battle of Eddington
10th century AD	991	Battle of Maldon takes place on the coast of Essex. Vikings defeat the Anglo-Saxons
	994	Danish raids led by King Sweyn
11th century AD	1016	Canute the Dane becomes King of England
	1066	William of Normandy becomes King of England

- There are dozens of stories and legends set in this period of English history. Try to get your child to read *King Arthur and His Knights of the Round Table* by Roger Lancelyn Green – or, if you can't manage that, buy or download the audiobook version read by Sean Bean and play it to them in the car. Bean is very good.

ANCIENT ISLAMIC CIVILIZATION

- If your child is doing the rise of Islamic civilization, you might want to take them to see 'The Islamic World' in Room 34 of the British Museum, where they can explore Islamic faith, art, calligraphy and science.

- Get your child to read *The Thousand and One Nights* – or read it to them. We recommend the Penguin Classics version *Tales from the Thousand and One Nights* by N. J. Dawood but there are some more recent versions written specially for children, such as *Aladdin and the Enchanted Lamp* by Philip Pullman and *My Sister Shahrazad: Tales from the Arabian Nights* by Robert Leeson. If your child really enjoys them – and who wouldn't? – ask them to write a short story in the style of *The Arabian Nights*.

Languages

If you haven't done so already, we recommend you read the introduction to Year 3 'Languages' on p. 233. In case you don't, it's important to repeat one paragraph here:

Given the range of time dedicated to language teaching that we expect to find across the country's schools, it's hard to say exactly what you should expect your child to learn in each year. If your child has less than an hour a week, your primary school may not be expecting to cover as much ground as we describe.

(For the 'Purpose of Study' and 'Aims' of the languages curriculum, see p. 469.)

The language content of the national curriculum in Key Stage 2 can be divided up under two broad headings, spoken and written.

Spoken language

Pupils should be taught to:

- listen attentively to spoken language and show understanding by joining in and responding

- explore the patterns and sounds of language through songs and rhymes, and link the spelling, sound and meaning of words

- engage in conversations; ask and answer questions; express opinions and respond to those of others; seek clarification and help

- speak in sentences, using familiar vocabulary, phrases and basic language structures

- develop accurate pronunciation and intonation so that others understand when they are reading aloud or using familiar words and phrases

- present ideas and information orally to a range of audiences

- appreciate stories, songs, poems and rhymes in the language.

As we've said before, your child's language teaching is likely to follow a scheme where new grammar and vocabulary is learnt in the context of a topic, such as 'My family'. Each topic will last about half a term. Possible examples of topics that may crop up in Year 5 are 'Food and drink', 'Music', 'On the way to school', 'At the beach', 'The four seasons', and 'The planets'. The weekly lesson will probably follow a pattern. After a warm-up game revising the previous week's progress, your child is likely to be introduced to new content. What follows will probably be different games, the format of which your child will become familiar with – singing, asking and answering questions, drawing and labelling pictures.

By the end of Year 5 your child will probably have been taught more formal conjugation of some regular verbs, so they will be able to say 'He likes', 'We want', etc., correctly, without learning each one by rote, or guessing. They may even be able to use the past tense for some verbs. They may learn the grammar surrounding the right word for 'some'. They'll possibly start building compound sentences, using connectives such as 'and' and 'but'. They might learn to express opinions (nothing too exciting, e.g. 'I like the summer because it is hot'). They could even go so far as to start using the future tense for a few verbs. They will probably learn some stock phrases such as 'I don't understand' or 'Please repeat that.' They may learn some directional vocabulary ('left', 'right', 'near', 'far'), or adverbial phrases of time ('five minutes later', 'then', 'after').

To give you an idea of the kinds of activities your child may take part in, here are some examples:

- Consolidate learning of vocabulary and grammar by reusing it in other contexts, e.g. revise vocabulary such as greetings and numbers throughout the day, and reuse familiar verbs and adjectives

- Use 'stalling strategies' to allow time to hesitate, e.g. use spoken expressions and gestures which allow for thinking time in the conversation

- Play Change the Meaning. Children take turns to change the meaning of a sentence they hear by changing just one element, such as a noun, verb or adjective. For example, the teacher says 'The pink cat is eating a green banana.' A volunteer says 'The pink cat is buying a green banana.' The class must identify not only which word has changed, but also what kind of word it is (noun, verb, adjective)

- Give a physical response to show understanding of an opinion, e.g. thumbs down for 'dislikes' and thumbs up for 'likes'

- Respond to a dictation by drawing, miming or acting out what they hear

- Listen to a story and identify a picture when they hear a description of it in the story, e.g. 'The big red monster ate the cake noisily'

- Answer more open-ended questions, as well as questions requiring yes/no answers

- Identify the type of passage being heard, e.g. a conversation, an advert, a news bulletin, a list of instructions

- Listen to longer passages of familiar language and identify specific details, e.g. name, place, quantity, cost

Written language

Pupils should be taught to:

- read carefully and show understanding of words, phrases and simple writing

- broaden their vocabulary and develop their ability to understand new words that are introduced into familiar written material, including through using a dictionary

- write phrases from memory and adapt these to create new sentences, to express ideas clearly

- describe people, places, things and actions orally and in writing.

By Year 5 your child is likely to have been taught most phonemes and, as with learning to read and write in English, once they have some phonic confidence and a list of familiar words to build from they will begin to find writing in the new language easier. By the end of Year 5 they should be able to spell an increasing number of words and phrases with confidence. There will be grammatical errors aplenty, but at this stage the focus will be on getting them expressing themselves in writing without too much attention to accuracy.

To give you an idea of the kinds of activities your child may take part in, here are some examples:

- Use the interactive whiteboard or Post-it notes to mask features of the text, e.g. the verbs. The children will then suggest ideas for the missing words, a bit like on *Have I Got News for You*

- Play a miming game. The teacher says a short phrase, e.g. 'A small dog is singing', 'A big rabbit is laughing'. The children respond by miming the phrase. They reverse the roles so that the teacher mimes and the children have to choose the word cards (and correct syntax) to describe what they see

- Work in groups. Arrange word cards, coloured according to what parts of speech they represent, into sentences

- Play Human Sentences by holding up cards and lining up in the correct order to form a sentence

- Jumble a conversation. Rearrange word cards to form a conversation

- Play Pass the Sentence Parcel. Listening to authentic music or songs, the children pass a bag around the circle containing word cards, which, when they're all out of the bag, can be used to form a familiar phrase or sentence. Each time the music stops, the child holding the bag takes out one word card, reads it aloud and places it in the middle of the circle. The music restarts and the game continues until all the words are in the middle of the circle. Children discuss with a partner what the sentence might be and try to place the words in the correct order

- Choose words from a list and copy them to match/ label pictures

- Use word cards or word lists to create a sentence for a speech bubble or caption

- Listen to a song and then look at a transcription of it with gaps. Children fill in the gaps with the correct words

- Use a computer program to create a greetings-card message

- Working in pairs, choose words from topic word lists. Then add them to the end of some simple sentence starters to form complete sentences, e.g. 'Here is . . .', 'This is . . .', 'I have . . .', 'He/she has . . .', 'He/she does not have . . .'

- Use a bilingual dictionary so they understand why it has two halves, i.e. one half consists of English words translated into the language in question; the other half contains words in the language translated into English

- Collect words that express greeting, surprise, apology, thanking, refusing

- List some things that typify the country, e.g. food, flags, dress, buildings, sport; and make comparisons with another country

- Drawing on the expertise of class members, learn about the currency of another country and read aloud prices from menus and price lists. Handle the money. Ask how much something costs and understand prices spoken in the language

- Send a shoebox with objects from your country to a school in another country, e.g. coins, sweet wrappers, a bus or train timetable, a school badge, a birthday card

What can you do to help?

All of the suggestions in the 'Languages' sections in the previous two chapters apply to Year 5.

● To help learn vocabulary (and how to spell foreign words), get your child to stick Post-it notes around the house labelling household objects. You could extend this to instructions in the language, such as a note telling family members to 'Wash your hands!' by the loo, or 'Don't forget your PE kit!' by the front door, or 'My room: Only friends allowed' on their bedroom door.

● Say grace in the language before starting meals (this could be secular). ('*Laissez-nous prier*' is 'let us pray' in French.) One French grace is: '*Bénissez nous, Seigneur, et bénissez le repas que nous allons prendre. Au nom du Père, du Fils, et du Saint Esprit. Amen.*' This means: 'Bless us, O Lord, and bless this meal we are going to eat. In the name of the Father, the Son, and the Holy Ghost. Amen.' A Spanish grace is: '*Te damos gracias, Señor, por estos alimentos que nos diste.*' This means: 'We thank you, Lord, for this food you gave us.'

Music

Throughout Key Stage 2 children will continue to sing and play instruments, listen to different genres of music and learn something about their history. In Year 5 teachers will probably try to broaden your child's musical vocabulary, introducing them to such phrases as 'melody', 'harmony', 'timbre', 'accents', 'pulse' and 'texture' and encouraging them to use them when describing their own or other people's compositions. (For the

'Purpose of Study' and 'Aims' of the music curriculum, see p. 470.)

The national curriculum divides up the content in Key Stage 2 as follows.

Pupils should be taught to:

- play and perform in solo and ensemble contexts, using voice and playing musical instruments with increasing accuracy, fluency, control and expression

- improvise and compose music for a range of purposes, using the interrelated dimensions of music

- listen with attention to detail and recall sounds with increasing aural memory

- use and understand staff and other musical notations

- appreciate and understand a wide range of high-quality live and recorded music drawn from different traditions and from great composers and musicians

- develop an understanding of the history of music.

By now your child should be able to sing confidently and expressively with attention to dynamics and phrasing, with good intonation and a sense of occasion, and to play the simpler accompaniment parts on glockenspiel, bass drum or cymbal. In Year 5 they'll be encouraged to follow the accompanying sheet music at the same time, relating the sounds to the different musical notations. They'll learn to use the top number of the time signature to say how many counts or claps should be made before they sing and they'll probably learn something about the different notes: the long (two-beat minims) and the very long notes (four-beat semibreves), the short (half-beat quavers) and the very short (quarter-beat semiquavers).

Your child may also be introduced to a range of rhythmic music from different parts of the world. They may explore how rhythms can be used repeatedly in cycles and how these rhythms can be made more interesting by adding different dynamics, durations and timbres. In this context, they might listen to music such as Bach's *Brandenburg Concertos*, as well as Indian and African drumming music. Your child will be shown that in much Western music, including most popular music, the listener is taken on a musical journey from the beginning to the end – the music has a linear progression. Other music, including music from Africa and India, does not progress in this way, but instead uses cyclical patterns that are constantly repeated. Your child may be told about the structure of a particular cyclical pattern or tala, e.g. 'Kaharwa', the most popular one in Northern India.

Another thing teachers like doing in Year 5 is rounds. The entire class might be taught to sing a round. When they can sing it confidently in unison they'll be divided into two and sing it in two parts, and then maybe three or four.

It's likely that your child will be played excerpts of Holst's *The Planets* to tie in with the work they're doing on Earth and space in science and the seasons in geography. The teacher may get them to discuss how planets in our solar system have acquired emotional signatures, e.g. Mars and war, Venus and love, and how these are expressed musically. The class may be asked to create a planetary 'soundscape', creating different textures by combining sounds.

It's likely your child will learn something more about

the history of music in Year 5, with references to the increasing sophistication of musical form over time. It's possible that the class will be divided into groups, with each group being given a particular period to research, with a set of specific questions to answer. When they've found out the answers they'll then present their findings to the rest of the class.

What can you do to help?

● Sometimes, children can understand music better if they can 'see' it. These apps and games are designed to teach children about music by illustrating how qualities such as colour, direction and speed can reflect elements of music like tone, pitch and rhythm:

The creators of the app Morton Subotnick's Pitch Painter (age 3+) compare it to finger-painting because it doesn't require formal training to make a final product. It's designed for three- to five-year-olds, but it can also be fun for older children. Create short pieces by moving your finger over a blank canvas. The lines help children internalize the properties of the music as they hear what they've created.

Scape (age 8+) is an iPad app that lets children generate ambient music as they combine shapes, colour and textures on a blank palette. Your child will be introduced to the idea that music has different 'moods' and encouraged to explore the tranquil sounds of an often-forgotten genre.

Sound Shapes (age 9+) is a platform game (i.e. you guide an avatar to jump between platforms and over obstacles) that creates a musical track as you play it. If your child makes a particular move in the game, the accompanying piece of music changes, resulting in a song that becomes deeper and richer as they progress through the levels.

- There are also a huge number of musical apps designed to get children composing, with varying degrees of help available. Some are better suited for children who already know standard notation (or who are willing to learn), while others are intended for children who prefer to experiment more freely:

Incredibox (age 8+) introduces your child to a bedroom full of sleepy-eyed hipsters who become their very own beatboxing crew. You can assign repeating musical elements (beats, melodies, voices) to each character and listen as the sounds layer on top of one another. Because all the sounds seem to 'fit' together, children will soon become confident enough to start experimenting.

GarageBand (age 10+) is a powerful app that allows kids to sequence pre-recorded loops, play virtual instruments and record live instruments and vocals. It's a sophisticated music-making tool that's surprisingly easy to use for kids who don't know formal notation.

Grammar and Punctuation

It's quite possible that you were never explicitly taught English grammar at primary school because in the seventies and eighties many schools didn't teach it. As so often in education, the fashion has now changed and your child will be taught some grammatical terms and some rules of grammar, alongside those of punctuation, and sit a SPAG (Spelling, Punctuation and Grammar) test in Year 6, as well as a similar test in Year 2. (See 'Reports and Assessment' on p. 52.) Explicit knowledge of grammar, says the national curriculum, gives us more conscious control and choice in our language. The idea is that every child should be taught Standard English, not because it's superior to, say, northern British English, but because it's the language of prestige and power and if children don't know it they could be handicapped later in life, particularly when it comes to professional advancement.

We've decided to put all the grammar and punctuation your child will be taught here, in one place, rather than in each year's English section.

Your child will learn to use and understand the

terminology through discussion, examples and lots of practice. Before they are tested in Year 6, they will do many practice papers so don't get too worried if some of these terms are new to you. By Year 6 they should be very familiar to your child!

Year 1

Your child will learn the meaning of the terms 'letter', 'capital letter', 'word', 'singular', 'plural', 'sentence', 'punctuation', 'full stop', 'question mark' and 'exclamation mark'.

They should learn that, to make a word plural, they add '-s' or '-es', and that when you add an ending to a word these additions are called 'suffixes'. Another example is adding the suffix '-ing' to 'learn' to make 'learning'. They'll learn that an addition to the beginning of a word is called a 'prefix', and that prefixes (like 'un-') can change the meaning of a word, e.g. 'unkind', or 'untie'.

They'll learn to separate words with spaces and that they need to end a sentence with a full stop, question mark or exclamation mark.

Year 2

In Year 2 full stops, capital letters, exclamation marks and question marks will be revisited. Your child will be taught to use commas in lists. The rule is to put a comma after every item in a list except the one followed by the word 'and'. So 'pants, socks, vests and shirts' is right, but 'pants, socks, vests, and shirts' is wrong. (This extra comma is known as an 'Oxford' comma and whether it should be there or not is a contentious issue among grammarians. Fights have been known to break out.) Your child will learn the word 'apostrophe' and how to use apostrophes in contracted forms, e.g. 'he's', 'can't', 'it's', and the possessive form ('Mary's coat').

Children will learn to use sentences with different forms: statement, question, exclamation, command (and what these words mean). They'll be asked, say, to change the sentence 'He shut the window' into a command ('Shut the window!'). They will learn to use the present and past tenses. Children find it quite hard to stick to one tense or to see that they have mixed tenses in a piece of writing, even after it's been pointed out. They may also learn that in the sentence 'She is drumming' or 'He was shouting' the form of verb is called the 'progressive' form and it is used to mark actions still in progress.

Your child should learn to identify 'nouns' (things or people), 'verbs' ('doing' words), 'adjectives' ('describing' words) and 'adverbs' (words describing how verbs are done, e.g. 'slowly') and know what these words mean. They'll learn to use 'when', 'if', 'that' and 'because' to create subordinate clauses, such as 'if I can find him' in the sentence 'I always stroke my cat if I can find him'. They'll use 'or', 'and' and 'but' to extend their sentences (but are unlikely to be told that using these is called 'coordination'). They'll learn to use the suffixes '-er' and '-est' in adjectives and that '-ly' turns an adjective into an adverb, e.g. 'suspicious' becomes 'suspiciously'. They'll be taught that 'the blue butterfly' and 'plain flour' are examples of 'expanded noun phrases' (i.e. an adjective attached to a noun).

Year 3

In Year 3 more prefixes will be introduced (embedding your child's understanding of the concept of a prefix) such as 'super-', 'anti-' and 'auto-'. Your child will learn when to use 'a' and when it should be 'an' (before a vowel, as in 'an igloo', but not before a consonant, as in 'a box'). They'll be taught that some words, such as 'solve', 'solution', 'solver', 'dissolve' and 'insoluble', form 'word families' where the words are all based on a common word and have related meanings. They'll learn that a 'conjunction' is a word that expresses time, place and cause, such as 'when', 'before', 'after', 'while', 'so' and 'because'. Some adverbs, such as 'then', 'next', 'soon' and 'therefore', serve the same purpose, as do prepositions such as 'before', 'after', 'during' and 'in'.

Your child will learn to use paragraphs to group related material. They are likely to be given passages with no paragraphs or commas, say, and told to mark where they should go. They'll start using headings and subheadings to organize their ideas (and improve their presentation).

Another tense will be introduced: the present perfect. So if asked to put the sentence 'He went out to play' (which is in the simple past, i.e. it's over now, finished and done) into the present perfect they'll write 'He has gone out to play' (where although you say 'he has', which sounds like the past, it's not over, because he's still out playing).

At this stage your child will learn to use inverted commas (quotation marks) to punctuate direct speech and should be encouraged to start a new line for each new speaker.

They will learn the term 'fronted adverbial' (a new one on us) to describe the use of an adverb to start a sentence in order to spice things up a bit or create a special effect. So they might write a sentence like 'Amusingly, the teacher had to look up what a fronted adverbial was.' (Or probably not.)

This year, they'll learn the term 'main clause' and then 'subordinate clause' (after starting to use them in Year 2) to describe a part of a sentence separated from the main part by a term such as 'when' or 'because'.

Year 4

In Year 4 if they haven't already, your child will learn the grammatical difference between -s used to show a plural and -'s or -s' used to show possession. So they'll be able, in theory, to use apostrophes correctly, even in sentences such as 'All the boys in the school thought the boys' toilets were inadequate' or 'St Paul's Girls' School' (even very well-educated grown-ups get that one wrong).

There will be firm instruction that, while your child may use terms such as 'I done' or 'we was' in colloquial speech, the Standard English forms are 'I did' and 'we were'.

More fronted adverbials may be introduced, as will the need to include a comma after using a fronted adverbial, e.g. 'Later that day, I heard the bad news.'

Your child will practise and become more used to using paragraphs to group related material, so that they'll have, say, an introductory paragraph to a story, followed by a paragraph that gets the action going, or one about mood and so on, until they end with a summing-up, moral-of-the-story-type paragraph.

More rules around direct speech may be introduced, such as using a comma after the 'reporting clause' and putting the final full stop (or exclamation mark, or question mark) within the inverted commas, e.g. 'The conductor shouted, "Sit down!" '. In this example, the 'reporting clause' is 'The conductor shouted'.

Year 5

Continuing their work on suffixes in Year 5, your child will learn that nouns or adjectives can be converted into verbs with suffixes such as '-ate', '-ize' (or '-ise') and '-ify', e.g. the adjective 'triangular' becomes the verb 'triangulate' and the adjective 'private' becomes the verb 'privatize'. They will learn the meaning and use of prefixes to verbs, such as 'dis-', 'de-', 'mis-', 'over-' and 're-', as in 'misrepresent' or 'disengage'.

They'll learn the term 'relative clauses' to describe sections of a sentence beginning with 'who', 'which', 'where', 'when', 'whose' or 'that'. In the sentence 'The cat, which was looking out of the window, gave an involuntary shudder', the phrase 'which was looking out of the window' is a relative clause. It's a clause because the sentence would be complete without this bit, and it's a relative clause because it starts with 'which'.

They'll be taught what a relative pronoun is. An example is the word 'that' in the sentence 'This is the house that Jack built.' In that sentence the phrase 'that Jack built' is a relative clause modifying the noun 'house'. The relative pronoun can provide a link between the two sentences 'This is a house' and 'Jack built the house', where the house referred to in each case is the same.

Your child will learn that the verbs 'might', 'should',

'will' and 'must' are called 'modal' verbs. In that order they indicate increasing degrees of possibility (something you 'must' do is more likely to happen than something you 'might' do). Another way of indicating degrees of possibility is to use adverbs such as 'perhaps' and 'surely'.

By now your child will be used to organizing their work into paragraphs. In Year 5 they may learn some techniques to build cohesion within a paragraph by using phrases or words such as 'then', 'after that', 'this' and 'firstly'.

New punctuation that your child will be introduced to this year, if it hasn't been introduced already, includes the use of brackets, dashes or commas to indicate parenthesis – a word or phrase inserted into a passage which is grammatically complete without it. They'll probably practise using commas to avoid ambiguity (and may be invited to insert commas into the sentence 'The panda eats shoots and leaves' to change its meaning in various ways). They'll learn what 'ambiguity' means.

Year 6

In Year 6 it's likely that some time will be spent looking at the use of different vocabulary in informal and formal speech and writing. Informally, they might, for example, use 'find out' where more formally the word 'discover' would be appropriate. Or 'ask for' might become 'request', and 'go in' might become 'enter'. There are sentence structures typical of informal speech, such as 'question tags', as in 'He's your friend, isn't he?' and more formal sentence structures such as 'If I were . . .' or 'Were they to come . . .' These last two are examples of the subjunctive form and your child may be taught that, too.

In striving to encourage your child to produce ever more interesting and varied writing, teachers are likely to focus on what are called 'cohesive devices' to link ideas across paragraphs. One example is the repetition of a word or phrase; another is the use of adverbials (phrases that give us more information about the verb), such as 'on the other hand' or 'in contrast'.

Your child should be taught that a string of dots (usually three) at the end of a sentence is called an 'ellipsis' and usually indicates an intentional omission of a word, sentence or whole section from a text which doesn't alter the text's original meaning. Ellipses can also indicate an unfinished thought, a slight pause and a nervous or awkward silence.

In Year 6 various layout devices will be used, such as headings, subheadings, columns, bullet points and tables to structure text.

The correct use of the semicolon (;), colon (:) and dash (–) to mark the boundary between independent clauses will be taught:

I drive a bus. (This is a 'simple sentence'.)

I am a doctor; my wife is a lawyer. (This is a 'compound sentence' made up of two independent clauses: 'I am a doctor' and 'my wife is a lawyer'.)

I want to be a nurse – but I need to receive my science degree. (This is a compound sentence made up of two independent clauses: 'I want to be a nurse' and 'I need to receive my science degree'.)

Colons and semicolons

Colons are used to introduce lists and semicolons are used to distinguish items within a list. An example is 'Topics discussed at the school council meeting will include: the Year 6 playground equipment, the new PE uniform and lunchboxes. The speakers will be: Mrs Higgs, Year 6 teacher; John Taylor, Year 5 council rep; Gerri Taylor, Year 4 council rep; and Mrs Jones, head teacher.'

The colon can also be used to introduce an explanation, conclusion or amplification of an earlier statement. This use of the colon separates and highlights the second statement, showing that it follows on from the first. An example is 'Tai chi is more than a form of physical exercise: it is meditation in movement.'

The semicolon represents a break within a sentence that is stronger than a comma but less final than a full stop. It enables the writer to avoid overuse of the comma and preserves the finality of the full stop. Semicolons are also used to link closely related sentences (and to separate items in a list, as already mentioned).

'I read the curriculum guide book in one evening. It was not very helpful' could become 'I read the curriculum guide book in one evening; it was not very helpful.'

Hyphens can also be used to avoid ambiguity: 'man eating shark' means something very different to 'man-eating shark'.

Your child will learn the difference between 'synonyms' (words with similar meanings, e.g. 'big' and 'large') and 'antonyms' (opposites, e.g. 'big' and 'small') and list examples.

Finally, they'll be shown that another way to vary the presentation of information in a sentence is by using the passive. So 'I broke the window in the greenhouse: I didn't know what to do,' could be changed to 'The window in the greenhouse was broken: I didn't know what to do.' One particularly irritating habit we've found in our children is their incorrect use of the passive when it comes to 'sitting'. 'I was sat on the bench . . .' they say, when they mean they were *sitting* on the bench. 'Who sat you there?' we ask, thereby confirming that we're about as annoying as parents can be.

Testing

In Years 2 and 6, as part of the statutory tasks and tests they do in English, your child will sit papers in spelling, punctuation and grammar referred to as the SPAG test in Year 6 (see 'Reports and Assessment' on p. 53). Sample papers for the SPAG test in 2015 include questions such as:

1. 'Liam and Dan _____ gone outside': choose the right word to fill the gap, from 'are', 'is', 'have'.
2. 'The teacher split _____ into teams. _____ were batting; the other team was fielding.' Choose the best pair of pronouns to fill the gaps, from 'them/they', 'us/we', 'her/she', 'them/I'.
3. Circle all the adverbs in this sentence: 'Excitedly, Dan opened the heavy lid. He paused briefly and looked at the treasure.'
4. You are looking over your work and decide to replace the word 'enormous' in this sentence: 'The castle was

enormous.' Choose another word with a similar meaning and write it in the box.

5. Change all the verbs (in a short passage) from the past tense to the present tense. One has been done for you.

6. Which of these should be written as two separate sentences? Tick one. 'I am eleven and my brother is eight'; 'Priya is my best friend she is very kind'; 'I like running, but I am better at swimming'; and 'My favourite lesson is science because it is fun.'

7. The word 'present' has more than one meaning. Write two sentences to show two different meanings.

8. Insert the missing inverted commas in this sentence: 'Following the Battle of Hastings, said the historian, William the Conqueror became King of England.'

9. Circle the preposition in this sentence: 'She waited until ten o'clock.'

What can you do to help?

● Practise changing a sentence from one tense to another. Use the wording on advertising hoardings, as in, put the sentence 'Because you're worth it' into the future and then into the past tense.

● Encourage your child to use longer sentences when, for example, writing thank-you letters, emails to grandparents and stories. For instance, 'It was hot. We went swimming' should be expanded to, say, 'Because it was boiling hot we were allowed to go swimming.'

● Play Greengrocer's Apostrophe. Give small prizes for spotting the wrong use of apostrophes. There's been an argument recently about whether councils should print road signs with or without apostrophes, e.g. St John's Street. Find out what your child thinks and see if they can find examples in your local area.

● Give small prizes to your child if they can find examples of whichever grammatical term they have learnt recently in a newspaper or magazine article. A fronted adverbial or a subordinate clause, for example. Offer slightly bigger prizes if they can find examples of grammatical errors.

● In the national curriculum the words 'grammar' and 'punctuation' are coupled with 'vocabulary', but no mention is made explicitly of the vocabulary your child is supposed to learn. Nevertheless, do what you can to expand your child's vocabulary. Draw attention to words they might not have come across before and work out together what they might mean. Ask your child to think of an alternative word which you or they could use in a description. Look up new words together and challenge each other to introduce them into a sentence during the following hour. (This game is just as good for adults as children, and seeing adults play it will reinforce the message that using new vocabulary is smart and fun.) See if you or your child can articulate what is meant by a concept such as 'pride'. Discuss the difference between 'envy' and 'jealousy'. Ask your child to explain what 'cool' or 'sick' means. They find this very difficult, which makes it all the more worth practising.

● Play Synonyms and Antonyms in the car: choose a word such as 'happy' or 'nice' and take turns naming synonyms, then antonyms. The first one to run out of ideas loses a life and chooses the next word. (Tell your child nouns aren't allowed because there aren't any synonyms or antonyms for nouns.) This is a good game to play on a walk, too.

● Get a copy of *Eats, Shoots and Leaves* by Lynne Truss. It also comes in a version for children with the subtitle 'Why, commas really *do* make a difference!'.

● If you want a reminder of some of the rules of grammar, we suggest you look at www.englishgrammar. org. There's also a good grammar checker (to help resolve any arguments): www.grammarly.com.

● There are lots of books about grammar that you can read if you need to bone up on it yourself. We recommend *Gwynne's Grammar* by N. M. Gwynne.

Year 6

Introduction

It's nearly over: the end is in sight. For your child it's the year when they rule the roost, top dogs at last. Their turn to lord it over the rest of the school, to use the special corner of the playground reserved for the elite, to stride around wearing badges saying 'House Captain', 'Monitor', 'Sports Captain' or even . . . 'Head Boy' or 'Head Girl'. Lots of schools have a 'buddy' system where older children are paired up with children in Reception and look after them in break, or read with them once a week, etc. In many schools this is a treat reserved for Year 6. It's hugely popular, with both sides getting a lot from the special relationship. Girls, of course, fall in love – 'Oh Mum, he/she is so cute!' – and even the boys enjoy the responsibility.

As a parent who may have made many 'school gates' friends and been to some degree involved in lots of aspects of your children's school life (those with the time and inclination, anyway) you will find secondary school a whole different kettle of fish. Your child will, in Year 7, relish their new status as quasi-adult and squirm at your attempts to escort them into school or get to know their new friends' parents. 'Mummm! You're so embarrassing!' So enjoy this last year!

There's still a lot of work to be done and the looming prospect of national curriculum tests in English and maths (still commonly known as SATs) will mean less time spent on the foundation subjects. There's no need for your child to be stressed about SATs: they will be well prepared because it's in the school's interest to get a good set of results. (See 'Reports and Assessment' on p. 53.)

Once these tests are over the final term should be filled with fun projects and activities, including some drama and art, for which there will have been less time in the run-up to the testing. There is usually a certain amount of pairing up. Child: 'Jude's going out with Sarah.' Parent: 'You're *much* too young to have a girlfriend or boyfriend. What does it actually *mean*? Do they hold hands or *what*?' Child: 'No. Eugh!' In some schools the head teachers 'ban' this sort of pairing up very effectively.

Your child should leave primary school feeling as if they've thoroughly outgrown it and itching to move on to their next adventure. However, at the same time, they're bound (the girls, at least) to shed dramatic tears at the thought of leaving.

Should I let my child have a mobile phone?

Parents have different policies about what age their children should be before they have a phone and there is no right answer to this question. It's not just a matter of personal preference. It will also depend on whether they're allowed to take phones into school, whether they're going to be travelling by themselves and the age at which most of their friends are allowed phones – though your child will probably be an unreliable source on that last point. They will tell you all the children in their class have phones from Year 3 onwards. In our case, we decided to give our children phones in Year 6, not least because they'd be using public transport every day when they started secondary school. If you give your child a smartphone it's important to be clear with them beforehand that, just because it's theirs doesn't mean they'll be able to get it out and start playing on it whenever they want or to keep it in their bedroom at night. But don't expect your children to observe these rules if you're a compulsive smartphone user yourself. If you've told your child that taking out a phone at mealtimes is impolite don't start doing it yourself.

English

The national curriculum doesn't differentiate between Years 5 and 6 in English. This is not because nothing new happens in Year 6, but because the type of learning that takes place in Year 5, with the emphases as described in Year 5 'English', remains the same. In Year 6 children will read and study more complex literature than in Year 5 and they will make further progress in their spelling, composition, comprehension and their ability to discuss texts.

We suggest that, if your child is in Year 6, you read Year 5 'English' on p. 312. We will add a little under the same headings as before.

- Reading = word reading; comprehension

- Writing = transcription (spelling and handwriting); composition; vocabulary, grammar and punctuation

We've tackled all of these subdivisions below, apart from the last, which is dealt with in 'Grammar and Punctuation' on p. 375. (For the 'Purpose of Study' and 'Aims' of the English curriculum, see p. 458.)

Reading

WORD READING

By now your child should be a fluent reader. Like anyone encountering a new piece of vocabulary, he or she may stumble over the emphasis if reading aloud, but as they read ever more widely and their vocabulary grows they will build up the etymology and morphology to read and interpret previously unmet words. By this we mean that when faced with a word they've never come across before, such as 'photosynthesis', they'll read 'photo' straightaway and then, after a moment or two, see 'synthesis'. They might know that 'photo' means something to do with light and that 'synthesis' means combining two things to make a new one, so they might be able to guess that 'photosynthesis' has something to do with making something from light. And this would be exactly right as it's how plants make food using the sun's energy. Your child will also be given the opportunity to rehearse reading passages out loud, be it their own work or texts in assembly, and will continue to hone their technique.

COMPREHENSION

Your child will continue to develop their understanding of how language, structure and presentation contribute to meaning.

Writing

TRANSCRIPTION

a) Spelling

Words such as 'committee', 'government', 'temperature' and 'disastrous' will be learnt.

There is a statutory word list for Years 5 and 6, which we reproduce here. At some point during Years 5 and 6 these words will appear on spelling lists to be learnt, if they haven't already. Your child may be asked to include the words in sentences to help them learn how to spell them.

WORD LIST: YEARS 5 AND 6

accommodate	bargain	criticize (critic + ize)
accompany	bruise	curiosity
according	category	definite
achieve	cemetery	desperate
aggressive	committee	determined
amateur	communicate	develop
ancient	community	dictionary
apparent	competition	disastrous
appreciate	conscience	embarrass
attached	conscious	environment
available	controversy	equip (-ped, -ment)
average	convenience	especially
awkward	correspond	exaggerate

excellent
existence
explanation
familiar
foreign
forty
frequently
government
guarantee
harass
hindrance
identity
immediate(ly)
individual
interfere
interrupt
language
leisure
lightning
marvellous
mischievous

muscle
necessary
neighbour
nuisance
occupy
occur
opportunity
parliament
persuade
physical
prejudice
privilege
profession
programme
pronunciation
queue
recognize
recommend
relevant
restaurant
rhyme

rhythm
sacrifice
secretary
shoulder
signature
sincere(ly)
soldier
stomach
sufficient
suggest
symbol
system
temperature
thorough
twelfth
variety
vegetable
vehicle
yacht

b) Handwriting

Your child should increase the legibility, consistency and quality of their joined-up writing. An average eleven-year-old, if writing something that requires little thought, should be able to cover a page of A4 in about fifteen minutes. But the variation from child to child is huge, not least because in Year 6 girls often go through a phase of teeny-tiny writing. They think it's neater. Discourage this, but don't worry about it too much; it hasn't lasted long in any of our children. It just frustrates the teacher who has to get a magnifying glass out to mark their work.

COMPOSITION

In this final year your child should continue to produce pieces of creative writing of increasing sophistication and length, be it prose or poetry. Their stamina for writing should increase so that writing a story that covers several sides of A4 is fairly routine. Children will be encouraged to use ever more varied vocabulary and grammatical constructions to alter the style of their writing to match different needs (descriptive prose, a formal letter, a report, an eyewitness account, etc.). There's also likely to be more focus on affecting the reader, e.g. using persuasive language as appropriate, or withholding information to create suspense in a narrative.

They will continue to learn to edit and evaluate their own work.

What can you do to help?

In this section we've put all these suggestions together, instead of putting them under each subsection as in previous sections, because the majority apply to all areas of English.

● Everything we said in Years 3, 4 and 5 still applies. Listen to your child reading aloud and read challenging texts to them. It could be anything: newspaper or magazine articles, in print or online.

● Encourage your child to research (using guide books) somewhere you might be taking them for the first time by asking them to find out some history, e.g. 'How old is the church?', or 'What are the ten best things to do when we get there?'

● Discuss books that you've both read.

- Help your child choose books to read. There's a lot of new, excellent literature for this age group. Try a book called *The Ultimate Good Book Guide*, which lists '600 Good Books for 8–12s'. Another good source is the website List Challenges (www.listchallenges.com), which has a surprising number of children's books. It also has a good book list for 'Young Adults', which some readers in Year 6 may be ready for. Another website designed to help is LoveReading4Kids (www.lovereading4kids.co.uk), which sorts books by age group and has books of the month.

- There are lots of children's book blogs. Try www.storyshack.org or www.bookzone4boys.blogspot.co.uk/. Your child should ask for recommendations from their peers, too, or be old-fashioned and try the local library for advice. And see our 'Key Stage 2 Reading List' on p. 455.

- Draw your child's attention to nuances in meaning between similar words. Look the words up together to show that even you can't always articulate these nuances without some help. Try and instil a pride in the English language, which has an unusually large word count. Select a new word from the dictionary every day and work it into conversation.

- Go to the theatre. By now your child will appreciate some adult plays, including Shakespeare. Shakespeare's Globe takes a play on tour around the country every year, usually performing to small audiences outdoors. The relaxed atmosphere is particularly engaging for a younger audience. See www.shakespearesglobe.com for details.

- Play word games such as Scrabble, Bananagrams, Snatch and Boggle.

● Do crosswords together, such as the one in First News, the weekly newspaper for children (www.firstnews. co.uk) or try Puzzle Choice (www.puzzlechoice.com/pc/ Kids_Choicex.html). The quick crossword in The Times is a good one to try together (perhaps leave the cryptic one for now . . .).

● Encourage your child to enter writing competitions. See the Booktrust for information (www.booktrust.org. uk/prizes).

Maths

As we said in the introduction to Year 5 'Maths', your child will learn to solve a wider range of problems using increasingly complex properties of number and arithmetic in the last two years of primary school. There'll be ever bigger numbers, more fractions and decimals, long division and long multiplication. They'll learn about percentages and ratios and even start using algebra.

The national curriculum sets out what your child should learn in Year 6 under the various headings below. (For the 'Purpose of Study' and 'Aims' of the maths curriculum, see p. 459.)

Number and place value

Year 5 dealt with numbers up to a million. In Year 6 your child should reach the dizzy heights of 10 million. The curriculum says they'll learn to read, write, order and compare numbers up to 10 million. (Why they should stop here is a mystery. Surely the sky's the limit once they've understood the system? We expect teachers will go further: children love to know that a 'googol' is a word in some dictionaries that means 1 with a hundred noughts after it.)

Your child will round any whole number to a required degree of accuracy (rather than to the nearest ten, hundred, etc.). They'll use negative numbers in context and calculate intervals across 0, e.g. between 412 and −762 the interval is 1174.

Addition, subtraction, multiplication and division

There is bound to be further practice at long multiplication with ever-bigger numbers (be prepared to revise all their times tables again).

Long division, that scourge of primary school maths, finally rears its (beautiful?) head. The national curriculum says that your child will be taught to 'divide numbers up to four digits by a two-digit whole number using the formal written method of *long* division, and interpret remainders as whole-number remainders, fractions, or by rounding, as appropriate for the context' *and* to 'divide numbers up to four digits by a two-digit number using the formal written method of *short* division where appropriate, interpreting remainders according to the context'. Let me translate. They should use both the old-fashioned method for long division (for something tricky like 975 divided by 17), and be able to recognize when they can get away with short division, even for a two-digit number, such as 357 divided by 17. Most of us could do 17 into 35 goes 2 remainder 1. Carry the 1. Now, 17 into 17 goes 1. Answer: 21.

No one we've met recently can remember how to do long division (okay, almost no one). And yet most people, if they really needed to find out how many tickets at £34 each they could buy for £1,475, would be able to work it out without a calculator if they had to. And your child deserves to be taught how, not only in case there's a Luddite rebellion and an end to the Machine Age, but because it furthers their understanding of numbers.

Long division is taught in two stages in most schools these days. The first method is often called 'chunking' and, once your child is proficient in this method, it segues nicely into the old-fashioned formal method you will have learnt at school. However, fashions in teaching change and chunking is on the wane so your child may not use it. By the end of Year 6 (or, rather, by the time they do their national curriculum tasks and tests) your child will be competent at the formal method. Let's hope so, anyway, because if they get a long division sum wrong in the statutory maths test at the end of Year 6 from 2016 onwards they will still get a half-mark if they show their working out using the formal method, but no marks if they use the chunking method.

We're going to explain 'chunking', because most parents won't know what it is. Take the following sum:

$$597 \div 22 = ?$$

We'll take a 'chunk' of 22s that we can easily calculate away from 597. We know that $10 \times 22 = 220$, so we'll start by deducting that:

$$
\begin{array}{r}
597 \div 22 \\
(10) \quad -220 \\
\hline
377
\end{array}
$$

We still have more than 220 left over, so we will repeat this step:

$$\begin{array}{r} 377 \\ (10) \quad -220 \\ \hline 157 \end{array}$$

We now have 157 left over. We know that $5 \times 22 = 110$ so we will now deduct that:

$$\begin{array}{r} 157 \\ (5) \quad -110 \\ \hline 47 \end{array}$$

We now have 47 left over. We know that $2 \times 22 = 44$. So we do the final step:

$$\begin{array}{r} 47 \\ (2) \quad -44 \\ \hline \text{r3} \end{array}$$

Adding all the chunks, there have been 27, and we're left with 3 over, so the answer is 27 r 3.

This can be much more concisely written in columns (see the second long-division example in the Appendix 'Addition, Subtraction, Multiplication, Division' on p. 476).

We're not going to explain the more formal version that we all learnt at school, but see the third example on p. 476 if you want a reminder.

This year your child will also learn to find common multiples (last year, it was common factors).

Multiples that are common to two or more numbers are said to be 'common multiples'.

Multiples of 2 are 2, 4, **6**, 8, 10, **12**, 14, 16, **18** . . .

Multiples of 3 are 3, **6**, 9, **12**, 15, **18** . . .

So, common multiples of 2 and 3 are 6, 12, 18 . . .

This year, your child will revisit common factors and relate them to finding equivalent fractions. This means they may be asked to make a fraction, say $^{45}/_{100}$, as small as possible (otherwise called 'putting it in its simplest form', or 'cancelling down', or 'simplifying'). $^{45}/_{100}$ is the same as (equivalent to) $^9/_{20}$, which is the answer you're aiming for. How should they get there? They look at the number 45 and at the number 100, and find a common factor (a number that 'goes into' both). In this case 5. Now they divide 45 by 5 to get 9 and divide 100 by 5 to get 20. So $^9/_{20}$ is an equivalent fraction to $^{45}/_{100}$.

Your child will be taught to undertake mental calculations with increasingly large numbers and more complex calculations. They'll use estimation to check answers to calculations and decide an appropriate degree of accuracy.

An important new skill will be to understand the need for brackets to fix the order of operations, e.g. $2 + 1 \times 3 = 5$ but $(2 + 1) \times 3 = 9$. So in the same way that leaving out commas can change the meaning of a sentence, leaving out brackets does the same in mathematics.

Fractions (including decimals and percentages)

Work with fractions should now include adding fractions with different denominators (the number on the bottom), starting with the relatively easy, e.g. $^1/_2 + ^1/_8 = ^5/_8$, and becoming harder, e.g. $^3/_7 + ^4/_8 + 2^2/_7$. Then comes multiplying and dividing, e.g. $^1/_3 \div 2 = ^1/_6$, and converting fractions to decimals, e.g. $^3/_8 = 0.375$. They'll learn to work backwards to solve problems, e.g. if $^1/_4$ of a length is 36cm, then the whole length is $36 \times 4 = 144$cm.

One model that's proved very helpful in visualizing maths problems is called the 'Singapore bar model'. We'll give one example. To solve a problem like this: Mary made 300 biscuits. She sold ¾ of them, and gave ⅓ of the remainder to her neighbour. How many did she have left?

If you represent the amounts by drawing bars, it's much easier to visualize what sum you need to do to get the answer.

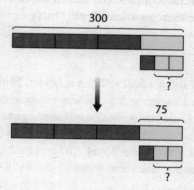

Answer: 50

Decimals should also be multiplied and divided, starting with, say, $0.4 \times 2 = 0.8$, and progressing to, say, 24×2.45, or £6.84 ÷ 5. (Each of these is slightly harder than the one before. Can you do these without a calculator? Your child will soon be able to show you how!)

Ratio and proportion

These important new concepts appear only in Year 6. Your child will probably draw shapes and scale them up, recognizing that every length has, say, been multiplied by 3. They may be taught to say that the lengths on the two shapes are 'proportional' to each other, and that they're in the ratio 1:3. An example of the kind of problem they're likely to be given is: 'If for every egg you need three spoonfuls of flour, how many spoons of flour will you need if you use four eggs?' Or 'If ⅗ of the class are boys and there are 25 in the class, how many boys are there?'

Another application of ratio could be to link percentages of 360° to calculating angles in pie charts.

Algebra

Algebra is not scary, it's fun. (Oh yes it is!) It's likely to be presented as a useful and quick way to write down 'missing number' problems, such as 'If Jenny gives you 2 sweets and now you have 14, how many did you have before?' could be written '? + 2 = 14', or you could use a letter for the question mark and write '$a + 2 = 14$'. That's all algebra is.

Your child should be taught to use symbols and letters to represent variables and unknowns in mathematical situations that they already understand, such as missing numbers, lengths, coordinates and angles or formulae in mathematics. They may have already written the perimeter of a rectangle as $2a + 2b$ (where a is the length and b is the width). They've used equivalent expressions such as $a + b = b + a$ (this is no different from saying that $3 + 2$ is the same as $2 + 3$).

It's likely they'll be asked to list possible values for a and b if, say, $a + b = 11$.

Measurement

In Year 6 your child should learn to connect conversion, e.g. from kilometres to miles, to a graphical representation as preparation for understanding linear/proportional graphs. This just means being able to use a graph like the one we've printed on p. 405 to read off, say, what 16km is in miles (10). They'll probably compare volumes of cubes and cuboids in cm³ and m³ (but converting from one to the other is something that even A Level Physics students struggle with).

They should get a feel for common conversions and be able to tell if an answer is sensible.

They'll calculate areas of shapes made up of combinations of rectangles and triangles.

Geometry

Your child should learn to draw shapes and nets accurately, using conventional markings and labels for lines and angles. They'll learn to describe the properties of shapes and explain how unknown angles and lengths can be derived from known measurements. They'll name parts of circles 'radius' (from centre to edge), 'diameter' (twice the radius) and 'circumference' (distance all the way around the circle).

These relationships might be expressed algebraically, e.g. $d = 2 \times r$ instead of diameter equals twice the radius; or $a = 180 - (b + c)$ for something to do with different angles drawn on a straight line.

They'll describe positions on the full coordinate grid (all four quadrants) and draw and translate simple shapes and reflect them in the axes. They'll draw and label rectangles, parallelograms and rhombuses, specified by coordinates in the four quadrants, predicting missing coordinates. These might be expressed algebraically, e.g. translating vertex (a, b) to $(a + 4, b - 9)$:

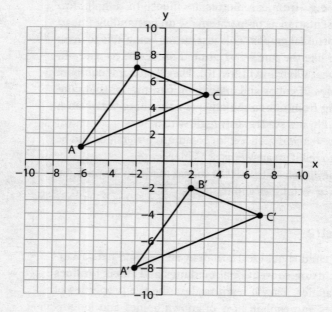

Here point A is at $(-6, 1)$ and it's been translated by $(4, -9)$ to end up at A′ which is at $(-2, -8)$.

Statistics

Your child should be taught to calculate and interpret the mean as an average and when it is and isn't appropriate to find the mean of a data set (it does make sense to find the mean height of children in the class, but it doesn't make sense to find the mean of a list of phone numbers). To find the mean of a set of, say, twelve numbers you add up all the numbers and divide by 12.

They'll probably apply their work on angles, fractions and percentages to the interpretation of pie charts. If a quarter of a pie chart is shaded in, it represents 25 per cent, and the angle in the circle will be 90°. If you had to shade a pie chart to show 60 per cent you'd shade $^{60}\!/_{100} = ^6\!/_{10} = ^3\!/_5$ of the chart. The angle in the circle would be three fifths of 360°. This is the same as $^3\!/_5 \times 360 = 216$ degrees.

Your child should learn to use and draw graphs relating to two variables, arising from their own enquiry and in other subjects, e.g. they'll connect conversion from kilometres to miles in measurement to its graphical representation:

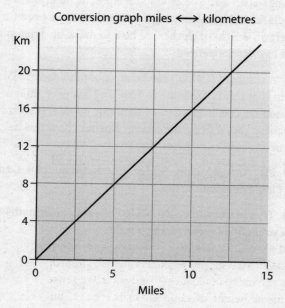

Conversion graph miles ⟷ kilometres

What can you do to help?

- In the car challenge your child to convert miles to kilometres. They could have started doing this in Year 3 or 4, depending on when they learnt their 8 times table: miles × 8 ÷ 5 = kilometres.

- Try to notice – and point out – the use of ratio in everyday life. It crops up in betting, whether in horse racing, in football matches or in the use of the doubling dice in Backgammon. (Of course we don't mean you should encourage your child to actually bet. Use matchsticks, or gambling chips at home to play Blackjack.) Ratio crops up in recipes, as mentioned before, and in calculating how much dye you need for a certain weight of clothes, or how to make up a quantity of two-stroke petrol.

- A standard (Calpol) medicine spoon holds 5ml. Point out that this is the same as $5cm^3$ and ask your child to visualize five little cubes of $1cm^3$ side by side. It's hard to believe they'd fit on the spoon. Not sure how this helps, but . . .

- Play Backgammon, Bridge, Chess and Sudoku. Games of logic help with maths.

- Try the website called NRICH (www.nrich.maths.org) if your child loves a maths puzzle.

Science

Living things and their habitats

Your child will have started some work on classifying animals and plants in Year 4. They should take it further in Year 6 and start subdividing the categories. In Year 4 they may not have included invertebrates; they will now. Through direct observations where possible, children will classify animals into commonly found invertebrates (such as insects, spiders, snails and worms) and vertebrates (fish, amphibians, reptiles, birds and mammals). They should discuss reasons why living things are placed in one group and not another.

Your child might find out about the significance of the work of scientists such as Carl Linnaeus, a pioneer of classification. By grouping living things into defined hierarchies and giving them individual names we create order, which makes it easier to study the chaotic world of nature. Carl Linnaeus is famous for creating the system of naming plants and animals that we still use today: we are *Homo sapiens*. *Homo* is the genus that includes modern humans and closely related species such as *Homo neanderthalensis* (Neanderthals), and *sapiens* is our species.

Your child's class is likely to use classification systems and keys to identify some animals and plants in the immediate environment, and it is likely to research unfamiliar animals and plants from a broad range of other habitats and decide where they belong in the classification system.

Animals (including humans)

In Years 3 and 4 your child will have learnt about the main body parts and internal organs (skeletal, muscular and digestive system). This year they should identify and name the main parts of the human circulatory system and describe the functions of the heart, blood vessels and blood. They should all, at the very least, learn that blood is pumped to the lungs where it absorbs oxygen, and then around the body, where the oxygen is used up. Some children may go into the detail of the four chambers of the heart, but this is usually taught at secondary school.

Children will continue previous work on how to keep their bodies healthy through good diet and exercise. In Year 6 they should also look at how some drugs and other substances can be harmful to the human body.

Your child may investigate some scientific research into the relationship between diet, exercise, drugs, lifestyle and health, perhaps producing a 'myth-buster' leaflet or educational poster. Health fascism is taught in primary schools as a matter of course.

Evolution and inheritance

A hot topic! The status of creationism and the theory of evolution in public education has been the subject of substantial debate globally. In the United States the Supreme Court has ruled that the teaching of creationism as science in public schools is unconstitutional. Here, On the Origin of the Species is included in the primary science curriculum for the first time and the government has made it clear that science lessons must teach the theory of evolution and not creationism. Creationism can only be taught in RE even in faith schools.

So, building on what they learnt about fossils in the topic on rocks in Year 3, your child should find out more about how living things on Earth have changed over time and that fossils provide information about living things that inhabited the Earth millions of years ago. They'll be introduced to the idea that characteristics are passed from parents to their offspring by considering different breeds of dogs, for instance, and what happens when, say, Labradors are crossed with poodles. They will also learn that variation in offspring over time can make animals more or less able to survive in particular environments, e.g. why giraffes' necks grew longer, or the arctic fox developed insulating fur. They are likely to compare how some living things are adapted to survive in extreme conditions, e.g. cactuses, penguins, camels. They might analyse the advantages and disadvantages of specific adaptations, such as being on two feet rather than four, having a long or a short beak, having gills or lungs, there being tendrils on climbing plants, flowers having bright colours and distinctive scents.

Scientists your child might study include Mary Anning (palaeontologist), Charles Darwin and Alfred Russel Wallace (who each independently came up with the theory of evolution through natural selection).

Light

In Year 3 your child will have played with mirrors and torches, looking at how shadows form and change. This year they'll explore the way that light behaves in more depth: how it travels in straight lines from a source, bouncing off objects and into our eyes. They'll draw diagrams (with rulers!) to show how shadows form, and make mirror-image drawings. They may use the idea that light appears to travel in straight lines to explain how a periscope works.

They might investigate the relationship between light sources, objects and shadows by using shadow puppets. They could extend their experience of light by looking at a range of phenomena, including rainbows, colours on soap bubbles, objects looking bent in water and coloured filters (but they probably won't learn why these phenomena occur – another thing they won't cover until secondary school). If you are fed up with fobbing off your child's scientific questions, try websites such as Explainthatstuff! (www.explainthatstuff.com/light.html) or HowStuffWorks (www.howstuffworks.com). But be aware: these sites are written for adults, so your child will need some help to understand them.

Electricity

Building on their work in Year 4, your child will again construct simple series circuits to see what happens when they try different components, e.g. switches, bulbs, buzzers and motors, and systematically isolate the effect of changing one component at a time in a circuit. They are likely to change the number or the voltage of cells (batteries), so they'll probably be introduced to the word 'voltage' as a measure of the energy provided. They will probably design and make a set of traffic lights, a burglar alarm or some other useful circuit. This time round, they'll learn how to represent a simple circuit in a diagram, using recognized symbols for each component. Scope for cross-curricular links with the work they're doing in DT here.

What can you do to help?

- Make a periscope if they haven't done so already at school (or even if they have). Hours of fun to be had hiding behind the sofa with the periscope poking up over the top to watch TV illicitly.

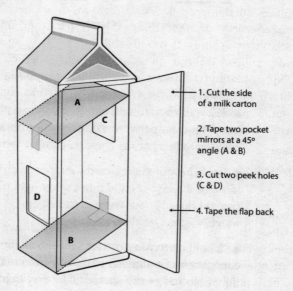

1. Cut the side of a milk carton

2. Tape two pocket mirrors at a 45° angle (A & B)

3. Cut two peek holes (C & D)

4. Tape the flap back

- Below is a key to classifying plants. Ask your child to adapt it for five of their soft toys, or their favourite Skylanders. Instead of 'Are there roots and stems?', the first question could be 'Does it have four legs?' If they've done it right you'll be able to use the key to tell them the name of any one of the toys.

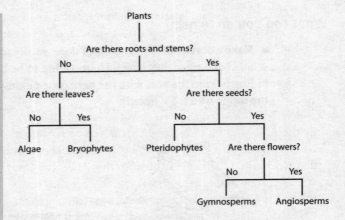

● Ask your child to find out what's special about mules (they're a cross between a donkey and a horse and they can't reproduce) or the zorse, zetland or zebroid.

● Learn how to make shadow puppets with your hands. It might make your child think about light travelling in straight lines . . . See www.youtube.com/watch?v=sPneQzqhh4g for inspiration.

● Take apart a cheap torch to show how the different components fit together to make a circuit. The battery, light bulb and switch should all be easy to identify, and you should be able to see metal strips linking them.

● The University of Manchester's children's site has a science section (www.childrensuniversity.manchester.ac.uk/interactives/science) which includes 'exercise' as a topic (lots of good muscle and digestion animations) and a section on the skeleton. There are games to play and it's well presented.

● The Natural History Museum in London has a fantastic dinosaur section that reinforces everything your child will have been taught about evolution. There are galleries on insects, mammals, etc. too, and beautiful fossils of all shapes and sizes.

Art and Design

By the time your child reaches Year 6 he or she should have been taught a good deal about art and design and discovered what particular form of art they're best at – or, at least, enjoy more than others. The teacher may leave them to their own devices more in lessons, trusting them to get on with the work they want to do. They'll probably have an opportunity to pursue projects over the course of half a term or a term, producing work that you'll genuinely want to keep, as opposed to just sticking it on the fridge for a couple of weeks. (For the 'Purpose of Study' and 'Aims' of the art and design curriculum, see p. 462.)

The national curriculum divides up the content in Key Stage 2 as follows.

Pupils should be taught to:

- develop different artistic techniques with creativity and experimentation, showing an increasing awareness of different kinds of art, craft and design

- create sketchbooks to record observations and use them to review and revisit ideas

- improve mastery of art and design techniques, including drawing, painting and sculpture, using a range of materials

- understand the work of great artists, architects and designers in history.

There's a unit in the old art and design curriculum which your child might be taught in Year 6 called 'A sense of place'. They will be asked to explore the landscape around the school as a starting point for some two-dimensional work, such as drawing, painting or photography. They might visit a local park or National Trust property for inspiration and note down some of the distinctive features, such as fields, walls, hedges, waterways and – if they're visiting a building – columns, windows, towers and doorways. There is scope here for cross-curricular links with geography and history.

If your child is doing this unit they may be shown some drawings from the sketchbooks of famous landscape artists for inspiration, such as Paul Cézanne and John Singer Sargent. There are also plenty of great British landscape artists they could be introduced to, such as John Constable, David Hockney, J. M. W. Turner and L. S. Lowry. They might also be shown the work of some famous landscape photographers, such as Ansel Adams.

What can you do to help?

● Take your child to see some great landscape paintings. You can find Constables at the National Gallery in London and in numerous museums and galleries in Colchester and in Ipswich (Constable country); Turners at Tate Britain in London and the National Maritime Museum in Greenwich; and Lowrys at The Lowry in Manchester, Tate Britain, the Walker Art Gallery in Liverpool and the Sunderland Museum.

● If your child has any interest in drawing cartoons or creating comic books, we recommend the book *Draw with the Cartoon Dude* by Dave Miller. It contains step-by-step instructions to drawing a vast range of things, from leaping horses to wizards, and the page opposite is always left blank so they can have a go at drawing the creature or character themselves.

● If you have any interest in knitting your child will have the fine motor skills now to take it up. There's a good beginner's guide at www.queenofdiy.com.

● There are plenty of great drawing apps out there, including SketchBook Express, Paper, Procreate, ArtRage and SketchBook Pro. David Hockney, among others, has shown what can be done on a tablet. For some examples of his iPad work, see www.hockneypictures.com.

● In our experience children are fascinated by public art, particularly if it has a vaguely illicit aura, such as the work of Banksy. A relatively benign form of this is Eyebombing, which involves sticking pairs of plastic googly eyes on inanimate objects found in public places, such as postboxes and paper-towel dispensers, with a view to transforming them instantly into cartoon characters. You can see some examples at www. eyebombing.com/archive.

Computing

In Year 6 it's possible that your child will be introduced to a text-based programming language such as Python, in preparation for Key Stage 3 (Years 7, 8 and 9), if they haven't been already, with the goal of making them 'secondary ready'. However, that doesn't mean they'll abandon the visual programming language they've been using up until now. They'll continue to use those coding skills and combine them with the new skills they learn in Year 6. Scratch, in particular, isn't considered a programming language suitable only for primary school children. If your child goes on to do a GCSE in computer science they will continue to use Scratch as part of that course. Nevertheless, the introduction of a text-based language will be a quantum leap forward. (For the 'Purpose of Study' and 'Aims' of the computing curriculum, see p. 463.)

The national curriculum divides up the content in Key Stage 2 as follows.

Pupils should be taught to:

- design, write and debug programs that accomplish specific goals, including controlling or simulating physical systems; solve problems by deconstructing them into smaller parts

- use sequence, selection and repetition in programs; work with variables and various forms of input and output

- use logical reasoning to explain how simple algorithms work and to detect and correct errors in algorithms and programs

- understand computer networks, including the internet; how they can provide multiple services, such as the World Wide Web; and the opportunities they offer for communication and collaboration

- use search technologies effectively, appreciate how results are selected and ranked, and be discerning in evaluating digital content

- select, use and combine a variety of software (including internet services) on a range of digital devices to design and create a range of programs, systems and content that accomplish given goals, including collecting, analysing, evaluating and presenting data and information

• use technology safely, respectfully and responsibly; recognize acceptable/unacceptable behaviour; identify a range of ways to report concerns about content and contact.

Computer science

We think it's likely that your child will create programs of increasing complexity in Year 6, using the visual programming languages they're used to and new text-based languages such as Logo, TouchDevelop and Python. Examples might include a program to create an animated rainbow, a random pattern-making program which produces Spirograph-like images, a program to make geometric shapes dance to different tunes and a program that writes absurdist poetry.

If your child is still being taught how to control physical systems via a computer program, it's possible they may do a unit in the old ICT curriculum which children used to be taught in Year 6 called 'Controlling and monitoring'. However, it's a mark of how much more advanced the current curriculum is that children are more likely to do this unit in lower Key Stage 2 (Years 3 and 4), particularly if they're working with Lego WeDo.

Digital literacy

In Year 6 your child should have a basic grounding in the staples of the subject, such as word-processing, spreadsheets, PowerPoint, search engines and computer networks, and the teacher may introduce them to some of the more controversial issues surrounding the World Wide Web, such as whether it's right for commercial companies or government intelligence agencies to track personal online activity. Are these invasions of privacy ever justified? Hopefully, your child's teacher will advise them to check the terms and conditions before signing up to any internet-based service!

Other units taught in Year 6 under the old ICT curriculum which may continue to be taught include 'Multimedia presentation' (PowerPoint), 'Spreadsheet modelling' (Excel) and 'Using the internet to search large databases and to interpret information' (search engines). As with 'Controlling and monitoring', though, these units – or something like them – are more likely to be taught in lower Key Stage 2.

Talking politics

Your child will have been introduced to lots of strategies for assessing the reliability of information they come across on the Web, but they probably won't have been introduced to the greatest source of unreliability of all – politics. Now might be a good time to tell them that, when it comes to politically contentious subjects – Brexit, immigration, taxation, crime and punishment, etc. – there are rarely such things as uncontroversial facts and figures. On the contrary, the relevant data in these areas is nearly always presented through a political filter, often in ways that are deliberately misleading. Or it's just flat-out invented. Your child may have been taught some basic facts in PSHE, such as who the prime minister is and what the different political parties are, but their teachers will probably have tiptoed around anything controversial, not least because schools are legally prohibited from engaging in any form of 'political indoctrination'. There's nothing to stop you teaching them about politics, though. In our experience, the best way to do this is to talk about politics at the dinner table, laying out both sides of the argument on a particular issue and inviting your child to take up a position and defend it. Some primary schools have debating clubs which your child can join and, if they don't, you can talk to the head teacher about starting one. Neighbouring independent schools will have debating clubs and may already have set up partnerships with other primaries in the area. If you want your primary to join in, a phone call between the two heads is probably all that's required.

What can you do to help?

● It might be the right time to let your child have their own computer. They will probably clamour for the latest laptop or tablet – and tell you that all their friends have one – but try not to give in to pester power. Just give them your old computer when you upgrade to a new one. As with phones, you'll have to set out some clear rules beforehand about when they can and can't use it, whether their siblings are allowed to use it and what social networks they're allowed to join, if any. Hopefully, some of the e-safety they've been taught at school will have stuck and they can be trusted to behave responsibly online. But if you're concerned you can contact your internet service provider and ask it to filter what you can access from your home – that's assuming the filters aren't on already. Most of the larger service providers, such as BT, now turn the filters on by default so if you became a customer from 2014 onwards, the content will already be filtered.

● If you think your ten- or eleven-year-old child is too young to be given their own computer, you could get them a Raspberry Pi instead. This is a very basic, credit-card-sized computer that has been designed to help children learn how to program. It plugs into a TV and can be used for many of the things a desktop PC can be used for, such as word-processing, creating spreadsheets, playing games and watching movies. Raspberry Pis cost about £50 and one benefit of buying your child one is that he or she can then go along to a Raspberry Jam – a local user group that meets every month so people can share information and demonstrate their programs. You can search for information about Raspberry Jams on Twitter, using the hashtag #RaspberryJam. There are groups in Preston, Cambridge, Sheffield, Durham, London, Manchester, Brighton, Nottingham, Bristol and Machynlleth, to name a few.

● You might consider letting your child open an Instagram account. Our children get a lot of pleasure from sharing photographs on this particular social network. There's a risk that they will start following someone who shares inappropriate content, but they can always unfollow them if that happens. Make sure your child turns on their privacy settings so no one can follow them without their consent. To do this, tap 'Edit your profile' next to the profile picture, scroll down to where it says 'Posts are private' and slide it to 'on'.

- If your child is racing ahead of their classmates and showing a real aptitude for programming, you could steer them towards the computer science section of the Khan Academy, the YouTube-based educational website created by Salman Khan (www.khanacademy.org/computing/computer-programming). They can take a number of online courses to advance their programming skills, such as 'Drawing and animation', in which they'll learn how to use the JavaScript language and ProcessingJS library to create drawings and animations. Codecademy (www.codecademy.com), which contains tutorials on working with several text-based programming languages, is also worth looking at.

- Another way to stretch your budding young coder would be to have them design a website using HTML code rather than the usual drag-and-drop building blocks. Html.net (html.net) offers free online tutorials.

- For a range of quite sophisticated apps and games designed to help children whose programming skills have already reached an intermediate level, see Year 5 'Computing' on p. 347.

Design and Technology

Don't expect much curriculum time to be devoted to DT in Year 6, as your child will be spending the lion's share of their time preparing for the all-important statutory tasks and tests that they'll take in May. That means DT, if it's taught at all, is likely to be combined with another subject, such as art and design or computing. Alternatively, what some schools do is to teach no DT during Year 6 until *after* the tests and then spend a week doing a DT project, such as 'Robot Wars'.

Your child may be given an opportunity to experiment with a 3D printer in their final year in school, if not before, assuming the school either has one or has access to one. That isn't as pie-in-the-sky as it sounds. At present, you can get one that's suitable for a school for about £1,000, but they're likely to fall in price over the next few years. We can envisage many PTAs deciding to raise money to buy a 3D printer – it may even rival 'playground equipment' as the most popular object of fundraising activities in years to come. (For the 'Purpose of Study' and 'Aims' of the design and technology curriculum, see p. 465.)

The national curriculum divides up the content in Key Stage 2 as follows.

When designing and making, children should be taught to:

Design

- use research and develop design criteria to inform the design of innovative, functional, appealing products that are fit for purpose, aimed at particular individuals or groups

- generate, develop, model and communicate ideas through discussion, annotated sketches, cross-sectional and exploded diagrams, prototypes, pattern pieces and computer-aided design.

Make

- select from and use a wider range of tools and equipment to perform practical tasks accurately

- select from and use a wider range of materials and components, including construction materials, textiles and ingredients, according to their functional properties and aesthetic qualities.

Evaluate

- investigate and analyse a range of existing products

- evaluate their ideas and products against their own design criteria and consider the views of others to improve their work

- understand how key events and individuals in design and technology have helped shape the world.

Technical knowledge

- apply their understanding of how to strengthen, stiffen and reinforce more complex structures

- understand and use mechanical systems in their products

- understand and use electrical systems in their products

- apply their understanding of computing to program, monitor and control their products.

Cooking and nutrition

- understand and apply the principles of a healthy and varied diet

- prepare and cook a variety of predominantly savoury dishes, using a range of cooking techniques

- understand seasonality, and know where and how a variety of ingredients are grown, reared, caught and processed.

Design

The reference to 'particular individuals or groups' (see above) means that your child will be asked to think about who a product is for before designing it. The suggestion that they should 'use research' before making something could be interpreted in a range of ways, not just surfing the Web to see what else is out there. The teacher might ask your child to conduct a survey among the group a particular product is aimed at or get them to fill out a questionnaire. For instance, if they're designing a pill dispenser they might go and interview some residents in a nearby old people's home.

Make

The national curriculum requires children to 'perform practical tasks accurately' and there's likely to be more emphasis on that in Year 6, by which time your child will have developed the fine motor skills needed to produce work that's polished and well-finished. One of our children made quite a smart-looking umbrella in Year 6. Children might be asked to make models of Viking long-boats to tie in with the work they're doing in history on Vikings.

Evaluate

If your child is doing 'Victorians' in history, they might well look at the work of some famous Victorian designers and engineers in DT, including Isambard Kingdom Brunel, Alexander Graham Bell (who invented the metal detector as well as the telephone) and George Stephenson.

Technical knowledge

There's a unit in the old DT curriculum called 'Controllable vehicles' which used to be taught in Year 6 that has been known to crop up again, although usually after children have done their SATs! It involves using construction kits and a range of materials and components to create a model vehicle (circus vehicle, carnival float, moon buggy) that's controlled by an electrical circuit. Your child will be expected to finish the vehicle to quite a high standard, using cladding and appropriate finishing techniques. There's scope for cross-curricular links with computing here – which may be combined with DT in Year 6 – and your child might have an opportunity to write a program that can control their vehicle.

Cooking and nutrition

In Year 6 your child may be introduced to the idea that our diet has changed over time. For instance, they might be asked to compare their diet today with the diet of children in the Anglo-Saxon era, looking at the crops and livestock of an Anglo-Saxon farmer. This would tie in with the work they're doing on late Anglo-Saxons in history.

What can you do to help?

● If your child has developed an interest in electrical systems, you could ask a grandparent to get them a subscription to Nuts and Volts, which bills itself as 'the magazine for electrical hobbyists'. It's not specifically aimed at children, but there's plenty of accessible material, such as articles on the Global Positioning System, amateur radio and all sorts of do-it-yourself projects. For a taste of the magazine's contents, check out its website: www.nutsvolts.com.

● There's a great website called Instructables (www.instructables.com) on which users post instructions on how to make stuff. Some of the things will be too challenging for an eleven-year-old, such as a robotic hand, but others should be well within their grasp – such as making a dragon out of paper and wire. It includes a section on 'Food' with instructions on how to make things to eat using unusual cooking utensils – brownies in flowerpots, for instance.

● Instructables has an entire section devoted to making trebuchets, a commonly used siege engine in the Middle Ages. Recommended: the desktop trebuchet made out of K'nex (www.instructables.com/id/How-to-Build-a-Trebuchet).

● If your child complains that trying to make, say, a robotic dinosaur is too hard, tell him about Jamie Edwards, a thirteen-year-old pupil at Penwortham Priory Academy who in 2014 built a nuclear reactor in his school science laboratory. You can watch a news report about this remarkable achievement on the BBC News website (www.bbc.co.uk/news/science-environment-

26450494). Jamie is the youngest person ever to bring about nuclear fusion.

● If your child enjoys making Viking longboats – or if they don't get an opportunity to make one at school – they can see some instructions on how to make one here: www.dailymotion.com/video/x2q7ms0_viking-ship-looledo-com-fun-kids-crafts-science-projects-and-more_lifestyle.

Geography

It's inevitable that your child will spend less time on geography in Year 6 than in previous years because their class teacher will be focusing on the statutory tasks and tests that they'll be doing in English and maths at the end of Key Stage 2. Nevertheless, children are expected to absorb so much geographical knowledge in primary school that there's bound to be quite a lot of the curriculum left to cover. As in Year 5, expect your child's teacher to smuggle in some of the higher-order thinking skills that were more of a feature of the old curriculum, inviting them to discuss issues such as inequality, poverty and fracking.

The national curriculum divides up the content in Key Stage 2 as follows.

Pupils should be taught to:

Locational knowledge

• locate the world's countries, using maps to focus on Europe (including Russia) and North and South America, concentrating on their environmental regions, key physical and human characteristics, countries and major cities

- name and locate counties and cities of the United Kingdom, geographical regions and their identifying human and physical characteristics, key topographical features (including hills, mountains, coasts and rivers) and land-use patterns; and understand how some of these aspects have changed over time

- identify the position and significance of latitude, longitude, the equator, northern hemisphere, southern hemisphere, the tropics of Cancer and Capricorn, the Arctic and Antarctic Circles, the prime/Greenwich meridian and time zones (including day and night).

Place knowledge

- understand geographical similarities and differences through the study of human and physical geography of a region of the United Kingdom, a region in a European country and a region within North or South America.

Human and physical geography

- describe and understand key aspects of physical geography, including: climate zones, biomes and vegetation belts, rivers, mountains, volcanoes and earthquakes and the water cycle

- describe and understand key aspects of human geography, including: types of settlement and land use, economic activity including trade links, and the distribution of natural resources including energy, food, minerals and water.

Geographical skills and fieldwork

- use maps, atlases, globes and digital/computer mapping to locate countries and describe features studied

- use the eight points of a compass, four- and six-figure grid references, symbols and key (including the use of Ordnance Survey maps) to build knowledge of the United Kingdom and the wider world

- use fieldwork to observe, measure, record and present the human and physical features in the local area, using a range of methods, including sketch maps, plans and graphs, and digital technologies.

Locational knowledge

In Year 6 your child will begin to explore the rest of the world, locating and naming the main countries in Africa, Asia and Australasia and identifying their main regions, their key physical and human characteristics and their capital cities. Again, they may compare a region of the United Kingdom in the present with that same region at some point in the past – the Danelaw, for instance, to tie in with the work they may be doing in history on Vikings. They might be asked to name and locate the key topographical features, including the East Anglian coastline, rivers, etc., and discuss how these features have changed over time. There's a unit in the old geography curriculum called 'Investigating rivers' which your child might be taught in Year 6, though it was about rivers in general and not individual rivers in a particular context.

Place knowledge

The teacher might ask your child to compare a region of the United States with a region of a South American country with significant similarities and differences, e.g. the coalmining region of Wyoming with the coalmining area of Santander in Colombia. What is the life expectancy of a miner in each region and what accounts for this? If your child does this they may be asked to write a diary, imagining what it would be like to be the child of a non-unionized miner in Colombia. Alternatively, your child might study the Amazon Basin and compare the Brazilian plan to build sixteen dams in the region with the dams of the American West.

Human and physical geography

In Year 6 your child's teacher may choose some of the more challenging items on the list above to focus on: climate zones, biomes (a large geographic region characterized by a dominant community of plants and animals) and vegetation belts, as well as coastlines, rivers and tides (physical geography). Your child may also study the unequal distribution of natural resources, focusing on energy and the impact that has on geopolitical power (human geography). They might explore some of the issues surrounding fracking and what the pluses and minuses are of the United Kingdom developing a fracking industry. Local issues are always popular, e.g. if your child's school is located in Hampshire the teacher might ask your child to consider whether a new national park in the South Downs is a good idea.

Geographical skills and fieldwork

In Year 6 as in earlier years, your child's teacher will almost certainly get your child to use maps, atlases, globes and digital mapping applications to locate the countries they're studying. Your child will probably learn about latitude and longitude in more depth and progress from using four-figure grid references to six-figure ones. At this point, they should be able to use Ordnance Survey maps to study different parts of the United Kingdom, and maps or an atlas to study other parts of the world. Your child will probably continue to use fieldwork to observe, measure and record the physical and human features in the local area, using a range of different methods, such as sketch maps, plans and digital technologies.

What can you do to help?

● Play Capital Cities. Each member of your family has to take it in turn to name different cities beginning with different letters of the alphabet, starting with 'A' for, say, Ankara. Each time it's someone's go they have to recite the entire list from the beginning before adding a new city.

● The Ordnance Survey website has 104 'Map Symbol Flashcards' which you can print out, half of which are the symbols for things such as 'Quarry', 'Site of Battle' and 'Public Convenience', and the other half the descriptions of what the symbols stand for. Your child can use these to play Pelmanism, in which you have to match the symbols with the correct descriptions, or Bingo. To play Bingo, divide the symbol cards equally between the players and keep the description cards yourself. As the caller, your job is to read out the descriptions and the first child to match all their symbol cards with the descriptions is the winner (www.ordnancesurvey.co.uk/education-research/teaching-resources/map-symbol-flashcards.html).

● It might be time to introduce your child to the international phenomenon known as 'geocaching'. Go to www.geocaching.com, become a member (it's free), type in your postcode and then record the GPS coordinates of your nearest geocache. Typically, a geocache is a waterproof container buried in the ground that contains a logbook and a pencil. The job of you and your child is to find it, dig it up, record the date and time that you found it in the logbook, then bury it again for someone else to find. You can download a free app from the Geocaching website that turns your mobile phone into a GPS tracker.

● A geography project your child might enjoy participating in is the Geograph, an attempt to photograph every grid square (i.e. every square kilometre) of Great Britain and Ireland. Your child can register for free on the website (www.geograph.org.uk) and then start uploading photographs. (They might want to make this a holiday project, photographing every square mile of an area within a ten-mile radius of where you're staying.) To date, over twelve thousand contributors have submitted more than 5 million images.

● Your child can watch a short video showing the Earth's orbit around the sun and explaining why we have different seasons on the BBC's Bitesize website (www.bbc.co.uk/education/clips/z6vfb9q).

● If you want to test your child's grasp of basic geographical knowledge, you can print out blank outline maps of the world's different countries and continents in the geography section of About.com (www.geography. about.com/library/blank/blxindex.htm). Start with an easy one like the United Kingdom and ask your child to draw the boundaries of the four nations that comprise it, and then move on to Europe and North and South America.

● If you live anywhere near Cornwall – or are going there on holiday – a trip to the Eden Project is worth making. The huge, dome-like structures are literally biomes, each simulating a particular climate with vegetation to match. So one is tropical, another is Mediterranean, etc. The most recent dome to be added, known as 'the Core', is devoted to education. The Eden Project's central educational message is that plants and people are interdependent, and lots of the plants on view are labelled with their medicinal uses. For a list of outdoor learning experiences, see the Eden Project's website (www.edenproject.com/whats-it-all-about/people-and-learning/young-people-and-education/mud-between-your-toes).

MNEMONICS AND MEMORY AIDS

There's a poem that can help you remember all fifty states of the United States:

Alabama and Alaska, Arizona, Arkansas,
California, Colorado and Connecticut and more.
Delaware, Florida, Georgia, Hawaii and Idaho.
Illinois, Indiana, Iowa, still thirty-five to go.

Kansas and Kentucky, Louisiana, Maine.
Maryland, Massachusetts and good ole Michigan.
Minnesota, Mississippi, Missouri and Montana,

Nebraska's twenty-seven, number twenty-eight's
　Nevada.

Next, New Hampshire and New Jersey,
And way down, New Mexico.
Then New York, North Carolina,
North Dakota, O-Hi-O.

Oklahoma, Oregon, Pennsylvania, now let's see.
Rhode Island, South Carolina, South Dakota,
　Tennessee.
There's Texas, then there's Utah.
Vermont, I'm almost through.

Virginia, then there's Washington and West
　Virginia, too.
Could Wisconsin be the last one in the forty-nine?
No, Wyoming is the last state in the fifty states that
　rhyme.

History

Expect your child to do less history in Year 6 as their
teacher prepares them for the statutory tests in English
and maths which they'll do towards the end of the academic year. Nevertheless, it's likely that your child will
study the Vikings – the fourth of the British history units
up to 1066 – and another aspect of British history, probably one their teacher is used to doing. The most popular
subjects in the old history curriculum were the Tudors
and the Victorians, so it will probably be one of those and
for the sake of completeness we've covered them both
below. In addition, the teacher may focus on more general historical questions in Year 6, such as the nature of

historical evidence and the basis on which we make judgements about the past. (For the 'Purpose of Study' and 'Aims' of the history curriculum, see p. 468.)

The national curriculum divides up the content in Key Stage 2 under the following headings.

- Changes in Britain from the Stone Age to the Iron Age

- The Roman Empire and its impact on Britain

- Britain's settlement by Anglo-Saxons and Scots

- The Viking and Anglo-Saxon struggle for the kingdom of England to the time of Edward the Confessor

- A local history study

- A study of an aspect or theme in British history that extends pupils' chronological knowledge beyond 1066

- The achievements of the earliest civilizations – an overview of where and when the first civilizations appear and a depth study of one of the following: Ancient Sumer; the Indus Valley; Ancient Egypt; the Shang Dynasty of Ancient China

- Ancient Greece – a study of Greek life and achievements and their influence on the Western world

- A non-European society that provides contrasts with British history – one study chosen from: early Islamic civilization, including a study of Baghdad c. AD 900; Mayan civilization c. AD 900; Benin (West Africa) c. AD 900–1300

If your child is doing the Viking unit in Year 6 they'll probably begin with the Viking raid on Lindisfarne Priory in 793, and go on to cover the growth of the Danish and

Norwegian marauding parties into an army, the settlement of the Danelaw, the creation of 'puppet' kings, Danegeld, the identification of the Viking invaders as a common enemy and the emergence of an English national identity, Alfred the Great, Athelstan, Edward the Elder, Ethelred the Unready, the return of the Vikings, King Canute, Edward the Confessor and the Norman Conquest. Quite a lot to cover in one term, but not as overwhelming as it sounds. The teacher will probably ask your child to write a diary as if they were a child at the time recording a Viking raid, maybe write a letter to another child explaining their day-to-day life in a Viking village and, possibly, write an essay explaining why the Vikings met with so little resistance (at least initially). They'll also do complementary work in DT, such as building models of Viking longboats.

The Tudors is a popular topic with many primary school teachers, so they'll have plenty of resources. Expect your child to focus almost exclusively on Henry VIII, learning about his court, the state of England at the time, the kinds of things he got up to every day (hunting, attending church, signing papers, dining in state) and why he married six different women. Why did he divorce Catherine of Aragon? Why didn't marrying Anne Boleyn or Jane Seymour solve his problems? Why did the marriage to Anne of Cleves fail? And why did he go on to marry Catherine Howard and Catherine Parr? Your child might also learn something about Henry's break with Catholicism and the establishment of the Church of England.

If the teacher covers the Victorians your child might learn what it was like to be a child in the 1840s, particularly a poor child, and what laws were passed in the period to protect children. They might be taught about schools in Victorian times, as well as the sort of work children were made to do out of school. More generally, they're likely to learn something about the Industrial Revolution, the growth of manufacturing and the technological innovations that drove those changes, such as the invention of the steam engine and the coming of the railways. Famous Victorians they might study include: Isambard Kingdom Brunel, Lord Shaftesbury, Lewis Carroll, Joseph Lister, Robert Louis Stevenson, Alexander Bell, Sir Robert Peel and Charles Dickens. Finally, the teacher might ask your child to think about some of the questions thrown up by the Victorian era. What was gained and what was lost in the transition from a rural, agricultural country to an urban, industrialized one? Was the price of 'progress' too high for some people? Could the nineteenth century be described as 'the Age of Improvement'?

History and politics

There's less emphasis on the development of higher-order thinking skills in the current history curriculum, partly for the reasons set out in the Introduction. However, it hasn't been expunged altogether. In the preamble to the history bit of the national curriculum it says teachers should encourage children 'to ask perceptive questions, think critically, weigh evidence, sift arguments and develop perspective and judgement'. By now, your child will have already been introduced to the idea that historical knowledge can be used in various ways to support or undermine contemporary political views. In Year 6 the teacher might spend a bit more time on this, asking your child to think about the relationship between history and politics. For instance, does learning that people have been coming from overseas to settle in Britain for at least two thousand years have any bearing on current debates about Brexit, immigration and national identity? The teacher may show the class some edited highlights of the opening ceremony of the 2012 Olympic Games and ask them whether the historical narrative at the heart of Danny Boyle's vision is consistent with their understanding of British history. The opening ceremony was ambivalent about the benefits of industrialization and portrayed the creation of the National Health Service and other social reforms as necessary correctives to unbridled capitalism. Is that narrative linked to a left-wing sense of British identity? Can the class think of an alternative narrative that would complement a more conservative outlook? Among historians, there's a debate about whether it makes sense to expect children to engage in these discussions in a meaningful way at such an early stage in their historical education. But some primary school teachers are firm believers in trying to get children to think analytically about the subject and will have been posing provocative questions about the nature of historical evidence, how to evaluate different sources and so on, throughout Key Stage 2.

What can you do to help?

VIKINGS

- The BBC's Bitesize site has a section on the Vikings which includes areas called 'Who were the Vikings?', 'Vikings at sea', 'Viking raiders', 'Beliefs and stories' and

'What happened to them?' (www.bbc.co.uk/education/topics/ztyr9j6).

● If you live near York, it's worth visiting the Jorvik Viking Centre, which is built on the site of the Coppergate Dig, an excavation that began with a discovery of small trenches beneath a branch of Lloyds Bank in 1972 and uncovered a quarter of a million bits of pottery and over twenty thousand individual objects. Children can walk along reconstructed Viking-age streets, explore Viking houses, visit four permanent exhibitions and view an artefact gallery.

● Roger Lancelyn Green's *Myths of the Norsemen* is a good introduction to the Norse myths but if you think it's a bit old hat you could try the *D'Aulaires' Book of Norse Myths* by Ingri and Edgar d'Aulaire. Your child may already be familiar with some aspects of the Norse myths, thanks to the popularity of Thor, the Marvel Comics superhero.

● You could encourage your child to read *The Hobbit*, pointing out that Tolkien was a professor of Anglo-Saxon at Oxford from 1926 to 1945. It's possible to see the Shire as an idealized Anglo-Saxon community and the enemies that Bilbo Baggins and his companions have to fight – the goblins, trolls, spiders, wargs, etc. – as proxies for Viking marauders.

THE TUDORS

● If you live in West London a visit to Hampton Court Palace would be a good way to introduce your child to Henry VIII. You can visit the king's apartments and see his crown, walk through some Tudor kitchens and get lost in the famous Hampton Court Maze. There's a permanent exhibition at the palace called 'Young Henry

VIII' which can also be viewed online (www.hrp.org.uk/younghenry).

● If you live near Liverpool it's worth taking a trip to the Walker Art Gallery to see the portrait of Henry VIII based on the Whitehall Mural painted by Hans Holbein. Children can stop by the Big Art children's gallery and dress up as Henry.

● In Portsmouth you can see the *Mary Rose*, Henry's warship, at the Mary Rose Museum in the Historic Dockyard. The *Mary Rose*, which first went into service in 1512, was discovered in 1971, raised from the ocean bed in 1982 and is now the centrepiece of one of Britain's newest museums. If you're planning a visit you should download the Mary Rose Museum app beforehand.

● Other Henry VIII exhibits in London include: a model of Henry in full battle armour at the Royal Armoury in the Tower of London (you can also see where some of his wives spent their final hours); a painting of Henry at the National Portrait Gallery; and a permanent exhibition called 'The Tudors' at the British Museum.

THE VICTORIANS

● The BBC's Primary History site has a section on Children in Victorian Britain which includes areas called 'Children in coal mines', 'Children at play', 'Children at work', 'Victorian schools' and 'Rich and poor families' (www.bbc.co.uk/schools/primaryhistory/victorian_britain).

● If your child is studying the Victorians you should consider a trip to the V&A, named after the queen and her consort (and built with the profits made from the

Great Exhibition of 1851, which was organized by Prince Albert and visited by 6 million people, almost a third of the British population at that time). Your child can kill two birds with one stone and pick up a Tudor 'Family Art Fun Trail' at the Learning Centre and explore the Tudor exhibits by searching for objects you might have found in Henry VIII's palaces.

● England is full of steam museums and steam railways. For a directory of both, see www.steamheritage.co.uk.

GENERAL

● The British Museum has an online resource called Ancient Civilizations (www.ancientcivilizations.co.uk) that enables children to explore the entire sweep of history, stretching back to 3500 BC, through a range of different lenses: religion, technology, trade, writing, buildings and cities.

● A good way to get your child to think about history and what historical artefacts can tell us about the past is to get them to create a time capsule and bury it in the garden or some nearby woods. Tell them to choose just a dozen things that, more than any others, will inform a person at some distant point in the future exactly what it was like to be a child in twenty-first-century England. But be warned: before they consign the capsule to its final resting place make sure they haven't included any valuable personal items belonging to you, such as your glasses!

● If your child is a confident reader it's worth trying to interest them in some historical fiction aimed at children. Some titles worth bearing in mind are:
The Stronghold by Mollie Hunter (1st century BC)

The *Eagle of the Ninth* by Rosemary Sutcliff (Roman)

The *Once and Future King* by T. H. White (Anglo-Saxon)

The *Door in the Wall* by Marguerite de Angeli (The Middle Ages)

Ivanhoe by Walter Scott (12th century)

The *Adventures of Robin Hood* by Roger Lancelyn Green (12th century)

Arthur: The Seeing Stone by Kevin Crossley-Holland (12th century)

Brother Dusty Feet by Rosemary Sutcliff (Tudors)

Cue for Treason by Geoffrey Trease (Tudors)

Children of the New Forest by Frederick Marryat (Civil War)

Kidnapped by Robert Louis Stevenson (Jacobites)

War Horse by Michael Morpurgo (First World War)

The *Silver Sword* by Ian Serraillier (Second World War)

Carrie's War by Nina Bawden (Second World War)

For a fuller list, see www.childliterature.net/childlit/historical/list.html

● Memrise (www.memrise.com), the free online learning tool we recommended in 'Times Tables' on p. 168, has a course called 'British and English Monarchs' in its 'History' section that your child might find useful. It lists different kings and queens and provides mnemonics to help your child remember when they reigned. For instance, if your child wants to remember the date that William the Conqueror became king, it suggests the following rhyme: 'In 1066 we were in a fix, William the Conqueror was playing his tricks.'

● A rhythmic couplet that can be used to remember Henry VIII's wives goes as follows:

'Kate 'n' Anne 'n' Jane, 'n' Anne 'n' Kate again 'n' again.'

(Catherine of Aragon, Anne Boleyn, Jane Seymour, Anne of Cleves, Catherine Howard and Catherine Parr.)

● To remember the fates that befell Henry's six wives, try this:

Divorced, beheaded, died,
Divorced, beheaded, survived.

MNEMONICS AND MEMORY AIDS

The Kings and Queens of England

Willie, Willie, Harry, Stee,
Harry, Dick, John, Harry Three,
One to Three Neds, Richard Two,
Harry Four Five Six . . . then who?

Edwards Four Five, Dick the Bad,
Harrys twain, Ned Six the lad,
Mary, Bessie, James you ken,
Then Charlie, Charlie, James again . . .

Will and Mary, Anne of Gloria,
Georges Four!, Will Four, Victoria,
Edward Seven next, and then
Came George the Fifth in 1910.

Ned the Eight soon abdicated,
So George Six was coronated,
(or a George was reinstated)
Then number two Elizabeth.
And that's all folks, until her death . . .

(And probably for the future:
Charles Three and now I'm out of breath!)

For reference, these are the kings and queens referred to in the above verse:

William I (1066–87), William II (1087–1100), Henry I (1100–35), Stephen (1135–54), Henry II (1154–89), Richard I (1189–99), John (1199–1216), Henry III (1216–72), Edward I (1272–1307), Edward II (1307–27), Edward III (1327–77), Richard II (1377–1399), Henry IV (1399–1413), Henry V (1413–22), Henry VI (1422–61, 1470–71)

Edward IV (1461–70, 1471–83), Edward V (1483), Richard III (1483–5), Henry VII (1485–1509), Henry VIII (1509–47), Edward VI (1547–53), Mary I (1553–8), Elizabeth I (1558–1603), James I (1603–25), Charles I (1625–49), Charles II (1660–85), James II (1685–8)

William III and Mary II (1689–94), William III (1694–1702), Anne (1702–14), George I (1714–27), George II (1727–60), George III (1760–1820), George IV (1820–30), William IV (1830–37), Victoria (1837–1901), Edward VII (1901–10), George V (1910–36)

Edward VIII (1936), George VI (1936–52), Elizabeth II (1952–)

Languages

If you haven't done so already, we recommend that you read the introduction to Year 3 'Languages' on p. 233. In case you don't, it's important to repeat one paragraph here:

Given the range of time dedicated to language teaching that we expect to find across the country's schools, it's hard to say exactly what you should expect your child to learn in each year. If your child has less than an hour a week, your primary school may not be expecting to cover as much ground as we describe.

(For the 'Purpose of Study' and 'Aims' of the languages curriculum, see p. 469.)

The language content of the national curriculum in Key Stage 2 can be divided up under two broad headings, spoken and written.

Spoken language

Pupils should be taught to:

- listen attentively to spoken language and show understanding by joining in and responding

- explore the patterns and sounds of language through songs and rhymes and link the spelling, sound and meaning of words

- engage in conversations; ask and answer questions; express opinions and respond to those of others; seek clarification and help

- speak in sentences, using familiar vocabulary, phrases and basic language structures

- develop accurate pronunciation and intonation so that others understand when they are reading aloud or using familiar words and phrases

- present ideas and information orally to a range of audiences

- appreciate stories, songs, poems and rhymes in the language.

Possible examples of topics that may crop up in Year 6 are 'Our school', 'Our world', 'Café life', 'The past and the present', 'At the theme park' and 'In the news'. The weekly lesson will probably follow a pattern. After a warm-up game revising the previous week's progress, your child is likely to be introduced to new content.

In Year 6 there will be plenty of recapping of the previous year's grammar and vocabulary. When they are ready the class will move on to conjugating some new verbs, possibly irregular ones. They may learn to tell the time and to use superlatives. They could learn the correct use of prepositions such as 'to' and 'from', and perhaps the possessive adjective.

Throughout, they will be revising and practising what they have learnt in previous years.

To give you an idea of the kinds of activities your child may take part in, here are some examples:

- Listen attentively to a story or spoken passage and retell the main ideas. Change key points of the story by substituting words such as nouns, pronouns, verbs, adjectives and adverbs, or suggest an alternative ending

- Memorize and perform a poem, song, story or sketch

- Give a 'live' talk (a multimedia presentation, a sketch, a poem, or a song) to the class, probably in a small group

- Listen to a spoken phrase or sentence and act out the meaning or point to a picture card illustrating the meaning. Your child may be asked to adapt the phrase by substituting a verb or noun, adjective, adverb, etc., to change the meaning

- Sustain a conversation within the class or with visitors, or via videoconferencing with native-speaking peers

- Play Hot Seating. One child who is in the hot seat starts a conversation/begins to say a rhyme/tell a story/describe something. At a given signal, e.g. a bell, another child must quickly take over as 'hot seater' and continue in the same vein

Written language

Pupils should be taught to:

- read carefully and show understanding of words, phrases and simple writing

- broaden their vocabulary and develop their ability to understand new words that are introduced into familiar written material, including through using a dictionary

- write phrases from memory and adapt these to create new sentences, to express ideas clearly

- describe people, places, things and actions orally and in writing.

In a logical progression from Year 5 your child will continue to practise their written communication in the new language, learning how to spell a growing number of words and phrases. They're likely to begin to innovate with language, too. Having parroted phrases in Years 3 and 4, and begun to adapt them and use them in sentences in Years 4 and 5, they might start to take more risks and realize that simply looking in dictionaries won't always help.

In Year 6 the activities may become more writing-intensive: writing an imaginary conversation between two people in a café, or a weather report, for example. Most schools are likely to make links with a school abroad so that everyone in the class is assigned a pen-pal. Your child will love getting a 'real' letter in basic English and they may even quite enjoy responding in the language they're learning. (Sending small items such as stickers or hair ties to and fro generally increases the pleasure of the exchange.) Some schools will set up a Skype link with the sister school, so your child may get to see and hear their pen-pal.

To give you an idea of the kinds of activities your child may take part in, here are some examples:

- Guess Who It Is. Children read short descriptions of people in the school or class or famous people and identify who they are. Include likes, dislikes, hair colour, age, where they live, etc.

- Read an email message from a partner school and reply to some of their questions on subjects such as hobbies, the weather, holidays, likes and dislikes

- Read a weather report and draw symbols on a map showing what the weather will be like in those regions/countries

- Read a familiar story or sing a familiar song. Using print-outs of the story or song, your child may try to answer some simple questions about it

- Read aloud a story, using a variety of voices and expression. Work in groups to record the story on to audiotape for others to hear

- Watch a video or listen to a song, break the sentences or lines down into separate parts and then try to reconstitute the text, or cut a sentence into words and reconstitute the sentence

- Create a sentence from given words and punctuation, looking for clues such as capital letters and full stops

- Produce a PowerPoint presentation for a Year 3 class studying the same language, building simple sentences for younger children to read

- Use a structure offered by a familiar poem or story to construct one of their own, e.g. 'This is the house that Jack built . . .'

- Create a wall on a theme from a different curriculum area, e.g. Henry VIII and his six wives. Give speech bubbles to characters to include personal information

- Work in pairs or groups to create a rhyming rap of four lines based on topic-specific vocabulary they've learnt

- Create a story using key elements from familiar stories in the foreign language, e.g. 'Once upon a time . . .', 'Fee-fi-fo-fum!', ' . . . and they lived happily ever after'

- Design and write a short presentation (make notes as prompts) and perform a role-play

What can you do to help?

Many of the suggestions in 'Languages' in Years 3, 4 and 5 apply to Year 6.

● Start the morning at home with a few greetings and some breakfast chat in the language. Say, for example, 'Good morning, did you sleep well?' to your child (and expect a response!). Whether they have learnt the grammar for such a stock phrase is irrelevant. Look it up, or ask someone who speaks the language well (their teacher, for example) for the right colloquial expressions. 'Please will you pass the butter?' and 'Would you like the milk?' are examples of easily learnt phrases that will encourage your child to use the language in a more fluid way than when they are trying to form a new sentence themselves.

● Play Twister in the language. This is the game played on a large plastic mat that is spread on the floor or ground. The mat has four rows of large coloured circles on it with a different colour in each row: red, yellow, blue and green. A spinner is attached to a square board and is used to determine where the player has to put their hand or foot. The spinner is divided into four labelled sections: right foot, left foot, right hand and left hand. This requires only the vocabulary of colour, body part and left/right. You can buy a Spanish version at www. alibaba.com/.

Music

By Year 6 your child should have become quite good at composing short pieces of music, either on their own or with others. They should have developed an ability to listen in a focused manner and pick out patterns and instruments in a piece of music. Hopefully, they'll be able to describe music using musical phrases and terminology. In this final year the teacher will introduce them to yet more musical vocabulary, including 'chord', 'mode', 'major', 'minor', 'metre', 'inversion', 'retrograde', 'ornamentation', 'variation' and 'form'. (In music, 'variation' is a formal technique where material is repeated in an altered form. The changes may involve harmony, melody, counterpoint, rhythm, timbre, orchestration or any combination of these.) (For the 'Purpose of Study' and 'Aims' of the music curriculum, see p. 470.)

The national curriculum divides up the content in Key Stage 2 as follows.

Pupils should be taught to:

• play and perform in solo and ensemble contexts, using voice and playing musical instruments with increasing accuracy, fluency, control and expression

• improvise and compose music for a range of purposes, using the interrelated dimensions of music

• listen with attention to detail and recall sounds with increasing aural memory

• use and understand staff and other musical notations

• appreciate and understand a wide range of high-quality live and recorded music drawn from different traditions and from great composers and musicians

• develop an understanding of the history of music.

In Year 6 your child will continue to listen to a wide variety of music across many genres, including classical, and hopefully learn to identify a range of musical devices and processes. They'll be expected to improvise using different melodies and rhythms and to perform with ever greater polish and confidence, either with instruments or using their voices.

It's possible that your child may spend a term studying a unit called the 'Overture'. This will involve listening to a wide variety of examples: classical overtures from baroque to the present day, modern musicals and Italian and French opera. They will learn how different themes can be used to provide dramatic contrasts or to describe different characters, events and moods. And they'll probably have a go at composing an overture of some kind themselves.

Your child might conceivably be introduced to the idea that some songs or tracks are more 'clichéd' than others and learn to distinguish between 'plagiarism', 'homage' and 'quotation'. The class may listen to some film music – the score of *The Magnificent Seven*, for instance – and reflect upon the mixture of originality and familiarity composers use to enhance the impact of a particular scene.

What can you do to help?

- You might want to consider enrolling your child at a local performing arts centre that offers after-school or weekend activities. Most will involve singing, dancing and acting. There are some nationwide schools, such as Stagecoach (check out its website at www.stagecoach.co.uk to find out the nearest location), and most areas will have good local offerings, such as the Music House for Children (www.musichouseforchildren.co.uk) in Shepherd's Bush. In Yorkshire, you could try Stage 84: www.stage84.com.

- If your child enjoys singing (and most do), get them to join a choir outside school. If you go to Big Big Sing (www.bigbigsing.org/find-me-a-choir), there's a good directory of local choirs and it should be possible to find one in your local area that welcomes children.

• Some children may be resistant to the idea of learning a musical instrument (because of the practice involved) but, thanks to the popularity of programmes such as *The Voice*, be open to the idea of being taught to sing. There are exams with grades for those who need this incentive, but our children enjoy singing just for the fun of it. A good teacher will allow them to choose their own repertoire and will teach in pairs or small groups which children often prefer.

Musical terms

a cappella: singing without instrumental accompaniment

adagio: slowly

allegro: briskly and happily

alto: high-pitched, lower than a soprano, higher than a tenor

andante: moderate tempo

arpeggio: notes of one chord played quickly, one after the other

bass: low, the lowest of the voices and the lowest part of the harmony

bravura: boldly

bridge: the part of a song that joins two parts

capo: the beginning

chord: three or more notes played at the same time

coda: the end, or closing section, of a song

common time: four beats per measure. Many songs have this timing, and it's indicated by a 'C' or half-circle.

crescendo: growing steadily louder

dissonance: a combination of sounds that sound unstable

dolce: sweetly

forte: loudly

harmony: several notes or chords combining to create a certain sound

improvisation: making up a song or tune as you go along

key: a collection of notes clustered around a certain note or class of notes that sound 'right' when played together

legato: smoothly, blending notes together

lento: slowly

metre: a pattern of strong and soft beats throughout a piece of music

octave: all the notes (C, D, E, F, G, A, B) as well as their sharps and flats

pizzicato: plucking the strings on a stringed instrument, rather than playing them with a bow

score: the written-down version of a piece of music, generally for a complex piece showing the music for a number of instruments

solo: a single musical instrument or voice

sonata: a piece designed to showcase the playing of a single instrument

soprano: the highest of the singing voices

sotto voce: quietly

staccato: each note is played sharply and by itself

stanza: the verse of a song

tempo: timing or speed of the music

tenor: the singing voice between the bass and the alto

vibrato: repeatedly changing the pitch of a note

Reading List

Some of these books may be too demanding for your child, while others may be considered a bit babyish, but this is a good list to be getting on with. Why not ask your child to see if they can read a dozen over the summer holidays between the end of Year 6 and the beginning of secondary school and offer them a reward if they manage it?

Adams, Richard: *Watership Down*
Ahlberg, Allan: *My Brother's Ghost*
Aiken, Joan: *The Wolves of Willoughby Chase*
Alcott, Louisa May: *Little Women*, *Little Men*
Alexander, Lloyd: *The Chronicles of Prydain*
Almond, David: *Skellig*
Ashley, Bernard: *Ronnie's War*
Barrie, J. M.: *Peter Pan*
Bawden, Nina: *Carrie's War*
Berry, James: *A Thief in the Village*
Blackman, Malorie: *Cloud Busting*
Buchan, John: *The Thirty-nine Steps*
Burnett, Frances Hodgson: *The Secret Garden*
Byars, Betsy: *The Midnight Fox*
Cooper, James Fenimore: *The Last of the Mohicans*
Cross, Gillian: *The Great Elephant Chase*
Crossley-Holland, Kevin: *The Seeing Stone*
Defoe, Daniel: *Robinson Crusoe*
Dickinson, Peter: *The Ropemaker*
Doherty, Berlie: *Street Child*
Doyle, Arthur Conan: The Sherlock Holmes series,
    The Lost World
Durrell, Gerald: *My Family and Other Animals*

Enright, Elizabeth: *The Saturdays*

Fine, Anne: *Flour Babies*

Forester, C. S.: The Horatio Hornblower series, *The African Queen*

Frank, Anne: *Diary of a Young Girl*

Gaiman, Neil: *Coraline*

Garfield, Leon: *Jack Holborn*

Gavin, Jamila: The Surya trilogy

Haggard, H. Rider: *King Solomon's Mines*

Higson, Charlie: *Young Bond: SilverFin*

Hoban, Russell: *The Mouse and His Child*

Hugo, Victor: *The Hunchback of Notre Dame*

Ibbotson, Eva: *Journey to the River Sea*

Jones, Diana Wynne: *The Homeward Bounders*

Juster, Norton: *The Phantom Tollbooth*

Kästner, Erich: *Emil and the Detectives*

Kipling, Rudyard: *Kim*, *The Jungle Book*

Laird, Elizabeth: *The Garbage King*

l'Engle, Madeleine: *A Wrinkle in Time*

Le Guin, Ursula: *A Wizard of Earthsea*

Lee, Harper: *To Kill a Mockingbird*

Lewis, C. S.: The Chronicles of Narnia

Lindsay, Norman: *The Magic Pudding*

Lively, Penelope: *The Ghost of Thomas Kempe*

London, Jack: *The Call of the Wild*

Mahy, Margaret: *Maddigan's Fantasia*

Mark, Jan: *Voyager*

McCaughrean, Geraldine: *Stop the Train!*

Morpurgo, Michael: *Kensuke's Kingdom*

Naidoo, Beverley: *Journey to Jo'burg*

Nesbit, E.: *The Railway Children*, *Five Children and It*

Nicholson, William: The Wind on Fire Trilogy

Pullman, Philip: His Dark Materials trilogy

Ransome, Arthur: *Swallows and Amazons*

Reeve, Philip: *Mortal Engines*
Scott, Sir Walter: *Ivanhoe*
Sedgwick, Marcus: *My Swordhand is Singing*
Shelley, Mary: *Frankenstein*
Stevenson, Robert Louis: *Treasure Island*
Sutcliff, Rosemary: *The Eagle of the Ninth*
Twain, Mark: *The Adventures of Huckleberry Finn, The Adventures of Tom Sawyer*
Tolkien, J. R. R.: *The Hobbit, The Lord of the Rings*
Verne, Jules: *Around the World in Eighty Days, Twenty Thousand Leagues under the Sea, A Journey to the Centre of the Earth*
Wells, H. G.: *The Time Machine, The War of the Worlds*
Westall, Robert: *The Machine Gunners*
White, E. B.: *Charlotte's Web*
Wren, P. C.: *Beau Geste*
Wyndham, John: *The Midwich Cuckoos, The Day of the Triffids*

Poetry anthologies

Duffy, Carol Ann: *New and Collected Poems for Children*
Heaney, Seamus and Ted Hughes (eds.): *The Rattle Bag*
Heaney, Seamus and Ted Hughes (eds.): *The School Bag*
Sweeney, Matthew (ed.): *The New Faber Book of Children's Verse*

Purposes of Study and Aims

English

The national curriculum in English covers Key Stage 1 to Key Stage 4 (Years 1 to 11).

Purpose of study

English has a pre-eminent place in education and in society. A high-quality education in English will teach pupils to speak and write fluently so that they can communicate their ideas and emotions to others and through their reading and listening, others can communicate with them. Through reading in particular, pupils have a chance to develop culturally, emotionally, intellectually, socially and spiritually. Literature, especially, plays a key role in such development. Reading also enables pupils both to acquire knowledge and to build on what they already know. All the skills of language are essential to participating fully as a member of society; pupils, therefore, who do not learn to speak, read and write fluently and confidently are effectively disenfranchised.

Aims

The overarching aim for English in the national curriculum is to promote high standards of language and literacy by equipping pupils with a strong command of the spoken and written word, and to develop their love of literature through widespread reading for enjoyment. The national curriculum for English aims to ensure that all pupils:

- read easily, fluently and with good understanding

- develop the habit of reading widely and often, for both pleasure and information

- acquire a wide vocabulary, an understanding of grammar and knowledge of linguistic conventions for reading, writing and spoken language

- appreciate our rich and varied literary heritage

- write clearly, accurately and coherently, adapting their language and style in and for a range of contexts, purposes and audiences

- use discussion in order to learn; they should be able to elaborate and explain clearly their understanding and ideas

- are competent in the arts of speaking and listening, making formal presentations, demonstrating to others and participating in debate.

Maths

The national curriculum in maths covers Key Stage 1 to Key Stage 4 (Years 1 to 11).

Purpose of study

Mathematics is a creative and highly interconnected discipline that has been developed over centuries, providing the solution to some of history's most intriguing problems. It is essential to everyday life, critical to science, technology and engineering, and necessary for financial literacy and most forms of employment. A high-quality mathematics education therefore provides a foundation for understanding the world, the ability to reason mathematically, an appreciation of the beauty and power of mathematics, and a sense of enjoyment and curiosity about the subject.

Aims

The national curriculum for mathematics aims to ensure that all pupils:

- become **fluent** in the fundamentals of mathematics, including through varied and frequent practice with increasingly complex problems over time, so that pupils develop conceptual understanding and the ability to recall and apply knowledge rapidly and accurately

- **reason mathematically** by following a line of enquiry, conjecturing relationships and generalizations, and developing an argument, justification or proof using mathematical language

- can **solve problems** by applying their mathematics to a variety of routine and non-routine problems with increasing sophistication, including breaking down problems into a series of simpler steps and persevering in seeking solutions.

Mathematics is an interconnected subject in which pupils need to be able to move fluently between representations of mathematical ideas. The programmes of study are, by necessity, organized into apparently distinct domains, but pupils should make rich connections across mathematical ideas to develop fluency, mathematical reasoning and competence in solving increasingly sophisticated problems. They should also apply their mathematical knowledge to science and other subjects.

The expectation is that the majority of pupils will move through the programmes of study at broadly the same pace. However, decisions about when to progress should always be based on the security of pupils' understanding and their readiness to progress to the next stage. Pupils who grasp concepts rapidly should be challenged through being offered rich and sophisticated problems before any acceleration through new content. Those who are not sufficiently fluent with earlier material should consolidate their understanding, including through additional practice, before moving on.

Science

The national curriculum in science covers Key Stage 1 to Key Stage 4 (Years 1 to 11).

Purpose of study

A high-quality science education provides the foundations for understanding the world through the specific disciplines of biology, chemistry and physics. Science has changed our lives and is vital to the world's future prosperity, and all pupils should be taught essential aspects of the knowledge, methods, processes and uses of science. Through building up a body of key foundational knowledge and concepts, pupils should be encouraged to recognize the power of rational explanation and develop a sense of excitement and curiosity about natural phenomena. They should be encouraged to understand how science can be used to explain what is occurring, predict how things will behave, and analyse causes.

Aims

The national curriculum for science aims to ensure that all pupils:

- develop **scientific knowledge and conceptual understanding** through the specific disciplines of biology, chemistry and physics

- develop understanding of the **nature, processes and methods of science** through different types of science enquiries that help them to answer scientific questions about the world around them

- are equipped with the scientific knowledge required to understand the **uses and implications** of science, today and for the future.

Art and Design

The national curriculum in art and design covers Key Stage 1 to Key Stage 3 (Years 1 to 9).

Purpose of study

Art, craft and design embody some of the highest forms of human creativity. A high-quality art and design education should engage, inspire and challenge pupils, equipping them with the knowledge and skills to experiment, invent and create their own works of art, craft and design. As pupils progress, they should be able to think critically and develop a more rigorous understanding of art and design. They should also know how art and design both reflect and shape our history, and contribute to the culture, creativity and wealth of our nation.

Aims

The national curriculum for art and design aims to ensure that all pupils:

- produce creative work, exploring their ideas and recording their experiences

- become proficient in drawing, painting, sculpture and other art, craft and design techniques

- evaluate and analyse creative works, using the language of art, craft and design

- know about great artists, craft makers and designers, and understand the historical and cultural development of their art forms.

Computing

The national curriculum in computing covers Key Stage 1 to Key Stage 4 (Years 1 to 11).

Purpose of study

A high-quality computing education equips pupils to use computational thinking and creativity to understand and change the world. Computing has deep links with mathematics, science, and design and technology, and provides insights into both natural and artificial systems. The core of computing is computer science, in which pupils are taught the principles of information and computation, how digital systems work, and how to put this knowledge to use through programming. Building on this knowledge and understanding, pupils are equipped to use information technology to create programs, systems and a range of content. Computing also ensures that pupils become digitally literate – able to use, and express themselves and develop their ideas through, information and communication technology – at a level suitable for the future workplace and as active participants in a digital world.

Aims

The national curriculum for computing aims to ensure that all pupils:

- can understand and apply the fundamental principles and concepts of computer science, including abstraction, logic, algorithms and data representation

- can analyse problems in computational terms, and have repeated practical experience of writing computer programs in order to solve such problems

- can evaluate and apply information technology, including new or unfamiliar technologies, analytically to solve problems

- are responsible, competent, confident and creative users of information and communication technology.

Design and Technology

The national curriculum in design and technology covers Key Stage 1 to Key Stage 3 (Years 1 to 9).

Purpose of study

Design and technology is an inspiring, rigorous and practical subject. Using creativity and imagination, pupils design and make products that solve real and relevant problems within a variety of contexts, considering their own and others' needs, wants and values. They acquire a broad range of subject knowledge and draw on disciplines such as mathematics, science, engineering, computing and art. Pupils learn how to take risks, becoming resourceful, innovative, enterprising and capable citizens. Through the evaluation of past and present design and technology, they develop a critical understanding of its impact on daily life and the wider world. High-quality design and technology education makes an essential contribution to the creativity, culture, wealth and well-being of the nation.

Aims

The national curriculum for design and technology aims to ensure that all pupils:

- develop the creative, technical and practical expertise needed to perform everyday tasks confidently and to participate successfully in an increasingly technological world

- build and apply a repertoire of knowledge, understanding and skills in order to design and make high-quality prototypes and products for a wide range of users

- critique, evaluate and test their ideas and products and the work of others

- understand and apply the principles of nutrition and learn how to cook.

Geography

The national curriculum in geography covers Key Stage 1 to Key Stage 3 (Years 1 to 9).

Purpose of study

A high-quality geography education should inspire in pupils a curiosity and fascination about the world and its people that will remain with them for the rest of their lives. Teaching should equip pupils with knowledge about diverse places, people, resources and natural and human environments, together with a deep understanding of the Earth's key physical and human processes. As pupils progress, their growing knowledge about the world should help them to deepen their understanding of the interaction between physical and human processes, and of the formation and use of landscapes and environments. Geographical knowledge, understanding and skills provide the frameworks and approaches that explain how the Earth's features at different scales are shaped, interconnected and change over time.

Aims

The national curriculum for geography aims to ensure that all pupils:

- develop contextual knowledge of the location of globally significant places – both terrestrial and marine – including their defining physical and human characteristics and how these provide a geographical context for understanding the actions of processes

- understand the processes that give rise to key physical and human geographical features of the world, how these are interdependent and how they bring about spatial variation and change over time

- are competent in the geographical skills needed to:

    collect, analyse and communicate with a range of data gathered through experiences of fieldwork that deepen their understanding of geographical processes

    interpret a range of sources of geographical information, including maps, diagrams, globes, aerial photographs and Geographical Information Systems (GIS)

    communicate geographical information in a variety of ways, including through maps, numerical and quantitative skills and writing at length.

History

The national curriculum in history covers Key Stage 1 to Key Stage 3 (Years 1 to 9).

Purpose of study

A high-quality history education will help pupils gain a coherent knowledge and understanding of Britain's past and that of the wider world. It should inspire pupils' curiosity to know more about the past. Teaching should equip pupils to ask perceptive questions, think critically, weigh evidence, sift arguments and develop perspective and judgement. History helps pupils to understand the complexity of people's lives, the process of change, the diversity of societies and relationships between different groups, as well as their own identity and the challenges of their time.

Aims

The national curriculum for history aims to ensure that all pupils:

- know and understand the history of these islands as a coherent, chronological narrative, from the earliest times to the present day; how people's lives have shaped this nation and how Britain has influenced and been influenced by the wider world

- know and understand significant aspects of the history of the wider world: the nature of ancient civilizations; the expansion and dissolution of empires; characteristic features of past non-European societies; achievements and follies of mankind

- gain and deploy a historically grounded understanding of abstract terms such as 'empire', 'civilization', 'parliament' and 'peasantry'

- understand historical concepts such as continuity and change, cause and consequence, similarity, difference and significance, and use them to make connections, draw contrasts, analyse trends, frame historically valid questions and create their own structured accounts, including written narratives and analyses

- understand the methods of historical enquiry, including how evidence is used rigorously to make historical claims, and discern how and why contrasting arguments and interpretations of the past have been constructed

- gain historical perspective by placing their growing knowledge into different contexts, understanding the connections between local, regional, national and international history; between cultural, economic, military, political, religious and social history; and between short- and long-term timescales.

Languages

The national curriculum in languages covers Key Stage 2 and Key Stage 3 (Years 3 to 9).

Purpose of study

Learning a foreign language is a liberation from insularity and provides an opening to other cultures. A high-quality languages education should foster pupils' curiosity and deepen their understanding of the world.

The teaching should enable pupils to express their ideas and thoughts in another language and to understand and respond to its speakers, both in speech and in writing. It should also provide opportunities for them to communicate for practical purposes, learn new ways of thinking and read great literature in the original language. Language teaching should provide the foundation for learning further languages, equipping pupils to study and work in other countries.

Aims

The national curriculum for languages aims to ensure that all pupils:

- understand and respond to spoken and written language from a variety of authentic sources
- speak with increasing confidence, fluency and spontaneity, finding ways of communicating what they want to say, including through discussion and asking questions, and continually improving the accuracy of their pronunciation and intonation
- can write at varying length, for different purposes and audiences, using the variety of grammatical structures that they have learnt
- discover and develop an appreciation of a range of writing in the language studied.

Music

The national curriculum in music covers Key Stage 1 to Key Stage 3 (Years 1 to 9).

Purpose of study

Music is a universal language that embodies one of the highest forms of creativity. A high-quality music education should engage and inspire pupils to develop a love of music and their talent as musicians, and so increase their self-confidence, creativity and sense of achievement. As pupils progress, they should develop a critical engagement with music, allowing them to compose, and to listen with discrimination to the best in the musical canon.

Aims

The national curriculum for music aims to ensure that all pupils:

- perform, listen to, review and evaluate music across a range of historical periods, genres, styles and traditions, including the works of the great composers and musicians

- learn to sing and to use their voices, to create and compose music on their own and with others, have the opportunity to learn a musical instrument, use technology appropriately and have the opportunity to progress to the next level of musical excellence

- understand and explore how music is created, produced and communicated, including through the interrelated dimensions: pitch, duration, dynamics, tempo, timbre, texture, structure and appropriate musical notations.

Appendices

How to Form the Letters of the Alphabet

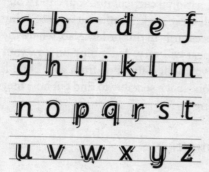

a b c d e f
g h i j k l m
n o p q r s t
u v w x y z

Lower case

A B C D E F
G H I J K L
M N O P Q R
S T U V W X
Y Z

Upper case

Addition, Subtraction, Multiplication and Division

This appendix sets out some examples of formal written methods of addition, subtraction, multiplication and division to illustrate the range of methods that could be taught in your child's primary school. These examples are taken from the national curriculum. Your child won't necessarily learn all these slightly different ways of doing things, and not necessarily in this order. Also, where the 'carried' digits appear will vary, depending on how your child is taught. If you do it differently from your child it can cause confusion, so it's sensible to find out how they do it before 'helping'.

Addition and subtraction

789 + 642 becomes

```
    7  8  9
 +  6  4  2
_____
 1  4  3  1
    1  1
```

Answer: 1431

874 − 523 becomes

```
    8  7  4
 −  5  2  3
_____
    3  5  1
```

Answer: 351

932 − 457 becomes

```
    8  12  1
    9̸  3̸  2
 −  4   5  7
_____
    4   7  5
```

Answer: 475

932 − 457 becomes

```
       1   1
    9   3  2
 −  4̸   5̸  7
    5   6
_____
    4   7  5
```

Answer: 475

Short multiplication

24 × 6 becomes	342 × 7 becomes	2741 × 6 becomes
$\begin{array}{r} 2\ 4 \\ \times\quad 6 \\ \hline 1\ 4\ 4 \\ \scriptstyle 2 \end{array}$	$\begin{array}{r} 3\ 4\ 2 \\ \times\quad\ 7 \\ \hline 2\ 3\ 9\ 4 \\ \scriptstyle 2\ 1 \end{array}$	$\begin{array}{r} 2\ 7\ 4\ 1 \\ \times\qquad 6 \\ \hline 1\ 6\ 4\ 4\ 6 \\ \scriptstyle 4\ 2 \end{array}$
Answer: 144	Answer: 2394	Answer: 16 446

Long multiplication

24 × 16 becomes	124 × 26 becomes	124 × 26 becomes
$\begin{array}{r} \scriptstyle 2 \\ 2\ 4 \\ \times\ 1\ 6 \\ \hline 2\ 4\ 0 \\ 1\ 4\ 4 \\ \hline 3\ 8\ 4 \end{array}$	$\begin{array}{r} \scriptstyle 1\ 2 \\ 1\ 2\ 4 \\ \times\quad 2\ 6 \\ \hline 2\ 4\ 8\ 0 \\ 7\ 4\ 4 \\ \hline 3\ 2\ 2\ 4 \\ \scriptstyle 1\ 1 \end{array}$	$\begin{array}{r} \scriptstyle 1\ 2 \\ 1\ 2\ 4 \\ \times\quad 2\ 6 \\ \hline 7\ 4\ 4 \\ 2\ 4\ 8\ 0 \\ \hline 3\ 2\ 2\ 4 \\ \scriptstyle 1\ 1 \end{array}$
Answer: 384	Answer: 3224	Answer: 3224

In the first example immediately above some people will choose to multiply 24 by 10 first, and then by 6, and some people will do it the other way round. It doesn't matter which, as the next two examples above show. Some people like to include a + symbol to show that (in, for example, the first long multiplication above) the 240 is added to the 144 to get the answer.

Short division

98 ÷ 7 becomes

```
    1 4
    2
7 | 9 8
```

Answer: 14

432 ÷ 5 becomes

```
      8 6 r2
      3
5 | 4 3 2
```

Answer: 86 remainder 2

496 ÷ 11 becomes

```
        4 5 r1
        5
1 1 | 4 9 6
```

Answer: 45 $\frac{1}{11}$

Long division

432 ÷ 15 becomes

```
        2 8 r12
1 5 | 4 3 2
      3 0 0
      1 3 2
      1 2 0
          1 2
```

Answer: 28 remainder 12

432 ÷ 15 becomes

```
          2 8
1 5 | 4 3 2
      3 0 0    15 × 20
      1 3 2
      1 2 0    15 × 8
          1 2
```

$\frac{12}{15} = \frac{4}{5}$

Answer: 28 $\frac{4}{5}$

432 ÷ 15 becomes

```
          2 8 . 8
1 5 | 4 3 2 . 0
      3 0
      1 3 2
      1 2 0
          1 2 0
          1 2 0
              0
```

Answer: 28.8

Some people like to put in a – sign to show that (in the first example above) the 300 is taken away from the 432 to leave 132.

The first two examples above show 'chunking' (see Year 6 'Maths'), and the final example shows the formal method of long division you will have learnt at school.

Glossary of Computing Terminology

algorithm: an unambiguous procedure or precise step-by-step guide to solve a problem or achieve a particular objective.

computer networks: the computers and the connecting hardware (Wi-Fi access points, cables, fibres, switches and routers) that make it possible to transfer data using an agreed method ('protocol').

control: using computers to move or otherwise change 'physical' systems. The computer can be hidden inside the system or connected to it.

data: a structured set of numbers, representing digitized text, images, sound or video, which can be processed or transmitted by a computer.

debug: to detect and correct the errors in a computer program.

digital content: any media created, edited or viewed on a computer, such as text (including the hypertext of a web page), images, sound, video (including animation), or virtual environments, and combinations of these (i.e. multimedia).

information: the meaning or interpretation given to a set of data by its users, or which results from data being processed.

input: data provided to a computer system, such as via a keyboard, mouse, microphone, camera or physical sensors.

internet: the global collection of computer networks and their connections, all using shared protocols (TCP/IP) to communicate.

logical reasoning: a systematic approach to solving problems or deducing information, using a set of universally applicable and totally reliable rules.

output: the information produced by a computer system for its user, typically on a screen, through speakers or on a printer, but possibly through the control of motors in physical systems.

program: a stored set of instructions encoded in a language understood by the computer that does some form of computation, processing input and/or stored data to generate output.

repetition: a programming construct in which one or more instructions are repeated, perhaps a certain number of times, until a condition is satisfied or until the program is stopped.

search: to identify data that satisfies one or more conditions, such as web pages containing supplied keywords, or files on a computer with certain properties.

selection: a programming construct in which the instructions that are executed are determined by whether a particular condition is met.

sequence: to place programming instructions in order, with each executed one after the other.

services: programs running on computers, typically those connected to the internet, which provide functionality in response to requests; for example, to transmit a web page, deliver an email or allow a text, voice or video conversation.

simulation: using a computer to model the state and behaviour of real-world (or imaginary) systems, including physical and social systems; an integral part of most computer games.

software: computer programs, including both application software (such as office programs, web browsers, media editors and games) and the computer operating system. The term also applies to 'apps' running on mobile devices and to web-based services.

variables: a way in which computer programs can store, retrieve or change simple data, such as a score, the time left or the user's name.

World Wide Web: a service provided by computers connected to the internet (web servers), in which pages of hypertext (web pages) are transmitted to users; the pages typically include links to other web pages and may be generated by programs automatically.

Taken from *Computing in the National Curriculum: A Guide for Primary Teachers* (NAACE).

Phil Bagge provides a useful glossary with more detailed explanations of some of these terms: see www.code-it. co.uk/csvocab.html.

Glossary of Education Terms and Acronyms

academy: state school funded directly by the Department for Education rather than a local authority. Governed by a charitable trust that employs the staff, owns the land and buildings and determines the admissions arrangements. Not obliged to teach the national curriculum.

AHT: assistant head teacher.

AP: alternative provision. Schools for children who have been excluded (see **PRU**).

baseline test: a test taken by some children in the first few weeks of Reception. A teacher-led assessment of your child's 'baseline' abilities in literacy, reasoning and cognition, not a formal exam.

BESD: behavioural, emotional and social difficulties (see **EBD**).

bulge year: an additional form of thirty children taken on in just one year that then works its way through the school like a mouse being digested by a python.

Common Entrance: a test taken by applicants to selective independent schools at the age of eleven or thirteen, depending on the year of entry.

community school: a local authority state school. The local authority funds the school, employs the staff, owns the land and buildings and determines the admissions arrangements.

convertor academy: a state school that was funded by a local authority but is now funded directly by the Department for Education. Governed by a charitable trust that employs the staff, owns or leases the land and buildings and determines the admissions arrangements. Not obliged to teach the national curriculum.

CPO: child protection officer.

CRB: Criminal Records Bureau. Anyone who works at a school, even in a voluntary capacity, used to have to be CRB checked. Now they have to be DBS checked (see **DBS**).

CSO: community support officer (usually a police officer).

DBS: Disclosure and Barring Service. Anyone who works at a school, even in a voluntary capacity, has to be DBS checked.

EAL: English as an additional language. A school with '30 per cent EAL' means 30 per cent of the pupils at the school speak English as an additional language, i.e. it's not the first language spoken in their homes. (Also known as EFL, as in English as a Foreign Language.)

EBD: emotional and behavioural difficulties. (Also known as **BESD**.)

11+: a test taken by applicants to grammar schools or selective independent schools for entry into Year 7.

ELG: early learning goal. What your child is expected to have learnt across a range of areas by the end of Reception.

EYFS: the Early Years Foundation Stage, covering the age range two (Nursery) to five (Reception).

EYFS Framework: a document setting out what children should be learning in Nursery and Reception classes.

EYFS profile: a summary of your child's attainment at the end of the EYFS (i.e. at the end of Reception) in no fewer than seventeen early learning goals (ELGs), with your child assessed according to whether they're 'emerging', 'expected' or 'exceeding' in each category. Non-statutory from 2016.

fair banding: a type of admissions policy whereby all the applicants to a non-selective state secondary are sorted into different bands according to their performance in a test. Typically, the top 25 per cent of performers are placed in the top band, the middle 50 per cent in the middle band, and the bottom 25 per cent in the bottom band. The school then applies its oversubscription criteria to each band, making sure it ends up with a broad mix of children from across the ability spectrum.

faith school: a state school with a religious ethos. Though funded by a local authority, most members of the governing body are appointed by a religious trust (which also owns the buildings and land). The governing body usually employs the staff and determines the admissions arrangements. In some (not all) faith schools, some places are reserved for children of a particular faith, hence the phrase 'On your knees to avoid the fees'.

FE: form of entry. A 2FE school is a school that has two forms of 30 children in every year group.

free school: see **sponsored academy.**

FSM: free school meal. A school with '25 per cent FSM' means 25 per cent of the children at the school are eligible for free school meals, i.e. they live in homes where the annual household income is below £16,190 (see **pupil premium**).

G&T: gifted and talented.

independent school: a private, fee-paying school.

inset day: a day set aside for staff training, usually just before term starts or just after term ends.

Key Stage 1: Years 1 and 2, covering the age range five to seven.

Key Stage 2: Years 3, 4, 5 and 6, covering the age range seven to eleven.

LSO: learning support officer, also known as a **TA** (see below).

middle school: a school for children aged nine (Year 5) to thirteen (Year 8).

MIS: management information system. All schools have a management information system that they use to store information about staff, pupils and parents, usually SIMS (School Information Management System).

NQT: newly qualified teacher.

PAN: published admissions number. The number of children on roll when a school is at full capacity, so the PAN of a 2FE primary is 420.

phonics check: a test that takes place in June of Year 1, designed to assess your child's phonics knowledge.

pre-prep: an independent school for children aged three (Nursery) to eight (Year 3).

prep school: an independent school for children aged eight (Year 4) to eleven (Year 6) or thirteen (Year 8). Some parents take their children out of state primaries at the end of Year 3 to send them to prep schools, hence the phrase 'Out the door in Year 4'.

PRU: pupil referral unit. Schools for children who have been excluded.

PSHE: personal, social and health education (also known as PSE, as in personal and social education).

public school: an independent school for children aged eleven (Year 7) or thirteen (Year 9) to eighteen (Year 13), usually boarding.

pupil premium: additional funding that schools get for each pupil on their roll who at some point in the last six years has been eligible for a free school meal.

SATs: Standard Assessment Tasks. What the national curriculum tasks and tests that children take in Years 2 and 6 used to be called, and in many schools still are.

SEAL: social and emotional aspects of learning.

SEN: special educational needs. Sometimes called SEND (special educational needs and disabilities).

SENCO: special educational needs coordinator. Sometimes called a SENDCO to include disabilities.

SLT: senior leadership team, usually comprising one or two deputy heads and a clutch of assistant heads. Also known as the SMT (senior management team).

SPAG: the spelling, punctuation and grammar test children take in Year 6 is known as the SPAG test.

Special Measures: a school judged by Ofsted to be failing or likely to fail to provide an acceptable standard of education will be placed in Special Measures.

special schools: schools that cater for children with special educational needs and disabilities.

sponsored academy/free school: state school sponsored and/or set up by a business, faith group, charity, university or a group of parents or teachers and funded directly by the Department for Education. Governed by a charitable trust that employs the staff, owns or leases the land and buildings and determines the admissions arrangements. Not obliged to teach the national curriculum. Schools of this type that opened before the change of government in 2010 are known as 'sponsored academies'; those that opened after the change of government are, for the most part, known as 'free schools'.

SRE: sex and relationship education, usually taught in **PSHE** classes.

TA: teaching assistant.

VLE: virtual learning environment. A web portal through which parents and children can access a school's learning resources from home.

voluntary aided school: a state school funded by a local authority, but in which the governing body employs the staff and determines the admissions arrangements.

voluntary controlled school: a state school funded by a local authority, but in which a charitable trust appoints some of the school governors.

WALT: We Are Learning Today. Often appears on children's homework followed by a one- or two-word description of the task covered in the homework.

He just wanted a decent book to read ...

Not too much to ask, is it? It was in 1935 when Allen Lane, Managing Director of Bodley Head Publishers, stood on a platform at Exeter railway station looking for something good to read on his journey back to London. His choice was limited to popular magazines and poor-quality paperbacks – the same choice faced every day by the vast majority of readers, few of whom could afford hardbacks. Lane's disappointment and subsequent anger at the range of books generally available led him to found a company – and change the world.

'We believed in the existence in this country of a vast reading public for intelligent books at a low price, and staked everything on it'
Sir Allen Lane, 1902–1970, founder of Penguin Books

The quality paperback had arrived – and not just in bookshops. Lane was adamant that his Penguins should appear in chain stores and tobacconists, and should cost no more than a packet of cigarettes.

Reading habits (and cigarette prices) have changed since 1935, but Penguin still believes in publishing the best books for everybody to enjoy. We still believe that good design costs no more than bad design, and we still believe that quality books published passionately and responsibly make the world a better place.

So wherever you see the little bird – whether it's on a piece of prize-winning literary fiction or a celebrity autobiography, political tour de force or historical masterpiece, a serial-killer thriller, reference book, world classic or a piece of pure escapism – you can bet that it represents the very best that the genre has to offer.

Whatever you like to read – trust Penguin.